ECONOMIC ELEMENTS
IN THE
PAX BRITANNICA

ECONOMIC ELEMENTS

IN THE

PAX BRITANNICA

Studies in British Foreign Trade in the Nineteenth Century

By

ALBERT H. IMLAH

NEW YORK / RUSSELL & RUSSELL

TO

H, A, J,

AND

M

PREFACE

Historians have a special interest in the light and shadow that the past can throw on the present; and it is an inexhaustible subject. But perhaps one may, for a moment in a preface, reverse the field and briefly suggest one single facet of the light that the present can throw on the past in relation to the central theme of this little volume. The course of world affairs in this century has been teaching us anew the close interdependence between politics and economics and not least, in international affairs, the significance of the policies of an economic center. Events in this century have certainly made it easier to appreciate — by contrast, alas — the importance of the part that Britain played in drawing the great powers towards paths of peaceful progress in the critical years after the Napoleonic Wars in the last century. At that time Britain was the leading industrial and financial power, enjoying a measure of island security and detachment yet intricately dependent on world conditions for the development of her economic opportunities. Readied for the role by centuries of involvement in European affairs and by a political system that somehow succeeded in effecting a working degree of harmony between short and long range political and economic interests, she was able to contribute significantly towards making the nineteenth century the most peaceful since the rise of European nation states.

In some respects a comparable opportunity was open to the United States after 1918. The defeat of Germany and the acceptance by the Allied Powers, largely on American insistence, of a comprehensive blueprint for international security and cooperation promised continuity for the better elements in nineteenth century development on a far more organized and systematic basis. Somehow the chance was muffed. Once the blueprint was drawn and accepted by the Allies, the United States withdrew from further part in the plans. Without the active participation of this great new industrial and financial power of the twentieth century, the system for international security and cooperation lacked body and heart; it proved to be a hollow thing that could cope successfully only with peripheral matters. Without the adherence of the United States to the alliance that had won the war, there was no obviously overwhelming power to make a fresh resort to war unthinkable in Germany or to temper, from strength, the penalties of defeat and thus render the choice of peaceful policies doubly sure. Moreover, without continuing commitment, the United States lacked the incentive to guide or even collaborate in liquidating postwar financial problems or to set an example of enlightened commercial policy to the world. America's former (and future) allies, like the vanquished enemy nations, were gravely handicapped rather than helped in recovery from the war. Certainly the world stage was not set for further natural development of their already interdependent economies. In this peacetime, it was each for himself; and all regressed towards limiting nationalist economic policies, a game in which the nations with the most to gain from a peaceful world order had also the most to lose from the disorder that their weakness and loss of common concert invited or even provoked. The penalty for all came within a single generation in another devastating general war.

With the contrasts that the twentieth century has inadvertently supplied, the positive values in the simple facts of Britain's continuing commitment to her allies after 1815 take on more solid meaning. It seems clearer now that Britain's active participation in the system of balance and concert of power for which she had bargained in the peace settlement was a major factor in shaping attitudes and policies in the first critical years of peace. With British adherence, there could be no doubt that the alliance was strong enough to contain France, and it became possible both to minimize the military element and to reduce the provocation to France by quickly liquidating the military occupation. Thanks to active British interest and British loans, general agreement was also reached in good time, cutting down the financial penalties of defeat imposed on France by the treaties. The political groundwork was laid for orderly international relations that enabled Britain to develop her economic potentialities and to demonstrate something of the vast possibilities for material and social progress by peaceful process and for peaceful ends. In this context it was possible within a decade for Britain to ease away from the older competitive power policies and to promote economic development in other countries as well as at home by moderating her trade regulations and tariffs, and by freeing the export of capital and machinery from political control. By the 1840's, Britain could begin the experiment of opening her ports wide to the trade and shipping of the world which made her the prosperous center of a highly international economy exerting a good deal of influence by example on the policies of other nations through the mid-century.

The logic of Britain's role in these developments after the Napoleonic Wars is briefly outlined in their interacting political and economic aspects in Chapter I. British commercial policy and experience, both under the postwar protectionism that failed to harmonize the primary interests of the nation and under the free trade program that became a central feature of the *Pax Britannica,* are examined more closely in Chapters V and VI.

The three middle chapters (II–IV) are concerned with the construction of statistical series on certain rather fundamental elements of British international economic relations. When these studies were begun nearly twenty years ago it was not possible to make any very close evaluation of the role of the British economy in world affairs in the early nineteenth century. There were no dependable series on the actual market values of British imports and re-exports before 1853; and there were no systematic data on British "invisible" trade — the earnings of shipping, business services, and foreign investments — or on the terms of trade until near the end of the century. Consequently it seemed necessary to undertake the long and laborious task of preparing estimates to fill in these gaps. The first constructions on these matters were published between 1948 and 1952. They have now been substantially revised in the light of further discussion and additional data, and it is this revision that prompts a second publication of these underlying statistical series with rather detailed accounts of the materials and procedures used in constructing them.

It may be useful to summarize the main changes that have been made in these estimates since they first appeared in print. For the real values (Chapter II), I have been able to strengthen considerably the coverage of commodities for the early years up to 1805, to add two more years at the beginning of the series, and to make a few minor corrections for later years. For the balance of payments and export of capital (Chapter III), I have recalculated shipping credits throughout, have made a somewhat bolder attempt to differentiate good years from bad in the matter of interest and dividend income prior to the "Coupon Act" of 1886, and have corrected a few minor errors here and there in other series. The terms of trade series (Chapter IV) have been completely recalculated to 1900. Breaking away from my earlier reliance on the old "official values" to 1865 and on the first Board of Trade series of absolute values for 1880–1900, I have prepared new volume series, with as complete coverage of the articles of trade as possible from available data and with much more satisfactory price weighting of commodities. I have also increased the list of commodities covered in the period 1865–1880.

It is a pleasure to record the assistance I have received in the course of preparing these studies. On the institutional side, of major importance first and last was ready access to the invaluable collections of *Parliamentary Papers* in the Harvard College Library and the Boston Public

Library. In 1942, the Social Science Research Council provided a grant for the checking of my worksheets for Table 2 by other hands; in 1953, the Fletcher School provided assistance towards a similar checking of the new worksheets for the terms of trade, and in the same year the Committee on Research in Economic History contributed funds for this cause and for the preparation of the charts. Two sabbatic leaves granted by Tufts University appreciably accelerated completion of the work. I am happy to acknowledge also the kind permission granted by *The Journal of Economic History, The Economic History Review, The South Atlantic Quarterly,* and the Trustees of Clark University to include here in revised form the matter previously published under their auspices.

Many individuals have also helped me in various ways in the preparation of these studies. I am particularly indebted to Professors Thomas S. Ashton, Robert E. Baldwin, Arthur H. Cole, Gottfried Haberler, George N. Halm, John R. T. Hughes, Leland H. Jenks, and Mrs. Anna Jacobson Schwartz for their readiness to discuss and advise on many questions which have arisen. Professor Halm read and made many useful suggestions on the semifinal draft of Chapters IV–VI. I am grateful also to Professor Charles P. Kindleberger for his cooperative interest in running down the sources of the divergences discussed in the Appendix. Miss Ruth Crandall carefully checked the large pile of worksheets behind Table 2; and Messrs. Ronald S. MacLean and George S. Sugden performed a like service for Table 8 and Appendix Tables II–IV. Mr. Walter F. Sharkey prepared the charts with skill and accuracy. Finally, but by no means least, my wife has not only tolerated my absorption in these matters but has also aided in many ways through the long processes of distilling the revised tables and text from the stacks of worksheets, and she has patiently assisted in all the various stages of proofreading.

ALBERT H. IMLAH

The Fletcher School of Law and Diplomacy
Tufts University
Medford, Massachusetts
July 1958

CONTENTS

TABLES

APPENDIX TABLES

CHARTS

ECONOMIC ELEMENTS
IN THE
PAX BRITANNICA

I

DISTINCTIVE ELEMENTS IN THE *PAX BRITANNICA*

The century after the defeat of Napoleon at Waterloo was remarkable for many things but not least for its relatively peaceful course and for its unparalleled economic and social progress. It was by far the longest period since the rise of the nation state that was free from general war. There were, to be sure, many local conflicts, and there were several wars involving major states, but each was brief and limited in scope. The nearest approach to a general war was the Crimean in the mid-century. It involved three great and two lesser powers but they engaged only relatively small proportions of their national resources in localized theaters of operations and for limited objectives. It did not assume anything like the proportions of the wars which opened and closed this remarkable era and which had dotted the preceding four or five centuries. Economic and social progress was extraordinarily rapid and, comparatively free from the restrictions which power competition imposes, was world wide. The new forces of steam power and machine production, which had their effective beginnings in Britain in the years of peace before the French Revolution and which required the wider area of the world itself and hence some measure of peace and international cooperation to reach their full potentials, improved the material basis of life and living in varying degrees virtually throughout the world. The political aspirations of people grew accordingly, and in this favorable climate of expanding prosperity and freedom from war, constitutional liberty had "time and space to work and spread."

These achievements were not, of course, the fruit of a single circumstance or the work of a single nation. They were the result of many conditions, of developing attitudes of people and policies of states, interacting amid many powerful counterforces and traditions. If British contributions to this era of peace and progress were sufficiently significant to warrant the term *Pax Britannica*, it was not because Britain was in any sense able to impose peace in a Roman manner by police power but because, mature in her nationalism and relatively free from constricting fears for her own security, and with parliamentary institutions, including freedom of speech and press, she was able gradually to find her way towards — and to set an example of — more intelligent policies suited to her complex but peaceful interests. In doing this she demonstrated the practical possibilities for orderly progress in organized human affairs. The military power of Great Britain was fully applied towards defeating Napoleon and thus making possible the peace settlement which launched this age; and it generally played its part in the balance of interstate relations thereafter. But what became distinctive in the *Pax Britannica* — the special contributions that Britain made towards setting Europe for a time on a different course — was rather more the influence she exerted on the attitudes of other people, and therefore on the policies of other governments, by her own liberal and highly rewarding policies.

THE PEACE SETTLEMENT

The starting point for the success of the nineteenth century in peace-keeping was the security formula worked out in the peace settlement of 1814–1815. It had three main elements which moderated and buttressed one another. First was the acceptance by the great states of the checks and restrictions of a balance of power among themselves. We have learned to think of balance of power as a particularly British principle, and the British once again made reconstruction of a "just equilibrium," as Lord Castlereagh preferred to call it, their chief objective in the peace settlement. To promote a satisfactory balance they were ready to hand back most of their overseas conquests. But this time balance of power was accepted — willingly in the West and somewhat reluctantly in the East — as a European principle designed to impose limitations not merely on France alone, but on each of the allies also, as was clearly illustrated by the combination of Britain, France, and Austria which checked Russian ambitions in Poland and preserved a balance in Eastern Europe.

As a security system, balance of power alone was far from perfect. It was not a guarantee of peace. It could not be expected to eliminate all war. Indeed its very maintenance depended — and fundamentally this is true for collective security systems also — on the known readiness of the major parties to use force if need be to prevent an aggressor, especially a Great Power, from acquiring additional resources with which to be able to impose its will on others. But it had this virtue, that as long as the Great Powers stood watchful to check unbalancing maneuvers by their fellows, it made war an untempting instrument for attaining advantage because there could be little prospect of easy success or profit in it. Hence, once it was established, it moderated fear and suspicion among the Great

Powers, protected the independence of the lesser states, and permitted a measure of unity and cooperation on matters of common interest.

The second element was the principle of legitimacy. The term is suggestive of the old absolute monarchical order of things, and this aspect has been so roundly denounced by liberal writers ever since that the kernel of virtue in the principle as it was intended in 1814–1815 has been almost lost from sight. We may discern its value more clearly if we call it legality or due process of law and place it in antithesis to the Paris mob and Napoleon's rule of force. This was a major part of the concept at the peace conference and in this reading it did not prohibit orderly change even from royal absolutism towards constitutionalism. The King of France could grant a constitution in 1814 and the King of Prussia could promise one. It was this conception of legality which, thanks largely to the developing foreign policy and domestic example of Great Britain, survived the severe test of the first postwar decade when the absolutist monarchies, impelled by fresh fear of subversion and revolution, invoked legitimacy in an ultraconservative sense to repress change and to make European society a static thing in which improvement could be possible only after the use of force and violence to overthrow existing government. As due process of law, legitimacy could supplement balance of power in imposing limitations on the use of force yet without blocking progress. In this sense, the treaties, "the Public Law of Europe," were contracts which could be modified with the consent of the signatories when circumstances and interests warranted change.

The third element was the unity, or Concert, of the allies. This took form in the Quadruple Alliance which was designed primarily to prevent a resurgence of French aggression but with provision also, in Article VI, for further top-level congresses of the sovereigns or their ministers to consult on their common interests and on measures "for the repose and prosperity of nations." This was a step in international organization and it was enormously useful in maintaining a united policy towards France in the first critical years of treaty management. Then later, converted by Metternich to the uses of repression, the more grandiose congress element collapsed under British opposition in 1823. What survived became known as the "Concert of Europe." It functioned through ad hoc conferences of the ambassadors of the Great Powers, sometimes consulting with representatives of the lesser states when their interests were directly involved. It met in the great capitals, most often in London, a kind of center of diplomatic gravity. It mediated disputes and legalized treaty changes when the more usual channels of diplomacy failed, and it contributed something towards making the "Public Law of Europe" viable and its maintenance practical. The Concert of Europe also gave some unity to the Great Powers and, while the *Pax Britannica* was in its heyday, helped to prevent balance of power from degenerating into mere competition for power.

There was, however, another important condition in this avoidance of competition for power, one for which it is commonly, but perhaps mistakenly, assumed that there is no satisfactory equivalent in this mid-part of the twentieth century. At that time there were five more or less balanced Great Powers. Each had such a wide variety of interests that every new problem that arose meant some change in the pattern of alignment. Particular groupings were not consolidated into permanent alliances. Controversy was not cumulative; the tensions of recurrent crises were not channeled between exactly the same sets of powers and bitterness was not brought to the boil. Even the deep and dangerous rift between Britain and the four absolutist governments on the Continent over the issue of restoring royal absolutism in Naples and Spain was soon dissolved by a totally new alignment when two absolutist governments, Russia and France, allied with Britain in behalf of autonomy for Greece. The Concert lived on.

Hardly less important than the general peace settlement was the treatment of the defeated aggressor. The first and second treaties of Paris, drawn before and after the Hundred Days, together contained in elementary form many of the punitive features of twentieth-century peace treaties. France was cut back territorially to nation-state proportions from the imperialist gains of the preceding twenty years and required to cede a few minor overseas possessions; she was pledged to pay an indemnity towards the costs of the Hundred Days; and to pay reparations also for certain private claims, the amounts to be determined later. There was restitution of art treasures, military occupation of territory at French expense; and Napoleon, who had been declared an outlaw, a war criminal, was banished to a kind of captivity at St. Helena. France, then, was confined within ethnic frontiers, yet, with her resources and her commercial empire, was still a formidable great power. But she was balanced and contained by the other Great Powers who, by their Quadruple Alliance, stood publicly pledged to act together if France again crossed her frontiers in aggression or if a Bonaparte returned to the throne.

As is the case with all formulas, the value of these two treaties depended on the way in which they were applied. Here the unity of the allies, cemented by British participation, made possible treaty application

that was firm, yet moderate, and rapid in execution. The Duke of Wellington as commander-in-chief kept the allied occupation troops under some
control. British bankers and their Dutch affiliates, with the unofficial en-
couragement of the British government, floated French loans in the British
and Dutch money markets which helped France to settle both the indemnity and the reparations bill in 1818 when the latter, under the arbitra-
tion of the Duke of Wellington, was written down to only one fifth of the
claims. Wellington, with the support of the British Foreign Secretary,
Lord Castlereagh, also persuaded the allies to terminate the military
occupation in 1818, two years ahead of schedule. At the same Congress
(Aix-la-Chapelle), the four victors formally admitted France to their top-
level conferences under Article VI while the security provisions of the
alliance against French aggression were secretly reaffirmed and the French
government was quietly informed of this significant fact. All this in three
years, by agreement among the allies who were reasonably assured by
their continuing solidarity of their own security, rather than as a result of
overt threats or intrigues by the French. The treaty provisions were
modified by consent, not by force or under compulsion, and the "Public
Law of Europe" gained strength where it counted most. French agitators
were left with little plausible basis on which to blame developing dis-
contents on treaty limitations. When France had her revolution in the
natural course of things a half generation later, it was for a more constitutional government, and militant, anti-treaty objectives were muted.
The contrasts to twentieth-century occasions emphasize that the achievements of allied unity in these first critical pattern-setting years after 1815
were of prime importance.

BRITAIN'S MEDIATING ROLE

The *Pax Britannica* operated within this context, which Britain herself
notably helped to establish. Obviously, Britain could not *impose* peace on
a balanced Europe. She could, to be sure, perform a certain police function
within her own spheres of special interest, but she lacked the preponderance of manpower or resources even to think of attempting alone to
impose peace on the nations of Europe. Her population, for example, was
less than that of any other Great Power except Prussia in 1815. Moreover,
the bent of her people lay towards creating and enjoying the comforts of
wealth, not towards military regimentation or war. Parliament, which
controlled the purse strings, showed, from the moment Napoleon's power
was broken, its characteristic aversion to maintaining military or naval

establishments above the bare minimum calculated to be strictly necessary for defense. At the same time, Britain's widespread commercial interests, like the far-flung empire, dictated considered effort towards maintaining peace and order in the world. Clearly something was required towards this end, but, as an island naval power vis à vis four great land powers, Britain could do little without the cooperation of one or more of the others. Happily for this cooperation, Britain's own chief instrument of defense, the navy, by itself could scarcely menace the essential security of any of the other great states. Only in conjunction with a major military force could it offer serious threat to any of the great land powers. This circumstance, combined with the moderate policies that commercial interests dictated, left fairly open to view broad bases of common interest.

Britain's role in the Concert of Powers was, therefore, essentially a mediating one. With good management and outside support her weight could often be a decisive deterrent to extreme or dangerous policies on the part of other states. But her statesmen discovered early in the 1820's that the opportunity to mediate was not automatic, and that success was certainly not inevitable. It depended to a large extent on the use she made of her resources and on the prestige and attractiveness of her policies to the peoples of other states when their governments were of a different mind. This discovery coincided happily with the turning point in British attitudes towards domestic reforms; and thereafter, for nearly forty years, Britain mediated with much broader effectiveness than her limited power resources, however shrewdly applied, could have made possible. To put it more precisely, she supplemented and strengthened her relatively weak military position for diplomatic mediation by exemplifying and promoting the attractive economic and social opportunities of the century which appealed to the peoples of Europe and of the world. This became a distinguishing feature of the *Pax Britannica* and a chief reason for the large measure of success which it achieved.

Britain was a "natural" for this role in Western Europe in a century ripening for liberal constitutionalism and material progress. Even before the reform era confirmed her progressive leadership, the freedom her people enjoyed in trial by jury, habeas corpus, freedom of the press, and government through remarkably stable parliamentary institutions had brought her closer than any other European nation to sober practice of the doctrines of the natural rights of man that were tried with explosive force in France in 1789 only to be subverted in later Revolutionary and Napoleonic years. Nevertheless, there was much still to be done to establish Britain as a thoroughly liberal nation. Parliament had become highly unrepresentative of population centers, while local government, equally unrepresentative, was corrupt and lethargic. The penal laws were harsh and the civil laws still held large inequalities. Although the press was free from censorship, newspapers were heavily taxed to keep them out of the hands of the common people. There was scope, then, for rather dramatic reforms when the time came. Perhaps her deliberative method of government by peaceful persuasion, though it meant long delays and "muddling" while divergent interests were reconciled into a majority will, supplied a useful kind of experience to the statesmen of a mediating power. Fortunately, the existence of a balance of power tended to make capacity for instant decision less imperative.

On the economic side, Britain seemed to hold in her hands the secrets of material prosperity and comfort. She was far ahead in the development and use of machine techniques, the giant among the trading nations, and the great financial center of the world of business. Even governments, including those of the Great Powers, now relied heavily on their credit standing in the London money market. But at the beginning of this peace period Britain held these rich possessions in a nationalistic spirit of monopoly. Export of machinery was prohibited by law and skilled artisans were forbidden to go abroad to practice or to teach their craft. Gold could be exported only under government license. Imports were subject to high protective, even prohibitive, duties and commerce was narrowly regulated by the intricate Navigation Acts. Here too, the material advantage both of Britain and of the world called for much more enlightened policy.

Britain's island immunity from direct attack made possible some of the sense of security and disinterestedness requisite for a mediator. Yet the logic of experience at this juncture of her history left little room for pushing her detachment to the point of isolation. For over a century every major European conflict had embroiled her sooner or later. Her swollen national debt and trebled scale of taxation were daily reminders of the consequences of the most recent involvement. Thus Parliament did not disavow the Foreign Secretary, Lord Castlereagh, when he committed Britain to the Quadruple Alliance of 1815 with its pledge of joint action against any recurrence of French aggression and its plan for continuing top-level Congresses of the allies. Castlereagh could join fully in the tasks of implementing the peace treaties through the first critical years, generally exerting his influence on the side of moderation with respect to the status and obligations of the former enemy state. He did not part company with the Congress System until the more permanent features of the settlement had been put into operation. When the split came, it was occasioned by other grave issues.

This selective summary may suggest that all was clear sailing for British mediation and leadership in the paths of peace. On the contrary, the seas ran high at times, and there were many obstacles to be circum-navigated. At the peace conference, Britain's prestige was unmatched. She had played a chief role in organizing and financing a succession of coalitions against Napoleon and, though allies had risen and fallen, she had held on to the final allied triumph. Her army under Wellington in Spain had, with the Spanish allies, been the first to breach French home defenses. Moreover, Castlereagh, and Wellington, had been careful not to overstrain British credit with the allies. But later, in the 1820's, when Britain reacted against the conservatism of the absolutist governments of the Continent, they began to look on the parliamentary monarchy of Britain as almost worse than a republic and to regard some of her political leaders as revolutionaries as invidious as the Jacobins. Increas-ingly, they detested her free-speaking Parliament and abominated her uncontrolled and "licentious" press. The power of her wealth aroused envy, and her government was constantly suspected of seeking commercial advantage for her nationals in every corner of the globe. As Englishmen took to continental travels again, they strode about, too often like lords of creation, free with criticism and generous with unsought advice; and there were times when the Foreign Office manifested similar propensities. These were, perhaps, the liabilities of the virtues. The most serious diffi-culty was the fact that the British themselves had no miraculous powers with which to achieve all at once the full harmony of domestic and foreign policy needed for their role. The path of enlightened self-interest is often a difficult one to find even with a free press and parliamentary institu-tions. Certainly it took the British a little time.

THE CRISIS OF THE TWENTIES

The satisfactory liquidation of the more onerous treaty obligations imposed on France had come none too soon in 1818. Made possible by the postwar unity of the allied powers, it barely preceded the first serious rift in that unity. The depression of 1819 brought discontent and agita-tion in many parts of Western Europe and fear of revolution soon replaced fear of France. Even in Britain a wave of alarm swept the governing classes into passing the notorious "Six Acts." Continental governments not only turned to more drastic domestic repression but also tried to convert the Congress System into an international instrument for rigid maintenance of "legitimate" royal governments, intervening to suppress constitutional movements in Naples and in Spain. Britain, as a constitutional state, rather naturally recoiled from this absolutist doctrine of intervention; but Castlereagh's protests — and those of his more articulate successor (1822), George Canning — were futile. By 1823 she stood alone and indeed in some peril. Flushed with their easy victories in Naples and Spain, the autocrats then talked of crossing the ocean to restore Spanish authority in the revolted colonies, a project loaded with danger to British interests. It was the first great crisis and it shattered the postwar Congress System. Surmounted successfully from the British point of view, it was a turning point, not only with respect to the issue of a static versus a developing society, but also with respect to the character of the *Pax Britannica* itself.

How Canning met the problem is well known. He gave a timely warning that the British navy would be used to prevent the departure of French or other non-Spanish troops from Europe. Using his power of oratory to rouse the nation, he left no doubt of Britain's capacity and will to act on a matter like this where she had the interests and, on the seas, the means to act decisively. Continental governments were given sobering bases for calculating the risks before they committed themselves. Thanks to British sea power, Canning could resolve that if France controlled Spain (by occupation with moral support by the three Eastern Great Powers) it would not be Spain "with the Indies." By extending de jure recognition in 1825 to the Spanish colonies which were in revolt, he insured their independence. In this way, as he claimed, he "called the New World into existence to redress the balance in the Old" and so gave other forces time to develop. Divergent interests in the Greek war of independence soon produced a new alignment of the powers, breaking the solidarity of the absolutists and enabling him to bring Britain, France, and Russia together in 1827 for a change in the status quo favorable to the Greeks. Then, in 1830, France had her revolution, ridding herself of the legitimist Bourbon Charles X who preferred rather "to saw wood than to be a king of the English type." Britain's voice was promptly given for recognition of the new government of Louis Philippe and there was scarcely even talk of foreign intervention. Belgian independence was also allowed, again after revolution. Here the treaties which had joined Belgians to the Dutch in 1814, mainly at British insistence, were ultimately adjusted by agreement of the Concert powers after many sessions of their ambassadors in London. Within the decade, then, the boundary where the status quo held sway had been rolled back to the Rhine without precipitating war. The somewhat spectacular top-level consultations of the Congress System were abandoned, but the Concert itself continued to function through the more patient processes of ordinary diplomatic channels and conferences of ambassadors.

Canning might, perhaps, have used the British money market directly and with effective results both to check the autocrats and to strengthen liberal forces. He might have brought financial pressure to bear on the continental allies,[1] or have given government support to loans to the Spanish-American insurgents. This would certainly have gained him great popularity among the holders of defaulted Spanish-American bonds. But he refused, and he checked the zeal of British agents when they sought special rights for British trade. In his view, and in that of a long succession of British Foreign Secretaries, financial pressure was not a suitable instrument of state policy. They considered it prudent to know all about the foreign loans floated by British bankers but they did not regard them as an interest to be promoted or controlled by the state, let alone to be used as a means of bringing pressure to bear on foreign governments.[2] To control credit for this purpose would only multiply the subjects of state rivalry and friction. The most striking case of noninterference, which arouses amazement today, was the flotation of a loan in the London money market for Russia while an enemy state during the Crimean War. It was in "the ordinary way of business" and ought not to be interfered with, wrote the Foreign Secretary, Lord Clarendon.[3]

Yet this freedom to an enemy state to borrow in Britain was little more than a continuation in wartime of a practice that had become accepted as normal and proper in the international conflicts that occurred during the preceding peacetime. In the crisis of the early twenties, the question whether or not to close the London money market to particular

---

[1] Parliament once pressed for collection on a loan to Austria that had long been in default, but it never insisted on the closing of the money market to European governments. Happily there was no great interallied war loan problem to be liquidated after 1815, British financial aid during the war — some £ 55,000,000 in all — having been given in the form of nonrepayable subsidies. Only one small loan, that to Austria, troubled postwar relations. It had been floated in the London money market with the interest guaranteed, and subsequently paid, by the British government. Under pressure from Parliament and public following Austrian intervention in the Italies in 1821, the British government asked for a settlement. In 1823 a lump sum payment of £ 2,500,000, about one-sixth of the principal and compounded interest, was accepted in full payment. Rothschild floated a new Austrian loan in Britain to provide the funds. See J. H. Clapham, "Loans and Subsidies in Time of War, 1793–1814," *The Economic Journal*, 22:495–501 (1917); and Charles Kingsley Webster, *The Foreign Policy of Castlereagh, 1815–1822* (London, 1925), pp. 401–402.

[2] Leland Hamilton Jenks, *The Migration of British Capital to 1875* (New York, 1938), pp. 39–44, 115–125.

[3] Sir Herbert Maxwell, *Life and Letters of the Fourth Earl of Clarendon* (London, 1913), II, 107.

governments does not seem even to have been considered in official circles. In 1822 and 1823, substantial loans were floated in London for the two foremost autocratic states, Russia and Austria. These loans probably contributed something towards maintaining bridges of common interest between the opposed camps. Certainly noninterference avoided expanding the areas of conflict between their governments.

The stabilization of European currencies and the gradual establishment of the gold standard during the century also served to reduce the areas of governmental interference. For, although initially stabilization usually required some form of governmental action, once effected, it reduced or eliminated the temptation or the need to intervene directly or indirectly with the day by day operation of the commercial exchanges. Quite possibly this development was of greater long-term benefit to social and political moderation within the nations and to orderly process between them than the principle of "legitimacy." In this matter, too, certain features of British policy and practice were generally helpful. British loans after 1815 enabled European governments more quickly to put their financial houses in order and to stabilize currencies. Britain's own early return to a gold-based currency also set an example. As early as 1817, the Bank of England resumed gold payment at current rates on small notes. Two years later, Parliament decreed progressive steps for return to cash payment, at the prewar rates (£3 17s.10½d. an ounce) to be effective after 1 May 1821. It was perhaps too sudden a return to the old standard, and it had the bad fortune of coinciding with and accentuating the deflation of prices in the depression of 1819–1821.

Yet this example by the leading industrial and creditor nation of the day could not have signified greatly in the long run had Britain, with her strong creditor position, drawn in and held an undue part of the world's stock of monetary gold. General acceptance of gold standards, and the successful functioning of the gold mechanism in the international exchanges, required adequate distribution of gold through the world trading community. Through the nineteenth century, Britain's great exports of goods and services were closely matched by her imports of goods and services from other lands — with less and less governmental regulation or tax burden after 1842 — plus the loans her investors placed abroad. The result was a remarkable degree of equilibrium in British balance of payments. There was only a modest net inflow of gold into Britain during the century (see Chapter III, Table 4) and at no time an excessive accumulation of it there. Under these circumstances, the gold mechanism could function effectively with almost no governmental intervention.

LEADERSHIP BY EXAMPLE

These years of crisis in the 1820's are notable for the beginning of reforms in British commercial policy which were to blossom twenty years later into the most constructive and fruitful features of British leadership. It was as though, standing alone and in danger, the British began to appreciate the value of winning the favor of people with commercial interests and liberal views in other lands not only for their help in war, if it came to that, but also to draw their weight into the balance for peace. Canning hinted at the importance of the unrest in other lands when, in 1823, he warned that the next war might be a war of opinions. He recurred to this theme more explicitly in 1826 after Britain had launched reforms which stood in striking contrast to the reactionary policies pursued from one end of the Continent to the other. It would be, he said, a terrible war, a civil war, in which "this country could not . . . avoid seeing ranked under her banners all the restless and dissatisfied of any nation with which she might come in conflict." But, as befitted the spokesman of a mediating power, his words shaped a reflective warning rather than a threat:

It is the contemplation of this new power in any future war which excites my most anxious apprehension. It is one thing to have a giant's strength, but it would be another to use it like a giant. The consciousness of such strength is, undoubtedly, a source of confidence and security; but in the situation in which this country stands, our business is not to seek opportunities of displaying it, but to content ourselves with letting the professors of violent and exaggerated doctrines on both sides feel, that it is not their interest to convert an umpire into an adversary. . . . The consequence of letting loose the passions, at present chained and confined, would be to produce a scene of desolation which no man can contemplate without horror.[4]

To set an example of orderly progress which could be emulated might be to effect, with British gradualness, a double conversion. It might win radicals from the sense of futility which breeds recklessness and violence, on the one hand, and restrain governments from extreme repression, on the other. If this assumes a little too much with respect to motivation, it is scarcely an exaggeration with respect to results. In any case, there were plenty of changes that Britain could make with advantage to her own interests. Most of the reforms which were made in these years had often been advocated and were sound in themselves. What was different after 1822 was the energy exerted, especially by Canning's friend William Huskisson, to prepare and to pilot the measures through Parliament.

[4] Thomas Curson Hansard, *Parliamentary Debates*, XVI (1826), 368–369. Other reportings of this significant speech, with slightly variant wording, are given in Harold Temperley, *The Foreign Policy of Canning* (London, 1925), Appendix.

The commercial reforms promoted by Huskisson in 1824–1825 checked a rising tide of protectionism. Britain had entered the peace period with import duties raised for the sake of revenue to much higher levels than had prevailed before the war. For the most part they were specific duties and, as prices fell after the war, the burden which they imposed on trade values increased greatly.[5] On the Continent, too, tariff rates and regulations multiplied. The channels of legitimate trade were being slowly choked, the economic opportunities of the era blocked, and governments entangled in competitive restrictions. The worst features of eighteenth-century mercantilism were being revived.

The danger lurking in this kind of economic nationalism is illustrated by the outburst of one bellicose member of the British Parliament after Prussia had imposed discriminatory duties on foreign shipping. Although in principle the Prussian measures were not very different from those which Britain herself maintained, he denounced them as "the insolent dictation of a petty German prince to which our rejoinder should have been from the mouths of our cannon." His absurd outburst gave Huskisson the opportunity to squelch such notions and he promptly grasped it in the House of Commons with an arresting statement of a vital condition for peaceful relations between equally sovereign states:

I hope I shall never bear any share in the councils of England when a principle shall be set up that there is one rule of independence and sovereignty for the strong and another for the weak; when, abusing its naval superiority, England shall claim for herself either in peace or war, maritime rights which she refuses to acknowledge in other states, or shall, under any circumstances, either neutral or belligerent, impose upon others obligations from which she claims, under the like circumstances, to be herself exempt. To act as if there were one rule of international law for ourselves, and a different rule for other states, would be not only monstrous injustice, but the only course, I verily believe, by which our maritime power could be brought into jeopardy. Such a pretension would call for and warrant a combination of all the world to defeat it; and it is only in such a combination, acting together in a just cause, that this country can have anything to apprehend.[6]

The British government itself had realized the unwisdom of continuing to levy the high duties that had been imposed during the war. But emotional reaction against the income tax, joined with unreasoned conceptions of commercial self-interest, led Parliament to maintain the high protectionist tariff rates and regulations after the war. In 1816 the Chancellor of the Exchequer, Nicholas Vansittart, had proposed to Parliament the retention of the income tax to cover the deficit and

[5] See Chapter V.
[6] Hansard, *Parl. Deb.*, New Series, XVII (1827), 656–657.

perhaps to permit some reductions in other war levies, but he was over-whelmed by a parliamentary revolt. The majority voted to abolish the hated income tax lock, stock, and barrel, even ordering that the records be burned. The tariff duties remained. Moreover, the war had built up many vested interests, both on farm and in factory, that were fearful of their position under peacetime competition. Although successive officials continued to recognize the evils of extreme protection, they felt powerless to effect correction. The President of the Board of Trade, Frederick J. Robinson, frankly admitted in Parliament in 1817 the harm which import restrictions worked on the British export trade but lamented that when-ever he proposed to lower the barriers half the manufacturers in the country presented petitions and sent delegations against any liberaliza-tion of the laws.[7]

Happily, the political temper changed for the better when the business upturn of the mid-twenties brought an increase in trade and in revenue. Moreover, where Robinson had preferred to let growling dogs lie, his successor at the Board of Trade, William Huskisson, advanced boldly. Carefully preparing the case and supported by committees, he stated confidently that to reduce restrictions was not only good in itself but would also go far to produce good will and fair treatment abroad.[8] He persuaded Parliament in 1824 to reduce prohibitive duties to more mod-erate proportions, to allow free export of gold instead of licensing, to allow artisans to emigrate to practice or teach their crafts, to permit more explicitly the export of machinery under license, and to breach the Navi-gation Acts themselves by reciprocity treaties with other states. Free emigration of artisans and freer export of machinery were symbols that the secrets of the Industrial Revolution were not to be made another subject of division and competition between nations. As far as the British government was concerned, they were to be open to all on equal terms. Similarly, free export of gold was a token of the availability of financial credit without political interference. The rapid industrialization of other countries dates from this year. Something was accomplished by the reciprocity treaties also, but the process of negotiation was slow and piece-meal and accompanied by close bargaining so that the results fell short of the needs. As Sir James Graham said in 1849 when total repeal of the Navigation Acts was under discussion, the principle of reciprocity made

---

[7] Hansard, *Parl. Deb.*, Second Series, XXXV (1817), 1046–51.

[8] Various speeches in 1824 as reported in Hansard, *Parl. Deb.* See also Alexander Brady, *William Huskisson and the Liberal Reform* (London, 1928), pp. 73–102; and A. L. Lingel-bach, "William Huskisson and the Board of Trade," *American Historical Review*, 43:759–774 (1938).

"the interest of others the measure of our interest — I had almost said it makes the folly of others the limit of our wisdom." [9]

These reforms were, perhaps, as much as the country would stand at the time. After two more severe depressions Parliament was ready in 1842 to try the explicit experiment of free trade accompanied by a revival of the income tax — rather more than the government program rejected twenty-six years before.

In the Whig interval of the thirties far-reaching political reforms added something to the meaning of the *Pax*. If habits of peaceful change in domestic political affairs are a requisite to orderly adjustments in international matters, this was a significant addition. The old Parliament, in which the landed interests were predominant, reformed itself. By putting into practice the principle of representation by population, it carried through by due process of law, without the use of force or violence, a veritable revolution which brought the middle classes into a fair share of political power. A train of further institutional adjustments followed in the wake of this Great Reform Bill. It was a signal example of the possibilities which constitutional reform offered for class conciliation and it undoubtedly did much to convince the middle classes in Europe that political change was not inevitably followed, as in 1789, by revolution or a reign of terror. This example, like machinery, was available for export — at the choice of the importer. When Lord Palmerston later tried to force the product on unwilling governments, his doctrinaire and complacent advocacy raised angry retorts from scions of the old order abroad. Yet the revolutions of 1848, which he had sought to forestall, lent point to his admonitions. Britain after her reforms was troubled by nothing more serious than the Chartist revival — another petition for a broader parliamentarianism. The Continent was in turmoil, and many a prince, even the King of Prussia, scurried for cover under the mantle of a constitution.

British colonial policy in this period also contributed something toward emphasizing conciliation and peaceful development. That the leading naval and imperial power had exploited so few of the opportunities to expand her empire at the peace settlement, and that she now began to grant more substantial privileges of self-government to several of her colonies beginning after the Canada Act of 1840, even to the point of allowing them commercial autonomy when the Navigation Acts were repealed in 1849, carried a meaning far greater than this brief reference may imply.

[9] Hansard, *Parl. Deb.*, Third Series, CIV (1849), 662.

But the free-trade program which Sir Robert Peel launched in 1842 [10] was, in the commercial sphere, the capstone of the *Pax*, establishing a clear-cut contrast to narrowly nationalist economic policies. In the first place, its very success assured the new policy long life in Britain itself and wide appeal abroad. It promoted a phenomenal growth in prosperity and social welfare in Britain. The market value of British exports increased 282 per cent in the twenty-five years after 1842, more than twenty times as rapidly as in the preceding quarter century. Imports grew even more in amount though less in percentage, since they started from a larger base. Here was exemplification, par excellence, of the alluring possibilities for material improvement by peaceful process, and it made the whole system appear desirable for imitation — at least until Germany offered a rival example of equally rapid growth seemingly stimulated by the results of her wars of unification and promoted after 1879 by protection. In the second place, to have the markets of this giant trading nation open freely and steadily to the products of other lands was an enormous stimulus to economic improvement throughout the world. It promoted economic development abroad in another way as well. Thereafter, the British could and did lend their capital more freely with a growing proportion of it invested in productive enterprise.[11] They lent with greater prospect of security, too, not only because of more productive use, but also because the prices of goods by which payments of dividends or interest might be made were not penalized by tariff duties. If British free trade contributed only a little to the phenomenal growth in the value of world trade in the rest of the century — a growth which can be estimated at well over 400 per cent from 1840 to 1872–1873 and at nearly 1400 per cent to 1913, in contrast to about 75 per cent from 1800 to 1840 [12] — it was still a great deal. To open wider economic opportunities was to ease both domestic and international tensions for all the trading nations.

In the fifties and sixties the *Pax Britannica* in this broad meaning of the term was complete and at its height, and several signs indicated some European acceptance of British patterns of development. Railways, telegraphs, and machine methods of production were widely installed with considerable assistance from British capital, and from British contractors, technicians, and experience. These developments not only increased productivity, but also multiplied the commercial classes and, raising their proportionate interest in national and international affairs,

[10] See pp. 150–155.
[11] See Chapters III and VI.
[12] See Chapter VI, Table 27.

affected the policies of their respective states. In France, Napoleon III professed devotion to the "conquests of peace" and departed from this formula only in matters which would not seriously impair good relations with Britain. A reciprocity treaty with Britain in 1860 was followed by a succession of such treaties reducing French tariff barriers with neighboring states. Before the decade ran out Napoleon converted the Second Empire into a limited monarchy. In the Italian peninsula Piedmont, aided by French arms and British sympathy, broke the hold of Austria and united Italians under a constitutional monarchy. It took a war to make this possible, but the annexations in this case were subject to the test of plebiscites. Force was not the sole arbiter. In the Germanies after 1848, Prussia seemed at first to have turned the corner with her essay in constitutionalism and with increasing freedom of trade under the *Zollverein* which she organized. The Austrian government remained as obdurate and unyielding at home until after 1866 as she had been in the Italies and the Germanies. Farther east Russia, after the Crimean War, moved in the direction of a new order with the abolition of serfdom, judicial reforms, and the establishment of provincial assemblies and municipal councils.

THE DECLINE OF THE PAX BRITANNICA

But even while the *Pax Britannica* was at the height of success the conditions of decay were forming. The seemingly swift but secretly prepared movement of French troops to Piedmont for use against Austria in 1859 spread a wide alarm for security in this age of swift orders by electric telegraph and rapid execution by means of steam transport. It was now, as one alarmed debater put it in the House of Lords, "a word and a blow." Military preparedness — and with it militarism — revived, a trend most thoroughgoingly exemplified by Bismarck's pushing through the army program in Prussia in defiance of the House of Representatives after 1862. Bismarck soon put the new Prussian army to use. His three short and successful wars not only brought the German Empire into being by 1871, and shook the old balance of power, but they also gave a new lease of life to the notion that war could be a useful and profitable instrument of national policy. In the German case, the use of force was circumscribed only by considerations of *realpolitik*. There were no plebiscites to test or validate the annexations made by force. The victor was absolute sovereign, although Bismarck and his King, unlike Napoleon I, could limit objectives. The Concert, and the concept of the "Public Law of Europe," were correspondingly weakened.

During these critical days of the late sixties, a second turning point in the century, the British government had little success in guiding the course of events. Palmerston and the Foreign Secretary, Earl Russell, to be sure, showed some of the old impulses in the Danish affair in 1864 but, lacking an ally — the French also were undecided and hesitant and felt that the brunt of war would fall on their army as it had in the Crimea if they joined with Britain for a firm stand against Prussia — with a divided cabinet, and with a public grown complacent in the satisfactions of material success, they stopped short of effective diplomacy; they failed to organize a concert of the Powers capable of qualifying the success of Bismarck's "blood and iron" program by assuring a reasonable settlement in the general interest by multilateral agreement; and their strong words of warning stood as the mere bluff and bluster Bismarck judged them to be. They knew better than to outrun the will of the British people, among whom the old concern for international balance and orderly process was relaxed by two generations of relative freedom from any very serious threat to either principle. There was, too, a kind of optimistic belief that sound sense, however unaided, must triumph in the end. At any rate, it is clear in retrospect that Britain did not perform her mediating role with unity or integrated purpose in this decade. She failed to rally other powers into a common front against violent change. Prussia was allowed to credit its success in forming the German Empire purely to superior force. Little wonder if, in the new lexicon of realism, the power state, with its sovereignty absolute, gained more attention.

Thereafter, the *Pax Britannica*, like the Concert and the concept of the "Public Law of Europe," although far from dead, was under increasing challenge. Each state, Britain included, had to take its own security into primary account in shaping its policies. Military preparedness became the order of the day, and on the Continent all of the Great Powers developed large conscript armies backed by reservoirs of trained reserves. A revival of trade restrictions soon followed also, accompanied by an increasing amount of effort by continental governments more directly to promote the business interests of nationals abroad, and by a scramble for overseas possessions, a scramble in which Britain participated and made large acquisitions even, contrary to past practice, in areas where interests were but thinly developed at the time. Empire building became competitive once more, linked with the revived concern for security, and stimulated by hopes for exclusive areas of commercial expansion in a world segmented by tariff systems.

Amid this revival of economic nationalism and imperialism, Britain adhered to her free-trade policy and she remained the great trading center of the world. The fact that her markets remained freely open to goods of other countries may well have modified the force or checked the growth of militant nationalist tensions in the world. London continued to be the prime and flourishing center of international finance, promoting economic development abroad and operating with relative freedom from political control. But London was far less the diplomatic center of gravity. It had yielded a kind of bipolar position to Berlin where very different traditions and conceptions of interest were in the ascendant. Under these circumstances "the restless and dissatisfied" of other lands looked less steadily to British models; governments and peoples were more ready to embrace nationalist or imperialist programs in the search for material advancement or for security. The promising concert of balanced powers which had so long promoted peace and had permitted a productive degree of internationalism in economic affairs yielded to fixed military alliances and competition for power. Europe and the world were moving to the first general war of the twentieth century.

II

REAL VALUES IN BRITISH FOREIGN
TRADE, 1796–1853

One cannot go very far in appraising Britain's role in the international
economy of the nineteenth century without more exact knowledge of
British foreign trade and services than has been available. It is well known
in general terms that British trade, and British services such as shipping,
insurance, and finance, played a large part in the economic life of the
trading world, but the values and rates of development of each are unduly
imprecise or uncertain, particularly in the first half of the century. While
it is scarcely feasible to bring all the elements in the complex international
economic life of Britain into precise focus, it is possible to map out some
of the major elements in rather close approximation and accordingly to
reduce the area of conjecture or speculation.

One of the elements which needs to be determined more closely is the
value of British merchandise trade in the first half of the century. The
"official" values which have long been used are not realistic measures of
current market values. They were started at the end of the seventeenth
century when the English began to keep records of their imports and
exports in terms of money values. Tables of prices were prepared first for
England, and subsequently for Scotland and for Ireland with the rates
based, it is said, on market conditions at the time. Some adjustments in
the initial valuations were made in the early years, but thereafter, for
over a century and a half, the same prices were used in calculating
"official" values.[1] For imports and re-exports they supplied the sole basis
for computing money values until 1854. For exports of domestic produce
and manufactured goods, however, a concurrent series of declared values
was begun when a convoy tax was imposed ad valorem in 1798; but this
series, though continued after the war, has been overshadowed by the
"official" valuation which attained something of the respectability of a
time-hallowed tradition. Year after year through peace and war, dearth
and plenty, high prices and low, the clerks meticulously multiplied their

[1] G. N. Clark, *Guide to English Commercial Statistics, 1696–1782* (London, 1938), pp.
8–12, 40–41.

quantities by these unchanging rates. British "official" trade values became progressively more useless as measures of current market values until the system was reformed in 1854[2] and historians and economists have been faced with frustration or distortion in any question dependent on a fairly accurate knowledge of the course, or the terms, or the balance of British trade in the period.

The problem of determining what British trade values actually were is not insoluble for the nineteenth-century part of the period. It is the purpose here to survey briefly the main features of the problem and the attempts that have been made to solve it, and then to present a set of estimated real values of British imports and re-exports beginning with the year 1796. This is as far back as it seems practical to go. Declared values of exports for co-ordinate use are not available until 1798 and it is scarcely possible to project estimates of the value of export goods, which were predominantly manufactured, more than two years further back with any confidence. If the import and re-export values constructed here are valid, Britain was, contrary to common assumption and in spite of her head start in applying machine techniques, an importing country throughout this period.

ERRORS DERIVED FROM THE OFFICIAL VALUES

It may be doubted whether the "official" values ever supplied a really correct picture of the state of British foreign trade. There were some curious discrepancies in the prices used that weaken confidence in their validity as a measure of market value at any time. Few articles were listed at precisely the same rate for each of the three kingdoms, and the differences are sometimes much larger than can be accounted for by the different dates at which the price tables for the three kingdoms were set up. In several cases also, the same commodities were put down for the same kingdom at radically different prices for import and re-export.[3] One might suppose that a large spread between the import and re-export valuations reflected the monopolistic colonial practices still generally prevalent when the tables took form. But why a large difference on some colonial articles and none at all on others? Such peculiarities suggest that ideas were as influential as facts in determining the price lists.

Whatever the original validity of the "official" prices, market values

[2] After a new method of valuation was set up in 1854, the old system was continued simultaneously and the results were printed annually until as late as 1869 in *Parliamentary Papers*, "Accounts and Papers (1) Financial: Trade and Navigation."

[3] The lists were published in *Parl. Pap.*, 1826 (385), XXII, 3–10.

changed a great deal during the five generations in which they were used. When price levels were high in the Napoleonic period, the declared value of exports in the aggregate regularly exceeded the "official" ratings — by as much as 80 per cent in 1803. Thereafter, with the fall in export prices which followed wider use of machine processes, and with postwar deflation, this relationship was gradually reversed. By 1854 the old "official" prices overvalued exports in the aggregate by 120 per cent. In the latter year when a new system was set up, re-exports were overrated in the "official" values by 60 per cent. Imports, on the other hand, were worth 19 per cent more by the new computed price method applied in 1854 than by the old system. Altogether, then, the "official" values utterly misrepresented the actual conditions of trade. Instead of the favorable balance of £ 119.8 million in visible trade shown by the "official" figures for 1854, there was in fact a negative balance of £ 36.6 million. The "official" values had become a caricature of market realities.

This unreliability of the "official" values — by the nineteenth century at least — has been too little appreciated and has done great harm. By recording the amazingly rapid and steady growth in the volume of British exports in value terms, and by showing always a favorable balance of trade, the "official" values confirmed, and seemingly justified, lingering mercantilist notions and may have contributed to delaying the adjustment of British thought and practice to the real needs for a healthy economic life.[4] They still confuse thought and teaching on the economic development of this most studied industrial country. To this day the "official" figures, even on exports on which the declared values are available from 1798, are quoted, often without any warning that, though useful perhaps as a rough over-all indication of quantity change, they are not to be trusted as measures of market value. Textbooks, special studies, and even seemingly careful statistical volumes, all too commonly use the "official" values, with the pound sterling sign prefixed, to indicate that exports doubled and redoubled in value in the first half of the nineteenth century.[5] Although

---

[4] Officials in the Board of Trade realized, of course, the limitations of these statistics. See, for example, George Richardson Porter, for many years head of the statistical department of the Board of Trade, *The Progress of the Nation*, 3 vols. (London, 1836–43), II, 98–100. Porter was chief statistician in the Board of Trade from 1834 to 1840. But the peculiar character of the "official" values was rarely explained in the annual publications seen by Parliament and public.

[5] Two examples will suffice. Walter Phelps Hall and William Stearns Davis, *The Course of Europe since Waterloo* (New York, 1951), p. 148, cite the official values of exports for 1821, 1831, 1841, and 1851 to demonstrate "an unparalleled record" of growth. Actually, the increase for a later thirty-year period, from 1841 to 1871, is almost as dramatic in real values as is this one in fictitious values. A very serious statistical case, widely quoted, is William Page, *Commerce and Industry* (London, 1919), II, 71. Page

the series of declared values of exports are probably reasonably reliable, as will be shown, they are all too commonly ignored.

It is not quite clear how to account for this persistent predilection for the wrong figures on exports. Possibly the preference for them is explained by the fact that the "official" values confirm the easy assumption that Britain's lead in developing machine techniques forced the growth of her exports as much in value as in volume. It may be forgotten that machine processes tended to reduce prices as well as costs. Or the taproot of the difficulty may be that word "official." It carries weight and gives a false sense of security even to those who should know its limitations.

It makes a good deal of difference which set of figures on exports one uses in interpreting this period in British economic history. By the "official" method of accounting, British commercial policies in the high protectionist period from 1815 to 1842, for example, seem to have been sound, successfully nursing British industries into increasingly vigorous life. The argument Bismarck used when he turned the German Empire toward protection in 1879 seems to be justified completely. England, "the mighty athlete," had entered the fray of free competition only after hardening her sinews under high tariffs. But if the declared values of exports are authentic, it may be concluded that Britain adopted her free-trade policy after a period of twenty-five years of relative stagnation in the values of her export trade. By these figures, exports of the United Kingdom in 1836, the best year in the decade before Peel's first free-trade budget, were worth only 3 per cent more than in 1815. Or to take depression years, they were scarcely 14 per cent more in 1842 than in 1816, an interval in which population rose by about 40 per cent and the real value of net imports increased by about 55 per cent. This suggests hardening of the arteries instead of the sinews and it more adequately accounts for the symptoms of rising social blood pressure which were evident at the time. Adoption of a free-trade policy may have been an escape from premature senescence.

THE DECLARED VALUES OF EXPORTS

The declared valuations begun in 1798 can be accepted as a fairly accurate statement of the real value of British exports. No one was in a better position to know the market value of their goods, many of them

---

cites the "official" values from 1815 to 1853 with the completely misleading notation that for the exports declared values are given "throughout": *ibid.*, II, xi. Even so careful a writer as Elie Halévy has been misled by this unfortunate error: *A History of the English People, 1830–1841* (New York, 1937), p. 284 n.

highly manufactured, than the exporters themselves. Indeed, this method affords the only practicable way to secure correct market values for manufactured goods; and when the system of recording trade statistics was overhauled in 1854, declared values were retained as real values for exports.[6] In the war years when the ad valorem convoy duty was in force there was possibly some incentive to understate value. After the war, there was little reason for undervaluation for most commodities,[7] and from 1813 on there was a penalty provided by law for fraudulent returns.[8] The declared values are not perfect. As late as 1859, the commissioner of customs complained of carelessness on the part of exporters in filing their returns, and more particularly of failure to notify the customhouse when goods declared for export were not shipped. But in his opinion the net effect of easygoing ways was not undervaluation but overvaluation.[9] All in all, we may fairly conclude that the declared values are reasonably reliable. They may overstate real values somewhat, but they err far less than the "official" figures.

THE PROBLEM OF IMPORT AND RE-EXPORT VALUES

The declared values, then, are fairly dependable as market values for British exports from 1798 on. If there were also reasonably reliable series on the real values of imports and re-exports for the same years, we might see the merchandise trade position of British as it actually was. Happily, British imports and re-exports were predominantly raw materials and foodstuffs. In contrast to Britain's exports, there were only a few imports whose market values were very much influenced by special factors of design or workmanship. It should be possible, therefore, with the aid of commodity price series, to compute the real values of imports and re-exports and thus to fill in this serious gap in our knowledge of the British economy before 1854.

Several attempts have been made at one time and another to estimate these real values. With the exception of the detailed computations of Thomas Irving and Robert Marshall for Great Britain and Ireland, respectively, as an average for the years 1796–1798 "agreeably to the prices

[6] *Parl. Pap.*, 1857 [2186], III, 121–122.

[7] The few heavy export taxes were specific duties, for example, 17s. on each cauldron of coal, affording no motive for misrepresenting real value because it had no bearing on the tax. Ad valorem export duties, payable for many years after 1815 on some commodities, were extremely light — 0.5 per cent — too trivial to encourage undervaluation. See customs schedules in *Parl. Pap.*, 1898, LXXXV.

[8] A fine of £ 20 and detention of the goods. — 53 Geo. III cap. 98.

[9] *Parl. Pap.*, 1859, sess. 2 [2540], XIV, 16–17.

current," [10] the early efforts made before the days of systematic studies of prices are not very reliable. In no case was a continuous series computed. When price series were available by the middle of the nineteenth century, interest in the subject had apparently died out. It was not until the marked revival of attention to international trade balances in the chaotic years after World War I that further efforts were made to resolve the riddle of Britain's real trading status in the earlier postwar era. In the 1930's two interesting attempts were made and published, one by Edward V. Morgan,[11] the other, covering a much longer period, by Werner Schlote.[12] A brief examination of the methods employed may throw some light on the procedures that are necessary. The results achieved by both are certainly better than the "official" returns, but both have avoidable flaws that reduce their reliability as estimates or approximations.

Morgan's series is based on a sample method of procedure. Using Norman J. Silberling's prices, he calculates the real values of some nineteen articles of import and ten of re-export for each year from 1805 to 1821. These samplings constitute a varying proportion of the total flow, ranging from 37 to 53 per cent for imports and from 22 to 37 per cent for re-exports, measured by "official" values. Assuming these are reasonably typical of the whole list, Morgan simply multiplies the total "official" value for each year by the ratio of his real to the "official" value of the sample.[13]

---

[10] *Parl. Pap.*, "Commercial Accounts," 1800, pp. 5–11, 43–51. Thomas Irving was inspector general of imports and exports for Great Britain; Marshall held the same office for Ireland.

William Irving, later inspector general of customs, also presented to Parliament statements on "actual values" of British imports and re-exports in the first decade of the nineteenth century, *e.g.*, *Parl. Pap.*, 1812 (63), (271) and (281), X. Although he stated to the Bullion Committee that he had secured his prices from merchants, he seems to have proceeded by rule of thumb thereafter, merely doubling the "official" value of imports and adding about 60 per cent to those of re-exports, then making a uniform deduction each year for what he considered to be "official" overvaluation of coffee. His very brief evidence rather suggests that he was anxious to show a favorable balance of trade: *Parl. Pap.*, "Bullion Report," 1810, III, 137–138, 144–146.

[11] E. V. Morgan, "Some Aspects of the Bank Restriction Period, 1797–1821," *Economic History*, 3:205–221 (1939).

[12] Werner Schlote, *Entwicklung und Strukturwandlungen des englischen Aussenhandels von 1700 bis zur Gegenwart* (Jena, 1938); translated into English with notes by William Henry Chaloner and William Otto Henderson as *British Overseas Trade from 1700 to the 1930's* (Oxford, 1952), pp. 30–34, 120–121. References here and elsewhere are to the English edition.

[13] Unfortunately, the series is marred by some statistical inconsistencies. British imports from Ireland seem to be included for the years 1805 to 1819 but excluded for the years 1820 to 1821; British re-exports to Ireland are included for 1805 to 1817 but excluded for 1818 to 1821; and in the export series of declared values, British exports to Ireland are included for 1805 to 1816 but United Kingdom figures used for 1817 to 1821. No notation is made of these curiously selected shifts.

Morgan's method is not well suited to the special nature of the problem. The valuations of the samples are tied to the qualities used in the price series without allowance for import of goods of other grades. A more serious weakness is that too few articles are included in the samples. The ratio of real to "official" value differs so much from commodity to commodity [14] that it is of paramount importance, if a sampling method is to be used, that the list be a large one. In fact, a sampling method is not satisfactory in dealing with this problem since it is uncertain, even improbable, that the ratio of the articles in the residue was approximately the same as that of the sample.

To control all the variables and to calculate real values with absolute precision is scarcely possible. Even if one could employ such a company of clerks as prepared the original "official" returns to work over the quantity of records in detail year by year, gaps in price data would still leave some elements of uncertainty. All that can reasonably be aimed at is an approximation by methods which should offer a fair degree of reliability or probability. Such an approximation is much more difficult to achieve, and the results more exasperatingly uncertain, for the investigator who limits his frame of reference to this early period alone. Silberling, working in these years, came to the conclusion, "after many attempts and much consideration," that it was "wholly impracticable to reduce official values to even approximate real values." [15] What is needed is a method that will control the major variables and will afford some check or test to indicate the degree of reliability attributable to the results. These requirements can be met by taking as the starting point the period from 1854 to 1869 when the old system was continued side by side with the new. Indeed, these years are the only satisfactory point of departure.

Schlote has in part taken advantage of this opportunity. His series, which extends from 1801 to 1860, uses 1854–1860 as base years. While he does not explain precisely all the steps and expedients he employed, he does state that his method takes account of (1) the quantities of the commodities of import and re-export each year from 1814 to 1860 as measured in the aggregate by the volume series which he prepared for other purposes, and (2) current values, which are determined, however, simply by means of William S. Jevons' general commodity index used in relation to the

---

[14] The price of West Indian cotton in 1805 was over three times the "official" rate of 7¾d. per pound, while that of East Indian cotton was over twice the "official" rate of 7d. On the other hand, the price of coffee in 1805 was rather close to the "official" rate of £ 7 per cwt. Ordinary Jamaica sold in bond at an average of only £ 7/16/-.

[15] N. J. Silberling, "Financial and Monetary Policy of Great Britain During the Napoleonic Wars," *The Quarterly Journal of Economics*, 38:229 (1924).

average of the new computed real values for his base years, 1854 to 1860.[16]

Schlote does not project these estimates constructed with Jevons' index beyond his base years to test them further against the real values.[17] However, these seven base years offer some pragmatic test of the adequacy of his method. The results, though much better than the "official" values, are only fairly accurate. The errors in these base years range up to 7.4 per cent on imports, up to 14.5 per cent on re-exports, and up to 23.5 per cent on the balance of trade. Had he utilized Jevons' index to its terminal date in 1865 to project his estimates forward through the years 1861 to 1865 when the American Civil War brought a wild rise in cotton prices, he would have put his method to stiffer test — a test much needed as a clue to the degree of reliability attributable to his estimates for the years of rapid price change during and after the Napoleonic Wars. Had he done so, much larger errors would most certainly have shown up with the use of Jevons' general index.

It is precisely this use of a general index with his two volume series that explains the size of the errors in some of the base years and that raises doubts about the reliability of the estimates for other years in the series. The two volume series themselves are open to some doubts.[18] But the use of a general commodity price index cannot produce very precise results with aggregate volumes. A general index, unless it is weighted — and here the weighting would have to be carefully revised year by year — averages prices. Components of small quantity importance in the actual flow of trade have as much influence in determining the average as do commodities of large volume. If prices of all articles moved always in the same direction and at the same rate, Schlote's method would be a more satisfactory one. They rarely do so. In this period prices sometimes varied as much in relation to one another as did the quantities imported or re-exported. To depend on a general price index, therefore, was to throw away a large part of the precision possible. Clearly, the particular price history of each article must be taken into account through each year of the series.

[16] To estimate values for the years 1801–1812 for which he did not have quantity data with which to construct his own volume series, Schlote adjusted and used the annual "official" values with Jevons' general index.

[17] Schlote does, however, compare the results by his method with Board of Trade values from 1854 to 1934, but using Augustus Sauerbeck's index, in the thought that this constitutes a "direct check" of his results with Jevons' index for the earlier period. As closely as one can judge from the rather small diagrams done in logarithmic scale, the errors run to 10 per cent or more on imports in the 1860's. As is to be expected, the errors are much higher on re-exports on several occasions. *British Overseas Trade*, pp. 32, 34.

[18] See Appendix.

DATA AND METHODS FOR CONSTRUCTING MARKET VALUES

As suggested above, there is probably no feasible method for solving with absolute accuracy this problem of real values of imports and re-exports. What is needed is a reasonable compromise between precision and practicability. The nature of the data dictates the lines of the compromise.

What we have to work with is as follows: (1) A series of "official" values itemized for most of the commodities of import and re-export and published regularly from 1804 to 1869.[19] These values, it will be recalled, were based on price tables drawn up much earlier and were sadly out of date by the nineteenth century. The degree of departure from real values differed markedly from commodity to commodity. The proportions each commodity bore to the total flow of trade varied greatly from year to year, as did also the proportions of the various qualities of some commodities. Moreover, in several cases the tables set very different rates on the same kind of article entering and leaving England, Scotland, and Ireland. Some allowance for these variables must be made in any use of the "official" values. (2) Real values computed by the customhouse on the basis of actual market prices from 1854 on. Thus the "official" and the real-value series overlap for a period of sixteen years. (3) Price series and quantity records for many, but not all, of the more important commodities of British import and re-export.

To take into account as many of these data as possible, I have used the following procedure: First, from the important articles of import and re-export for the years just following 1854, forty-six commodities or groups of commodities of import and twenty-six of re-export were ultimately selected in accordance with (1) the availability of relevant price series over at least a substantial part of the half century when real values were to be determined and (2) the accuracy of the results when tested against the computed real values from 1854 to 1869. Second, using the years 1858–1860 as base years,[20] the annual "official" value of each commodity was multiplied by the ratio of the real value computed by the customhouse to the "official" value for the base years.[21] To allow for price

[19] Reported annually in *Parl. Pap.*, "Accounts and Papers (1) Financial: Trade and Navigation."

[20] In a very few cases, 1854–56 were used as base years.

[21] By using a price ratio based on the new computed real values of 1858–60, instead of the simpler method of quantity multiplied by price current, some allowance was made — the same as that by the customhouse in those years — for the different qualities of a commodity imported and re-exported. Undoubtedly the proportions changed from year to year, but it is not possible to make very exact allowance for this except in a few cases like coffee, cotton, sugar, and wool, where data on country of origin afforded an indication of quality and permitted more adequate annual allowance. There is sometimes

change from year to year, the figure thus obtained was multiplied by the price index pertaining to it in order to arrive at the real value for each year. Next, the "official" values of these commodities were added together for each year and this total was subtracted from the total "official" value of the imports and re-exports respectively to secure the "official" value of the residue or remainder, the articles not treated with separate ratios and indexes. The "official" value [22] of this residue was then similarly multiplied by its price ratio for the base years 1858–1860 and by a general price index to determine its real value for each year. Finally, the estimated real values of the commodities and of the residue were added, making the total estimated real value for each year.

The commodities separately treated in this way represented a fairly high proportion of the total volume. Measured by "official" values, they constituted 81 per cent of imports and 80 per cent of re-exports in 1869, and 83 per cent and 81 per cent respectively in 1854. As the distance from the base years grew, the number of commodities and groups of commodities separately treated declined for various reasons.[23] By 1814, it had fallen to thirty-five for imports and twenty for re-exports, still representing, however, a high proportion of the totals — 81 per cent and 80 per cent, respectively. In 1805, thirty-three import commodities or groups constituted 77 per cent of the total whereas seventeen re-exports constituted 72 per cent. By 1798 imports were down to thirty, constituting 67 per cent of the total "official" value, and re-exports were down to fourteen, 53 per cent of the total.[24] Both imports and re-exports dropped off further in number by 1796, namely to twenty-one and twelve re-

---

another limitation on strict accuracy. This derives from the fact that the prices of the various qualities of a commodity do not always move in the same direction or at exactly the same rate as the prices of the single quality used in the price series.

[22] "Official" values had to be used here since they supplied the only ready means of making some allowance for the differing relative values and the differing standards of measurement of the variety of components. "Official" values also took account of those articles admitted by value rather than by quantity, though the amount here was very small.

[23] Most of the articles dropped between 1804 and 1840 were either latecomers in trade or were trivial in importance, too small to be listed separately in the annually published returns by "official" values in the early years. With each change, the price ratio of the residue was recomputed to allow for the price ratio of the commodity thus dropped from separate treatment and added to the residue.

[24] Measured by real values or estimated real values, the proportions represented by the commodities computed in separate series diverged slightly from proportions by "official" values. The proportions of real values are as follows:

	1869	1854	1814	1805	1798	1796
Imports (%)	79	83	83	80	70	70
Re-exports (%)	81	75	76	65	56	57

spectively, but the proportions of the totals remained fairly steady at 69 and 51 per cent.

The test years were invaluable in indicating the need for some variety in the treatment of the different commodity series. For most articles, the "official" values are a fair measure of changes in volume from year to year and could be used instead of direct quantity figures, thus simplifying a little the bookkeeping involved in computing the residue each year. In cases where "official" rates of valuation differed appreciably for England, Scotland, and Ireland, with notable variations in the flow to these sections, it was necessary to use quantity figures, recording also the "official" values for use in computing the residue. It was necessary also, because of wide fluctuations of flow and price over the years, to break down some commodities into separate series by quantity and by country of origin such as: East Indian and other cotton; British and foreign sugar and coffee; Australian, Saxon, and Spanish wool. And it was clearly necessary to treat separately related items with quite disparate prices, such as saltpeter and cubic nitre (1840–1869); raw, waste, thrown, and manufactured silk; and copper ore, regulus, and bricks (1833–1869). In a sense, this meant covering over sixty commodities of import rather than the forty-six referred to above. By and large the decisions were made on a pragmatic basis. Quite elaborate breakdowns were tried with some articles and found to be less successful in the test years.

Perhaps the most important matter was that of the price series. For the years from 1846 to 1869, the problem was not very difficult. Augustus Sauerbeck's individual commodity indexes, based on monthly quotations,[25] were suitable for the majority of the articles covered. Thomas Tooke's quarterly quotations were also used for some articles from 1846 to 1857 and a sequence was made for the later years from the computed average prices used by the customhouse after 1853. In these few cases, 1854–1856 were used as base years to promote consistency for the earlier years, though somewhat at the expense of the test years. For the residue of imports and re-exports, treated as a lump, Sauerbeck's general index was modified by removing certain irrelevant articles, such as coal, and by strengthening others. As was to be expected, this residue offered the greatest difficulty, chiefly because of variations in volume of component articles (and therefore of ratios) from those of the base years. In the test years it showed the largest departures from accuracy, though less deviation proportionately than some of its components like currants and oranges,

[25] A. Sauerbeck, "On the Prices of Commodities and the Precious Metals," *Journal of the Statistical Society*, 49:632–648 (London, 1886).

which refused to yield satisfactorily to separate treatment through lack of sufficiently relevant price series. The law of averages does give some aid when other expedients fail and when not called on too often.

For the years before 1846, the problem of price series was more difficult. There were no price indexes for separate commodities, such as Sauerbeck's, ready at hand. Jevons' group indexes are of little value for application to particular commodities. It was necessary to construct a price index for each commodity treated. For this purpose chief reliance was placed on the series of monthly quotations for many commodities in bond or with duties deducted which were prepared by Arthur David Gayer, Walt Whitman Rostow, Anna Jacobson Schwartz for their study, *The Growth and Fluctuation of the British Economy, 1790–1850*,[26] and which were generously lent in typescript for this purpose.[27] Transfer to these was made on the basis of the estimated real values for the five years 1846–1850. For corn, the prices of the *English Gazette* were used, but were modified by a rough deduction to allow for duties under the sliding scales, taking for this purpose the rates applicable to foreign grains when prices were high, for colonial grains when prices were low. For tea, the average import price series prepared by the customhouse was used throughout.[28] Tooke's quarterly quotations were again resorted to for a few commodities. For rice, Arthur H. Cole's prices for Charleston and New York ordinary were used from 1830 to 1850. For the residue, Silberling's general index [29] was applied without modification.

THE TEST YEARS

Within this framework the same methods and procedures were applied for the years 1796 to 1853 as in the test years 1854–1857 and 1861–1869. The innumerable arithmetical operations have been checked carefully by other hands to eliminate clerical errors.[30] The test years should, therefore, furnish some indication, though by no means a guarantee, of the degree of reliability which can be attached to the estimates of real values in the other years of the series.

[26] (Oxford, 1953).

[27] I am particularly indebted to Mrs. Schwartz for the loan of these series over a period of several years for recurrent reference, and for much valuable advice also.

[28] *Parl. Pap.*, 1898, LXXXV, 203–205.

[29] Arthur Harrison Cole, *Wholesale Commodity Prices in the United States, 1700–1861* (Cambridge, Mass., 1938), I, 154; II, 168, 359; N. J. Silberling, "British Prices and Business Cycles, 1779–1850," *Review of Economic Statistics*, 5:219–262 (1923).

[30] I am indebted to the Social Science Research Council for a grant-in-aid which made this possible. I am indebted also to Miss Ruth Crandall for the care and patience with which she performed almost the whole of this arduous task.

In two major respects these test years supply a rather severe trial of the adequacy of the methods used for coping with the variables involved. First, it was a period of very rapid changes. Steam navigation, just coming into its own on the busier freight routes, was beginning to multiply the sources of supply as well as the range of quality and price of British imports. The completion of the British free-trade policy, which made the whole United Kingdom a kind of free port, combined with the wider application of machine processes on the Continent, promoted a tremendous growth of British re-exports — an increase of 153 per cent by value from 1854 to 1869. Second, the Crimean War and especially the American Civil War brought violent price fluctuation in several important articles of British trade. Chief among these, raw cotton made up fully 17 per cent of the total value of British imports and 37 per cent of the value of re-exports in 1860. As supplies fell off, prices rose to fantastic heights, by 1865 averaging 440 per cent above the 1860 level, with a frantic searching for new sources of supply of all qualities.

In Table 1 and the following charts, the estimates of real value of imports and re-exports so constructed are compared with the new real values computed by the customhouse for the base and test years. The percentages of error are small. With respect to the balance of trade they are more substantial, however, but the percentages here are calculated, of course, not on the total value of trade flow, but on the balance itself, a much smaller base. In terms of pounds sterling, or in comparison with the total value of British foreign trade, the amounts themselves are small. The old "official" values are given also in Table 1 since they are rarely seen for the years after 1853. They show decisively their own inadequacy as measures of value in all categories.

The errors in the constructed real values for the test years are relatively small. For imports, the estimates correspond almost exactly with the real values computed by the customhouse in years of moderately stable or declining prices even when there was considerable change in volume relationships. The largest errors occur in years when many prices advanced rapidly, as in 1854, 1857, and 1861–1864, producing excessive estimates.[31] On an average of the thirteen test years the estimates on imports exceed real values by less than 0.75 per cent. For re-exports the errors are larger with a less distinguishable pattern of deviation, although they tend to be

---

[31] Possibly because importers succeeded in buying a little ahead of the price rise. In the method followed here, the imports and re-exports for the year as a whole are related by the price index to the annual average of the monthly quotations. A precision method would require at least monthly quantities with monthly quotations.

TABLE I. BASE YEARS AND TEST YEARS IN CONSTRUCTING REAL VALUES [a]

(All values in millions of pounds)

	Old "Official" Values				Real Values Prepared by the Customhouse				Constructed Real Values					
	Imports	Exports	Re-exports	Balance	Imports (computed)	Exports (declared)	Re-exports (computed)	Balance	Imports	(per cent error)	Re-exports	(per cent error)	Balance	(per cent error)
1854	124.1	214.1	29.8	+119.8	152.4	97.2	18.6	−36.6	154.1	(+1.1)	18.7	(+0.5)	−38.2	(+ 4.4)
1855	117.3	226.9	31.5	+141.1	143.5	95.7	21.0	−26.8	143.3	(−0.1)	20.4	(−2.9)	−27.2	(+ 1.5)
1856	131.9	258.5	33.4	+160.0	172.5	115.8	23.4	−33.3	172.6	(+0.1)	22.9	(−2.1)	−33.9	(+ 1.6)
1857	136.2	255.4	30.8	+150.0	187.8	122.1	24.1	−41.6	192.2	(+2.3)	24.3	(+0.8)	−45.8	(+10.1)
1858	138.2	271.7	33.9	+167.4	164.6	116.6	23.2	−24.8	165.2	(+0.4)	22.9	(−1.3)	−25.7	(+ 3.6)
1859	145.6	297.4	37.2	+189.0	179.2	130.4	25.3	−23.5	177.7	(−0.8)	25.4	(+0.4)	−21.9	(− 6.8)
1860	164.7	315.7	43.5	+194.5	210.5	135.9	28.6	−46.0	208.9	(−0.8)	29.1	(+1.7)	−43.9	(− 4.6)
1861	171.2	289.3	50.2	+168.3	217.5	125.1	34.5	−57.9	223.3	(+2.7)	34.5	(0.0)	−63.7	(+10.0)
1862	160.7	240.6	51.0	+130.9	225.7	124.0	42.2	−59.5	229.2	(+1.5)	42.1	(−0.2)	−63.1	(+ 6.1)
1863	171.9	258.2	54.9	+141.2	248.9	146.6	50.3	−52.0	256.2	(+2.9)	50.4	(+0.2)	−59.2	(+13.8)
1864	174.0	267.2	55.0	+148.2	275.0	160.4	52.2	−62.4	279.7	(+1.7)	53.7	(+2.9)	−65.6	(+ 5.1)
1865	181.8	301.6	62.4	+182.2	271.1	165.8	53.0	−52.3	268.6	(−0.9)	54.1	(+2.1)	−48.7	(− 6.9)
1866	201.2	348.5	64.4	+211.7	295.3	188.9	50.0	−56.4	292.9	(−0.8)	51.8	(+3.6)	−52.2	(− 7.4)
1867	201.1	361.8	64.8	+225.5	275.2	181.0	44.5	−49.7	273.1	(−0.8)	46.0	(+3.4)	−46.1	(− 7.0)
1868	220.9	381.1	69.5	+229.7	294.7	179.7	48.1	−66.9	294.4	(−0.1)	49.0	(+1.8)	−65.7	(− 1.8)
1869	224.3	389.0	67.1	+231.8	295.5	190.0	47.1	−58.4	296.9	(+0.5)	48.6	(+3.2)	−58.3	(− 0.2)

a Comparison of the old "official" figures for the trade of the United Kingdom, of new customhouse figures, and of those constructed by use of price ratios and price series, in the base years (1858–60) and the test years (1854–57, 1861–69).

CHART I. BASE YEARS AND TEST YEARS : IMPORTS

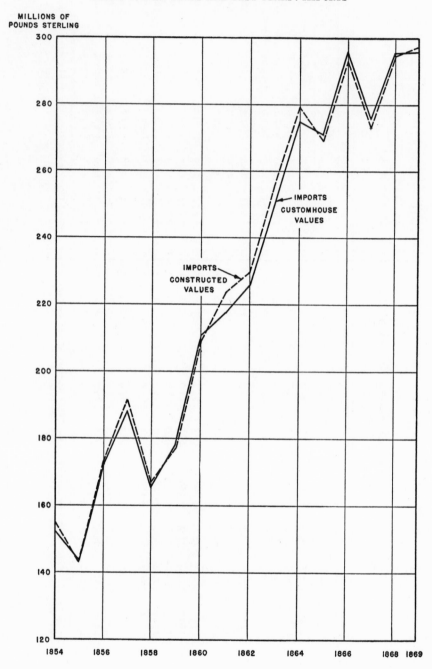

MILLIONS OF
POUNDS STERLING

IMPORTS
CUSTOMHOUSE
VALUES

IMPORTS
CONSTRUCTED
VALUES

CHART 2. BASE YEARS AND TEST YEARS: RE-EXPORTS

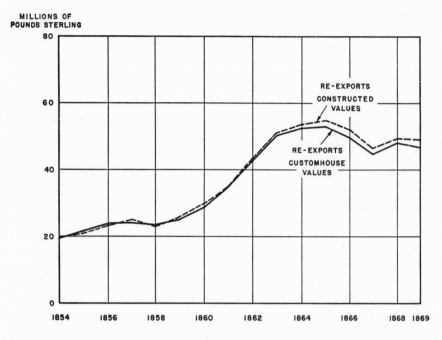

MILLIONS OF
POUNDS STERLING

RE-EXPORTS
CONSTRUCTED
VALUES

RE-EXPORTS
CUSTOMHOUSE
VALUES

80

60

40

20

0

1854   1856   1858   1860   1862   1864   1866   1868 1869

CHART 3. BASE YEARS AND TEST YEARS: MERCHANDISE TRADE BALANCE

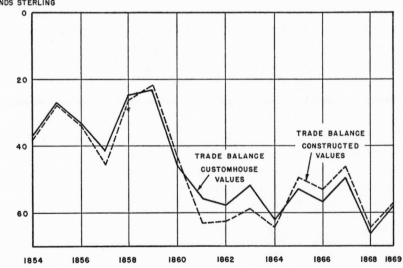

MILLIONS OF
POUNDS STERLING

0

20

40

60

TRADE BALANCE
CONSTRUCTED
VALUES

TRADE BALANCE
CUSTOMHOUSE
VALUES

1854   1856   1858   1860   1862   1864   1866   1868 1869

[35]

largest and on the plus side in the later years when volumes were greater. The average error for re-exports in the test years is 1.5 per cent.

It would, however, be too sanguine to suppose that the same degree of accuracy shown in the test years is sustained throughout the series. For the years 1840 to 1853, when the data are fully equal to those of the test years, the same degree of accuracy may be assumed. For the years from 1814 to 1839, some reduction of data and the increasing distance from the base years make it wiser to assume that the error may be larger. The largest errors will occur in boom years such as 1818, 1825, and 1836, when the estimates on imports may be excessive by possibly as much as 3 or even 4 per cent. But for an average of any five-year period between 1814 and 1839 the error on imports probably should not reach 2 per cent. On re-exports we must assume that error on a five-year average may reach up to 4 per cent, but it will have a corrective influence with respect to retained import values and the trade balance.

In the war years of the series, from 1796 to 1814, there is some increase in the probable margin of error beyond that offered by the diminution of the data and the further distance from base. Prices were high and fluctuating and there were scarcities which may have drawn a higher proportion of goods of lower quality into British trade. Moreover, because declared values for Irish exports are not available until 1805, it is necessary to estimate these by means of a price index and the "official" values, and add them to those of Great Britain in order to preserve continuity for the series on the United Kingdom. For 1796–1797, the market values of British exports are estimated also, but with the guidance of the values computed at the time by Thomas Irving [32] without which it might be rash to attempt to do so. All in all, the probabilities are that errors in the estimates for these war years may run as high in the direction of overvaluation as in boom years later. Comparison with Irving's and Marshall's averages for the triennium 1796–1798, adjusted as closely as possible to cover only the international trade of the United Kingdom,[33] suggests that the estimates constructed here may be excessive on imports by about 4 per cent for that triennium, and on re-exports by as much as 10 per cent. The error on re-exports partly offsets that on imports with respect to the balance of

---

[32] See above, pp. 24–25. Thomas Irving's and Robert Marshall's calculations for Great Britain and Ireland respectively were not indexed and were discovered late in the preparation of this study in the course of turning the pages of the *Parliamentary Papers*, volume by volume, in the hope of finding more data on individual commodities for the final years of the 18th century.

[33] Irving's and Marshall's figures on exports exclude Anglo-Irish trade, as do Marshall's on imports and re-exports; but Irving's on imports and re-exports for Great Britain include trade with Ireland and it is necessary to adjust these for comparison.

TABLE 2. REAL VALUES IN THE FOREIGN AND COLONIAL TRADE OF THE
UNITED KINGDOM, 1796–1853

(All values in millions of pounds)

Year	Imports constructed values	Exports declared values	Re-exports constructed values	Balance of trade
1796..........	39.6[a]	30.1[a]	8.5[a]	− 1.0[a]
1797..........	34.4[a]	27.5[a]	9.3[a]	+ 2.4[a]
1798..........	49.6	32.2[b]	11.3	− 6.1
1799..........	50.9	36.8[b]	9.4	− 4.7
1800..........	62.3	37.7[b]	14.7	− 9.9
Av. 1796–1800	47.4	32.9	10.6	− 3.9
1801..........	68.7	40.6[b]	12.9	−15.2
1802..........	54.7	45.9[b]	12.9	+ 4.1
1803..........	53.9	36.9[b]	9.1	− 7.9
1804..........	57.3	38.2[b]	11.0	− 8.1
1805..........	61.0	38.1	10.0	−12.9
Av. 1801–1805	59.1	39.9	11.2	− 8.0
1806..........	53.3	40.9	9.2	− 3.2
1807..........	53.8	37.2	8.3	− 8.3
1808..........	51.5	37.3	6.5	− 7.7
1809..........	73.7	47.4	14.3	−12.0
1810..........	88.5	48.4	12.5	−27.6
Av. 1806–1810	64.2	42.2	10.2	−11.8
1811..........	50.7	32.9	6.7	−11.1
1812..........	56.0	41.7	9.1	− 5.2
1813..	Records destroyed by fire			
1814..........	80.8	45.5	24.8	−10.5
1815..........	71.3	51.6	16.8	− 2.9
Av. 1811–1815	64.7	42.9	14.4	− 7.4
1816..........	50.2	41.7	12.6	+ 4.1
1817..........	61.0	41.8	10.1	− 9.1
1818..........	80.7	46.5	12.3	−21.9
1819..........	56.0	35.2	10.2	−10.6
1820..........	54.2	36.4	10.4	− 7.4
Av. 1816–1820	60.4	40.3	11.1	− 9.0
1821..........	45.6	36.7	9.5	+ 0.6
1822..........	44.6	37.0	7.8	+ 0.2
1823..........	52.0	35.4	7.2	− 9.4
1824..........	51.2	38.4	7.5	− 5.3
1825..........	73.6	38.9	8.2	−26.5
Av. 1821–1825	53.4	37.3	8.0	− 8.1

[a] British and Irish trade reduced to represent the United Kingdom on an overseas basis and real (market) values estimated.
[b] Market values of Irish exports (to foreign and colonial parts) estimated 1796–1804 and added to British declared values.

[37]

TABLE 2. (*Continued*)

Year	Imports constructed values	Exports declared values	Re-exports constructed values	Balance of trade
1826.........	50.4	31.5	7.3	−11.6
1827.........	58.8	37.2	6.8	−14.8
1828.........	57.3	36.8	6.5	−14.0
1829.........	54.1	35.8	6.6	−11.7
1830.........	55.9	38.3	5.6	−12.0
Av. 1826–1830	55.3	35.9	6.6	−12.8
1831.........	62.0	37.2	6.7	−18.1
1832.........	52.5	36.5	7.3	− 8.7
1833.........	58.9	39.7	6.9	−12.3
1834.........	64.7	41.6	8.0	−15.1
1835.........	68.0	47.4	9.2	−11.4
Av. 1831–1835	61.2	40.5	7.6	−13.1
1836.........	84.4	53.3	9.3	−21.8
1837.........	70.1	42.1	9.0	−19.0
1838.........	80.1	50.1	9.2	−20.8
1839.........	90.8	52.2	10.2	−28.4
1840.........	91.2	51.4	10.0	−29.8
Av. 1836–1840	83.3	49.8	9.5	−24.0
1841.........	83.9	51.6	9.9	−22.4
1842.........	76.4	47.4	8.4	−20.6
1843.........	71.0	52.3	7.8	−10.9
1844.........	78.9	58.6	8.0	−12.3
1845.........	88.4	60.1	9.3	−19.0
Av. 1841–1845	79.7	54.0	8.7	−17.0
1846.........	87.3	57.8	9.2	−20.3
1847.........	112.1	58.8	11.7	−41.6
1848.........	88.2	52.9	8.4	−26.9
1849.........	101.4	63.6	12.1	−25.7
1850.........	103.0	71.4	12.0	−19.6
Av. 1846–1850	98.4	60.9	10.7	−26.8
1851.........	109.5	74.4	12.5	−22.6
1852.........	110.0	78.1	13.0	−18.9
1853.........	148.5	98.9	16.8	−32.8
Av. 1851–1853	122.7	83.8	14.1	−24.8

MILLIONS OF
POUNDS STERLING

CHART 4. THE MERCHANDISE TRADE BALANCE OF THE UNITED KINGDOM IN REAL VALUES, 1796–1853

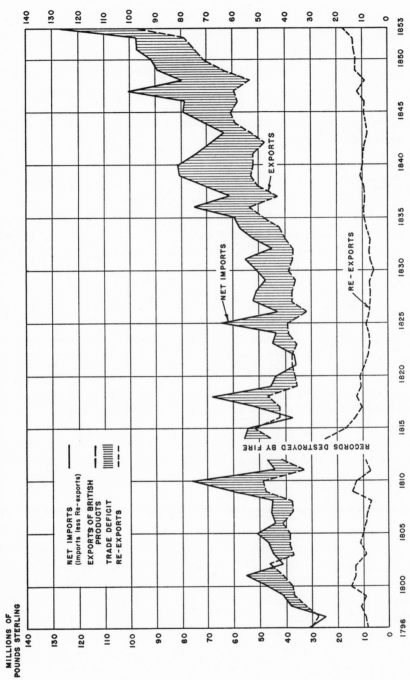

NET IMPORTS
(Imports less Re-exports)

EXPORTS OF BRITISH
PRODUCTS

TRADE DEFICIT

RE-EXPORTS

NET IMPORTS

EXPORTS

RE-EXPORTS

RECORDS DESTROYED BY FIRE

trade so that the difference from the Irving-Marshall results is small in absolute amount. Where the latter indicate an average annual negative balance of £ 1.0 million, these constructed estimates show an average negative balance of £ 1.6 million.[34] Furthermore, the Irving-Marshall method, using average quantities and prices for the triennium, which included one year with larger quantities and higher prices, may slightly understate the values.

CONCLUSIONS

It will be obvious from these constructed real values that many questions relating not only to the British balance of trade but also to British balance of payments and terms of trade in this period need reconsideration. Indeed much of the rationale of Britain's industrial and financial development in relation to the world trading community should be examined afresh.

It is unmistakably clear that, on balance, Britain was an importing country throughout this half century. The import surpluses, which are shown by the new valuations from 1854 on, did not begin as a consequence of the freer trade policies launched in the forties, but in fact preceded them by many decades. By the same token, the rate of growth in the value of British imports under free trade has been exaggerated by use of the old records. In only five years after 1796 is a favorable balance of visible trade shown by the estimates presented here. Even if one resorted to the rather extreme procedure of discounting the import estimates each year as in every case too high to the full limit of probable error which can be assumed for a single year, no quinquennial period would show a positive balance. There seems to be no escape, therefore, from the conclusion that Britain's new industrial system did not create export surpluses. Her phenomenal accumulation of overseas credits in the nineteenth century cannot be explained by the time-honored assumption that machine-made exports supplied the credits, an assumption that did not take into sufficient account the fall in export prices and that had, indeed, no other bases than a certain measure of *post hoc, ergo propter hoc* logic and that word "official" attached to the old valuations. In this first half of the century, as later, Britain's invisible credits — the earnings of the merchant marine, the commercial commissions, the savings of her experts and technicians and colonial officials abroad, and the income from her foreign in-

[34] In contrast, the "official" values, which understate the market values of imports at this time and overstate those of exports, indicate a favorable balance of trade averaging about £ 4.5 million a year for the United Kingdom in 1796–1798.

vestments — made up the deficit on her visible trade and supplied whatever new capital was invested overseas. These will be examined in more detail in the next sections, and some of the questions which these estimates raise with respect to terms of trade and to tariff policies will be considered in later pages.

III

BRITISH BALANCE OF PAYMENTS
AND EXPORT OF CAPITAL, 1816–1913

One of the emptier pages in the history of British economic life in the nineteenth century is that which deals with the balance of payments with the outside world. It is clear enough that the British balance of payments was generally favorable after the close of the Napoleonic Wars. The ability to invest large sums abroad attests that large credit balances were earned. But how large these credit balances were in any given year or period, and how they were earned — by what kinds of exports, visible and "invisible," and in what proportions — is not known even in rough approximation except, perhaps, for the later part of the period.[1] Ideas with respect to the international accounts of this great trading and capital exporting community are unduly vague and imprecise for this century of significant international development. For the first part of the century, the size of British credit balances and of the amount of capital export have generally been exaggerated, partly because of the assumption, which the "official" valuations of merchandise trade seemed to confirm, that British factories produced huge export surpluses at this time.[2] Even when the merchandise trade statistics had greatly improved, after 1853, the uncertainty concerning the "invisibles" which offset the huge trade deficits left room for some very large errors.

It is possible to be much more definite in these matters. By drawing on the findings and procedures of investigators who have worked on various facets of the problem, by extending them over a longer period, and by filling in the remaining gaps on the basis of more or less guided assumptions and conjectures, one can construct annual balance-of-payments state-

[1] Several attempts have been made to estimate the British balance of payments for particular periods towards the end of the century. The most systematic and comprehensive, covering the years 1870–1912, is that of Charles Kenneth Hobson, *The Export of Capital* (New York, 1914). The accuracy of certain of Hobson's methods is questionable, and his results, as will be shown later in this chapter, cannot be accepted as very close approximations.

[2] Jenks, by his study of actual security issues, was the first to moderate these exaggerated notions. He showed that British foreign investments in 1854 were scarcely half the accepted estimates: Leland Hamilton Jenks, *The Migration of British Capital to 1875* (New York, 1938). The first edition of his book was published in 1927.

ments for the United Kingdom beginning with the year 1816 [3] with some assurance that the main items are measured fairly closely, and that other items are adequately allowed for. The balances so constructed measure the growing volume of foreign investment which, in turn, can be checked at certain points with the more credible results achieved by other investigators who have made different approaches to the problem. These comparisons, which will be made in some detail later in this chapter, are reassuring. They suggest that any errors in the annual estimates for particular items in the balance sheet are relatively small or are cancelled by compensating errors in other items in the same year or in proximate years. The statement presented here should, therefore, constitute a fairly close representation of British international accounts, at least for any five-year period, and it should mark more clearly and continuously the rate of growth in British foreign investments through this century.

The data, methods, and assumptions employed in constructing this balance-of-payments statement must be described in some detail. As presented together in Table 4 below,[4] each of the known or estimated items of payment is arranged in continuous series running from 1816 to 1913 inclusive. In each series the object is to show the balance of credit or debit, not the gross earnings or payments. Thus the "Balance of visible trade: Merchandise" is the value of exports and re-exports less that of imports. Since the value of exports was regularly below that of imports through this century, the entry in almost every year of the series is a negative quantity, a debit. "Net credits from shipping" represents the credits due to the United Kingdom after allowing for the expenditures of British shipping abroad. Similarly, the final series, the "Accumulating balance of credit abroad," represents the net amount of British capital abroad after deducting the foreign capital placed in Britain. Some items of debit and credit, temporary or recurrent, are not specifically covered in these accounts. It is assumed that these about cancelled one another in any group of years. The data and procedures will be described series by series in the order in which they were constructed and appear in Table 4.

THE BALANCE ON VISIBLE TRADE: A. MERCHANDISE

The import and re-export values constructed for the preceding chapter were used for this series from 1816 through 1853 along with the declared values of exports. As was shown, these estimates compare very favorably

---

[3] It is hardly possible for earlier years. Estimates of invisible income for the period of the Napoleonic Wars, and earlier, would be almost purely conjectural and subject to a wide and incalculable margin of error.

[4] See pp. 70–75.

with the new computed values in the test years from 1854 to 1869 when the old and new systems of valuations overlapped. They tend to be a little high in boom years, however, so that in a year like 1825 the trade deficit may have been a little smaller than is shown in the table. But it is likely that any overestimate of the value of imports is offset by a similar tendency to high estimates for re-exports in the same boom years and by somewhat inflated values placed on exports in subsequent depression years. Export prices frequently fell very fast in the early part of the century and, lacking up-to-the-minute news of market conditions which the electric telegraph later supplied, exporters may have been a little optimistic in declaring values for the goods which they shipped to their agents for sale abroad. The five-year average should even out the inaccuracies of particular years.

For the period from 1854 to 1913, the trade values as reported in the *Statistical Abstract for the United Kingdom* were used. In these, the export values continued to be based on declarations made by exporters. Import and re-export values were computed, until 1869, on the basis of prices supplied by dealers. Thereafter, the latter were also compiled from declarations made by the importers and re-exporters. These returns are not absolutely perfect or complete. Exporters, for example, sometimes failed to notify the customhouse when goods declared for export were not shipped; and other deviations from strict accuracy occurred.[5] But the values can scarcely be improved on and can certainly be used for all practical purposes.

Several relevant items affecting the balance of payments are not covered in this series. Bullion and specie are not included. Values of new ships sold abroad were not included until 1899, and those of old ships were not included at any time in the period. The values of diamonds and other precious stones were not recorded. These omissions will be allowed for in other series.

THE BALANCE ON VISIBLE TRADE: B. GOLD AND SILVER BULLION AND SPECIE

Although records were made of the quantities of gold and silver bullion and coin exported, none was kept of imports before 1858. The export quantities can be valued quite accurately by using the Bank of England purchase prices of gold and silver. But to place the annual value of imports up to that year, we must resort to estimates. Some help is found, however,

[5] *Parl. Pap.*, "Third Report of the Commissioner of Customs," 1859, sess. 2 [2540], XIV, 16–17. See also Stephen Bourne, *Trade, Population, and Food* (London, 1880), pp. 15–26; Robert Giffen, "On the Use of Import and Export Statistics," *Journal of the Statistical Society (JSS)*, 45:185–188 (1882).

in the Bank's quarterly statements of bullion holdings, in the Bank purchase rates, and in the Mint returns, and, for the years 1852 and 1853, Tooke's estimates of imports.[6] It is fairly clear from these data

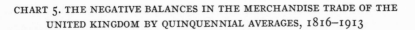

CHART 5. THE NEGATIVE BALANCES IN THE MERCHANDISE TRADE OF THE UNITED KINGDOM BY QUINQUENNIAL AVERAGES, 1816–1913

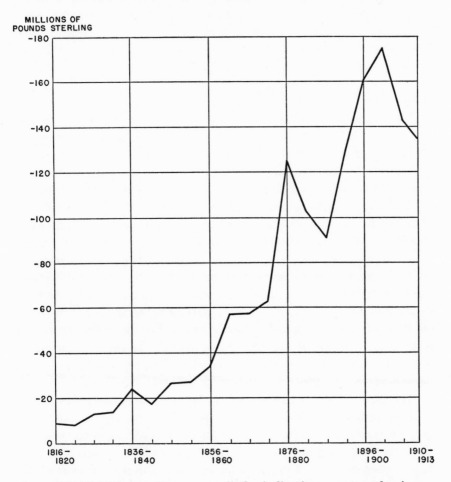

that, while British supplies grew a little, indicating some predominance of imports, the net gain of bullion was relatively small before the 1850's.[7] There does not seem to have been any large reserve of gold built up in the United Kingdom in this period and, indeed, gold was rather frequently in

[6] Thomas Tooke and William Newmarch, *A History of Prices* (New York, n.d.), V, 302.

[7] Mint figures on new coinage may suggest a much larger balance of imports than is shown here by the minus signs. But some of this new coin was subsequently exported from the kingdom in one way or another and some was merely a reminting of old coins.

short supply. The Bank reserves sank perilously low in 1819, in 1825, in December 1836, and in 1839–1841.

Beginning in 1858, records of import and export values of gold and silver coin and bullion are available in the *Statistical Abstract*.

It should be noticed that, in this balance sheet, gold and silver coin and bullion are combined. This series will, accordingly, differ from others covering a single component as, for example, gold bullion alone. Also, appropriate to the purpose here and in contrast to the system in some series constructed for other uses, export balances are indicated by a plus sign and import balances by a minus sign.

THE BALANCE ON VISIBLE TRADE: C. SHIP SALES

There is no record of the ships sold or transferred to foreign or colonial registry [8] before 1855. This is probably not a serious lacuna in respect to the balance of payments. It seems rather likely that, in the first half of the century when wood and sail prevailed, British purchases (from the maritime colonies in British North America, for example) about balanced British sales. Increasing use of steam and steel gradually altered this situation, however. British export of ships gained in importance while import of ships declined. Happily, the beginning of the records which permit rough computation of values corresponds fairly satisfactorily in point of time with this change. Accounts of the new ships transferred to other registry begin in 1855 in terms of number and tonnage of sail and of steam. From 1899 on, values on these were declared and are included in the "Balance on visible trade: Merchandise." For old ships, records by number and tonnage of sail and of steam begin in 1886, a date which probably marks closely enough the time when British purchases of foreign or colonial vessels, other than small or special craft, virtually ceased.

The construction of this series may be summarized as follows:

1855–1885: New ships only. For the years 1855 to 1879 inclusive, Stephen Bourne's estimates of values are used.[9] From 1880 on (to 1898) the values are computed from the tonnage records by means of a price index, based on a series of prices for new steamers per ton dead-weight as reported by Sir Robert Giffen,[10] used in relation to the average export prices for the years 1899–1901 as given in the *Statistical Abstract*.

1886–1898: New and old ships. Values of new ships are computed by

[8] The point is sometimes made that many so-called sales were merely transfers to British owners doing business under foreign or colonial registry. Such transfers meant, however, that capital values were placed outside the United Kingdom.

[9] Bourne, *Trade, Population and Food*, p. 65.

[10] "The Excess of Imports," *Journal of the Royal Statistical Society* (*JRSS*), 62:48 (1899).

the method noted above. Values for old ships are calculated, without price index, at £5 per ton for steam and £2 per ton for sail, rates which are considered low enough for most of these years to provide some margin to offset British purchases of foreign or colonial vessels.

1899–1913: *Old ships only*. These were calculated at the flat rates noted above.

THE BALANCE ON BUSINESS SERVICES: D. PROFITS ON FOREIGN TRADE
AND SERVICES

Several sorts of income from foreign and colonial sources are included under this heading. The most important are the profits made by British firms which handled the marketing and purchasing for much of the British export and import trade and did other business abroad. The export values used for the "Balance on visible trade: Merchandise" are taken f.o.b. at home ports. Separate allowance must therefore be made for profits made by British firms in handling consignment goods abroad. Import values, on the other hand, since they are taken c.i.f. (*i.e.* including cost, insurance, brokerage, commissions, and freight to British ports), already include such profits, but on the wrong side of the ledger. To the extent that profits were made by British firms in the purchasing of goods for import this debit entry must be offset by a credit entry. Included under this heading, also, is international income from banking, engineering and other technical services abroad, and from British administrative services charged to colonial governments, as well as from the savings, or pensions, of colonial and Indian officials when they retired to Britain. There was, of course, some offset in the net earnings of foreign firms and individuals rendering comparable services in Britain.

The question is, how much to allow year by year for the balance of earnings in these items? There are no records which are at all comprehensive, and we can only make a rough allowance in accordance with estimates developed by informed investigators. Jenks, drawing on the work of Bourne, Giffen, William Newmarch, and Ernest Seyd, allowed a flat 5 per cent on the total value of imports and of British produced exports for foreign trade profits per se for the period from 1854 to 1880.[11] I have used essentially the same formula, but with two modifications which seemed appropriate for the longer period and for the somewhat broader coverage of profits and services. First, I have included re-exports in counting the trade values because there was surely a profit in this trade beyond

[11] *Migration of British Capital*, pp. 412–414.

what is shown in the trade valuations, at least until 1870.[12] This slightly more liberal allowance seems further justified in view of the wide variety of services included under this heading. Second, it seemed illogical to assume that the same rate of earnings held throughout this longer interval. I have raised the rate to 5½ per cent for the years 1816–1818 on the assumption that rates of profit were still inflated from the war period. This increase may be somewhat too conservative as to amount and duration.[13] At the other end of the series I have assumed that profit margins, as well as the relative proportions of the business done by British firms, fell with the rise in the volume of foreign trade and with keener international competition towards the end of the century. I have, therefore, reduced the rate allowed to 4½ per cent beginning in 1880, and to 4 per cent beginning in 1893.

THE BALANCE ON BUSINESS SERVICES: E. INSURANCE, BROKERAGE, SHIPPING COMMISSIONS, ETC.

The propriety of making allowance for a net balance of earnings in this category will be obvious.[14] Again there is some guidance towards constructing a series of approximate values. Robert Giffen, followed by Jenks, estimated earnings in this category at 2½ per cent on the total value of British foreign trade, including bullion, for the period 1854–1880.[15] I have, however, excluded bullion values, insured though they certainly were, by way of making some allowance for foreign insurance underwriting in Britain, a business which grew in importance about contemporaneously with the growth in the value of bullion movements. I have also raised the rate to 2¾ per cent for 1816–1818, and have reduced it successively to 2¼ per cent in 1880 and to 2 per cent in 1893 to allow for increased competition, and for the rising proportions of British trade carried in foreign vessels after the turn of the century and presumably more commonly insured with foreign companies. The credits entered here are, therefore, exactly one half of those shown under "Profits on foreign trade and services."

[12] The estimated values used here up to 1854, and the new computed values used from 1854 to 1869, do not include allowance for profit. Beginning in 1870, when declared values came into use for re-exports, profit may be included.

[13] See below under "Accumulating balance of credit abroad."

[14] Hobson questions whether a credit for insurance should be allowed against the value of imports "since the valuation of the Board of Trade includes insurance charges": *Export of Capital*, p. 188. He forgets that the valuation for imports is entered on the other side of the balance-of-payments ledger and that insurance premiums received by British companies on British imports constitute a credit item against this debit.

[15] "The Use of Import and Export Statistics," *JSS*, 45:207,209, 221–222 (1882).

THE BALANCE ON BUSINESS SERVICES: F. NET CREDITS FROM SHIPPING

If the estimates presented here are reasonably close to the mark, British net credits from shipping, including the international earnings of the British merchant marine and the expenditures of foreign and colonial ships in British ports, constituted the most important class of Britain's invisible income for almost two thirds of this century. Not until the 1870's did income from foreign investments begin to surpass them. Throughout the century the international earnings of the British merchant marine made very large contributions towards balancing the mounting deficit in visible trade.

The values required as earnings of British shipping for balance-of-payments purposes must be clearly defined. They are not simply the profits of British shipmasters. What is wanted here is the annual amount of the freight charges on those British imports and exports which were carried in British bottoms, as well as the freight and passenger charges earned by British ships in the carrying trade of other countries, after deducting in both cases all outlay abroad. The inclusion of all freight charges on British imports carried in British vessels, subject only to deduction for expenses abroad, is necessary to balance the freight element in the debit entry of imports valued c.i.f. (cost, insurance, freight). The freight charges on exports are included because they were, presumably, added to the cost of the goods (which were valued f.o.b. in the United Kingdom) to the importing country. They are comparable to earnings in the carrying trade between foreign countries.[16] In addition, it is fairly relevant to include in this series allowance for a credit item not covered elsewhere in these accounts — the expenditures of foreign and colonial ships in British ports.

At least two attempts have been made to estimate British ship earnings for balance-of-payments purposes for later parts of this century. A brief review of the methods employed will throw light on the difficulties of the problem and on the reasons for the procedures used here. The first was made by Robert Giffen when he was head of the Statistical Department of the Board of Trade. Giffen took samples of freight earnings and of expenditures abroad from a considerable number of shipping firms for the year 1880 and concluded from these that a fair average allowance for net earnings for balance-of-payments purposes would be £ 5 per registered ton for sailing ships and £ 15 for steam. Applying these rates to the whole

[16] It will be clear that earnings of foreign ships in the British import and export trade do not need to be considered in these accounts of British balance of payments since the debit charges on imports are already covered in the import valuations c.i.f., while the freight charges on exports normally become a part of the total cost of the goods at the destination abroad.

net registered tonnage without deduction for the coasting trade, he calculated net earnings at £ 60 millions for that year. As a check on this estimate, he also computed the difference between the total import and export
valuations of the chief trading countries of the world for the year 1879.
This difference, £ 162 millions, is attributable to (a) insurance, brokerage,
and commissions, and (b) freight charges. He allowed £ 32 millions for
(a) and put the British share at half. The remaining £ 130 millions represented freight charges, and he allocated 55 per cent of this, or £ 71½
millions, to British ships in accordance with their tonnage relationship
to total world tonnage. He also calculated that one sixth of this amount
should be deducted as a fair allowance for outlay abroad. The result,
£ 59½ millions for the year 1879, is, because of a smaller total tonnage,
slightly more than the estimate of £ 5 per registered ton for sail and
£ 15 for steam which he reached by the other method for 1880.[17] This
second method of calculation is open to some doubt, but it tends generally to confirm the first estimate. One difficulty lies in the lack of uniform-
ity in national systems of trade valuation at this time. Another is that
this method makes no allowance for land transit in international trade.
Possibly, however, Britain, as a rather centrally located island, with a
very large share of total world trade and with a large part of her shipping
in steam,[18] received more than her tonnage share of sea-borne freight,
passengers, and mails. Further, Giffen includes in his calculation for 1879
ships under colonial registry assumed to be owned in Britain. Their
income should properly be classed as income from foreign investment.
Giffen applied his 1880 estimate of earnings per ton of sail and steam
arbitrarily to the annual figures for registered tonnage from 1854 to 1881
without allowing for fluctuations in freight rates or shipping activity. His
object in constructing the series was mainly to show that large credits
were earned to offset the great excess of imports over exports.

Giffen made another survey for the year 1898, but used a smaller sample
so that his findings have a more tentative character. Net earnings, after
outlay abroad, he wrote, "could hardly be put now at more than 4 l. per
ton annually" for sail, or "more than 12 l. per ton" for steam, taking "one
year with another." He put the total earnings at between "70 and 80
millions" at that time.[19]

[17] "The Use of Import and Export Statistics," JSS, 45:206–223, 259–270 (1882), and
discussion, 284–296.
[18] See Table 23.
[19] "The Excess of Imports," JRSS, 62:11, 46–55 (1899).
The Board of Trade estimate of £ 90 millions for the year 1901 is frequently cited.
It was not the result of a fresh study of the question, but was simply Giffen's "hardly

The second notable attempt was made by Charles K. Hobson in his *Export of Capital*. Hobson estimated net ship earnings from 1870 to 1912 by means of the annual net registered tonnage figures and a combined freight rate and "increasing efficiency factor" index used in relation to estimated earnings in a base year, 1907. To establish earnings for this base year Hobson made three sets of calculations and took an average of the results.[20] By means of the "increasing efficiency factor" Hobson allows 4 per cent annually from 1870 to 1912 for growth in earning capacity due to the change from sail to steam and to technical improvements in the capacity of steam vessels. It seems likely that, with the growing amount of competition, both British and international, a large part of the improvements made in the efficiency of steamships was passed on to consumers in the lower charges mirrored in Hobson's freight-rate index. Use of a freight-rate index seems sound when it can be based on broadly representative samples. But rates varied enormously from month to month, route to route, and article to article. Finally, it is not enough to use registered tonnage figures without reference to the foreign trade activity of the vessels registered. For this, some co-ordination with annual clearances is needed. Hobson's estimate for 1880 is 12½ per cent below Giffen's, perhaps mainly from the operation of the "increasing efficiency

---

more than" formula for 1898 applied to the registered tonnage of 1901 without allowance for change in freight rates or shipping activity. Cf. *Parl. Pap.*, 1903 [1761], LXVII, 101.

[20] *Export of Capital*, pp. 171–187. Two of his methods are like Giffen's. One is to consider that British ship earnings are indicated by the British share, on the basis of tonnage proportions, of the difference between the total valuations of world imports and of world exports. He ignores insurance, brokerage, and commissions as constituting part of the difference, and, like Giffen, makes no allowance for inland transport which was more important by 1907, with the result that he arrives at his highest figure, £ 97 millions for 1907, by this calculation. The second is a sampling method, by which he puts net earnings at £ 86 or 90 millions. Here, average income per gross ton is calculated from the gross receipts of eleven British steam shipping companies, with about one eighth of the British gross tonnage in 1907, but apparently without considering sailing vessels which constituted slightly over one eighth of the net registered tonnage in 1907, but over four fifths in 1870. Hobson deducts one third for expenditure of British ships abroad, which seems too high to leave sufficient allowance for expenditures by foreign ships in British ports, also a variable factor. The third method is to consider what the merchant marine must have earned in 1907 to meet expenses and to pay an assumed dividend of 5 per cent on an assumed capital of £ 160 millions, a procedure which does not appear to distinguish adequately between the domestic earnings of the companies and the international earnings of the merchant marine. By this method he estimates earnings at £ 80 millions. He uses £ 90 millions as a rounded average of the three estimates. This average compares rather closely with the estimate of £ 91.9 millions constructed here for British ship earnings and foreign expenditure in British ports for 1907 by working from the 1880 base with very different methods of accounting for the known variables. Divergence between Hobson's series and the one constructed here develops and becomes considerable as one moves away from Hobson's base year.

factor." His estimate is excessive to an extreme degree in 1912 when a serious strike occurred and the freight-rate index rose nearly 40 per cent. The efficiency factor, the freight-rate index, and the registered tonnage returns used without consideration of clearances in foreign trade, do not seem to produce very reliable results.

It is much easier to find the faults in these two series than to construct a better one by methods which can be applied throughout this century with what data are available. Consideration of these two efforts threw a good deal of light on the problems, however, and led to the conclusion that, while the data are not available to include all factors with year by year precision, the major variables can be taken into account sufficiently to produce fair approximate values. Giffen's estimates of average earnings per net ton of sail and of steam, after outlay abroad, seem fairly reliable for the year 1880. They make the distinction between sail and steam which is so necessary for the greater part of the century, and they are based on a wider sample than his tentative estimates for 1898. They offer the further advantage of being more proximate to the mid-point of the period to be covered. However, the net registered tonnage records to which Giffen applied his net ton averages are not alone a suitable guide because they do not distinguish between ships in domestic service in and about the home islands and those in foreign trade. This is a particularly important matter through the period of transition from sail to steam. In sailing days, and before the British railway network was completed, the coastal trade used a much larger part of the net registered tonnage than in 1880 when hardly more than 10 per cent was exclusively so engaged.[21] While this variable can be controlled by considering the ratio of clearances in foreign trade to net registered tonnage, it is simpler and equally precise to use the clearance records directly. For this purpose, Giffen's estimates of the international earnings per ton of sail and of steam for 1880 were applied to the net registered tonnage which engaged in foreign trade in that year, and the respective totals for sail and steam were then equated with the average of entries and clearances of each in cargo from and to all foreign and colonial ports. The allowances so calculated were £ 3.85 per ton for sail, and for steam ships, which made much more frequent and, on the average, much shorter voyages, £ 2.79 per ton. These rates were then used annually with the average of the tonnage entered and cleared in cargo from 1827 on, when these records begin. For 1816–1826, these rates are adjusted to accord with the records which

---

[21] After allowing for the fact that the "home trade" classification of the net registered tonnage included ships plying to north European ports all the way from the Elbe to Brest.

then made no distinction between ships entered and cleared in cargo and in ballast.

As a check on price change — in default of freight-rate and cost indexes for which there are too few dependable data over this long period — the results were modified by means of the import price index described in Chapter IV and shown in Table 8. The use of this index may appear to be the doubtful element in this combination. Although it includes the factor of freight charges, it also contains much more and is only a crude measure of the ups and downs of freight rates. At first glance, the results seem high in boom years in the first half of the century, and in the later years also, when freight rates fell more rapidly than average import prices. Further consideration gives some reassurance, however. There is much evidence to indicate that freight rates responded even more quickly to prosperity than did average import prices in the early years, while the faster fall of freight rates towards the end of the century was probably largely the result of increased efficiency of steam engines and other improvements which raised cargo carrying capacity beyond what is shown by the tonnage records. While this price index will not ensure precise annual values, it should, in conjunction with the other factors considered, produce fairly dependable five-year averages.

Another element of imprecision is the matter of British earnings in the carrying trade abroad between third countries. On this there are no adaptable records. These earnings are presumably covered by the estimates for the base year, 1880, but it seems unlikely that British activity abroad held throughout the century to a constant proportion of British carrying in and out of the home ports.[22] However, the imprecision here may be a relatively small matter with respect to international credits, as distinct from profits of shipowners, because the freight charges in this trade were doubtless partly offset by larger expenditures abroad.

The expenditures of foreign and colonial ships in British ports also require attention. Since the foreign share in the British carrying trade fluctuated, tending to rise appreciably in years and periods of rapid growth in trade, this expenditure cannot have remained throughout in the proportions of 1880. The figures on total tonnage, and on the percentages which were British and foreign, for a few selected years through the century (Table 3) will indicate both the range of fluctuation in the proportions and the great growth in foreign shipping activity. For this purpose, tonnage in cargo and in ballast is appropriate.[23]

---

[22] See also pp. 171–175.
[23] Tonnage data, to 1840, are taken from *Parl. Pap.*, 1852–53 (1012), XCVIII; there-

TABLE 3. FOREIGN MERCHANT SHIPPING IN THE PORTS OF THE UNITED KINGDOM, SHOWING PERCENTAGE OF TOTAL ENTRIES AND CLEARANCES BY TONNAGE IN SELECTED YEARS, 1816–1913

| | Entered in cargo and ballast | | | Cleared in cargo and ballast | | |
| | | Foreign | | | Foreign | |
	Total tonnage (millions)	Tonnage (millions)	Per cent of total	Total tonnage (millions)	Tonnage (millions)	Per cent of total
1816....	1.80	.38	21	1.74	.40	23
1818....	2.65	.76	29	2.45	.73	30
1820....	2.12	.45	21	1.98	.43	22
1825....	3.10	.96	31	2.70	.91	34
1830....	2.94	.76	26	2.86	.76	27
1840....	4.66	1.46	31	4.78	1.49	31
1850....	7.10	2.40	34	7.40	2.66	36
1860....	12.18	5.28	43	12.52	5.49	44
1870....	18.11	5.73	32	18.53	5.84	32
1880....	29.07	8.58	30	29.66	8.80	30
1890....	36.78	10.06	27	37.45	10.25	27
1900....	49.22	17.78	36	49.31	18.04	37
1910....	66.66	27.02	41	67.37	27.20	40
1913....	82.15	35.55	43	82.66	36.01	44

The change from sail to steam was another variable affecting foreign ship expenditure for which statistical allowance should be made since steam vessels were much more subject to expenses for fuel and for repair of engines and machinery when in British ports than were sailing ships. By 1913, nearly 96 per cent of foreign entries were in steam.

The credits attributable to expenditures by foreign shipping in British ports can be estimated with some approximation by means of tonnage allowances and a price index. In the base year 1880, the allowance worked out amounts in all to £ 5.2 millions — about the equivalent of the potential international earnings at Giffen's rates of that part of British net registered tonnage then engaged in the coastal carrying trade. For sailing vessels, an average of 8s. per ton was allowed on the 5.56 million tons entered in cargo and in ballast; for steam ships, which also took coals and sometimes repairs, 20s. per ton was allowed on the 3.02 million tons entered in 1880. From 1898 on, I have reduced the tonnage credit on steam by steps in order to allow for probable reduction of repair in

after from the *Statistical Abstract*. These records do not include ships sailing under government contract, a matter of some importance in war years as in 1854–56 and 1899–1902. For British proportions in cargo only in selected years, see Table 22.

British ports consequent on the considerable development of facilities elsewhere in the world. The tonnage allowances made each year are also modified by the net import price index.

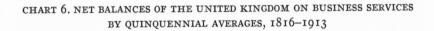

CHART 6. NET BALANCES OF THE UNITED KINGDOM ON BUSINESS SERVICES
BY QUINQUENNIAL AVERAGES, 1816–1913

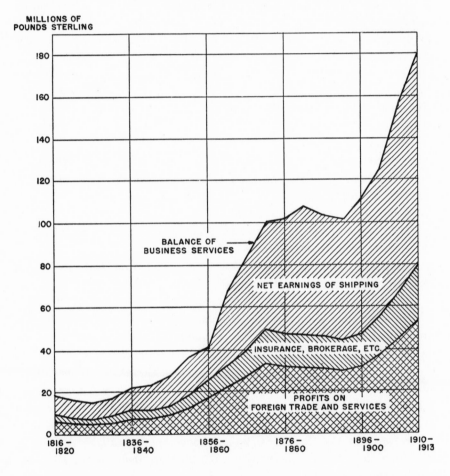

The credits allowed in this way for expenditure by foreign shipping in British ports changed a good deal over the century. In the earlier years they were very small both in amount and in proportion to the totals entered in this series. In 1816, for example, at £ 0.35 million, they were less than 4 per cent of total estimated shipping credits; and in the boom year 1825, at £ 0.75 million, they were just under 7 per cent. They grew into significant sums in the course of the century, however, and the trend in the proportions also was generally upward. By 1900 they amounted to £ 12.2 millions, or nearly 18 per cent of total estimated shipping credits, and in 1913, to £ 23.1 millions, or nearly 21.5 per cent of the total.

THE BALANCE ON OTHER CURRENT ITEMS: G. EMIGRANT FUNDS

The hundred years preceding the first World War was the great century of emigration from Europe. In the first half of this period a very large proportion of the emigrants came from the British Isles. Few of them crossed the seas without some reserve of funds (as well as personal effects and equipment which, however, do not affect the balance of payments) to tide them over the first days of looking about. By the rather conservative estimates constructed here, the net balance of money carried out of the United Kingdom in this way, though small in any one year in relation to other accounts, amounted during the century to over £ 136 millions. The cumulative effect of omitting these annual debits would, therefore, be considerable. If they were not taken into account, they would, at compound interest, distort the estimates of the amount of credit accumulated abroad by several hundred millions by 1913.

There are no records of the actual amounts of currency carried out of the country by British emigrants during the century. There are, however, accounts of the numbers of persons who emigrated from the United Kingdom each year throughout the period.[24] These data have some limitations in the early years. No distinction was made until 1861 between emigrants of British origin and those who were merely passing through British ports from other European countries, but it may be assumed that the number of the latter was relatively small in the days of sailing ships when continental emigration was light (except from the Germanies in the fifties) and when passage on fast American vessels could be taken from all the major European ports. Rough adjustment, on the basis of 1861 returns, is made for these from 1857 to 1860. No records of the reverse flow, the return to Britain of the homesick or disappointed, is available until 1876, but from that date on the numbers reported are deducted to allow for funds brought back.

The next question is, how much money did the "average" British emigrant carry with him for his start in the new world? This is a more difficult matter. Yet there is some contemporary testimony. The *Liverpool Mail* stated in 1837 that two thirds of British emigrants to the United

---

[24] Taken, up to 1856, from the "Seventeenth General Report of the Emigration Commissioners," *Parl. Pap.*, 1857, sess. 2 [2249], XVI, 57; thereafter, from the *Statistical Abstract*.

States took passage in the faster American ships at £ 5 per head, and carried out a good deal of hard money, the Irish carrying the larger sums, the English the smaller. It put the average at £ 15 per person.[25] A dozen years later, Mr. T. W. C. Murdoch, Chairman of the Land and Emigration Committee, testified that large sums were carried out by the Irish, even by those receiving public aid. One man on relief was found, on his arrival in Canada, to have £ 70 in his possession. On one ship, the *Ocean Monarch*, 320 emigrants had £ 10,000, an average of over £ 30 per person.[26] Perhaps these were somewhat unusual cases, noteworthy rather than typical; but there can be no doubt that in the aggregate large amounts were carried out by emigrants. Funds were also sent out by emigration societies. It will scarcely exaggerate this debit item to allow £ 15 per capita as the net balance of funds taken out through emigration for the years 1816 through 1846.

In due course funds began to flow back to the United Kingdom in the form of remittances from former emigrants. Beginning in the mid-century, there is a certain amount of information on this subject also. Murdoch, after checking with several banking houses, though not on this occasion with Baring's, the most important of those doing business with the United States, reported that not less than £ 464,000 was sent to the United Kingdom in the year 1848.[27] Thereafter, similar surveys were made annually by the Emigration Commissioners. These show a total of some £ 17 millions returned from 1848 to 1871, inclusive,[28] in annual amounts which correlate rather closely with the tides of emigration. In the light of these reports, it seemed proper, as a net balance calculation, to reduce the allowance in 1847 to £ 12 per capita, and in 1850, when remittances increased sharply, to £ 10, which rate is continued to the end of the series. It is likely that remittances rose more rapidly after the mid-century than the reports reveal, for the channels of transmission multiplied. But it is also probable that the average sums carried out by emigrants rose similarly.

[25] Cited by *The Financial Register of the United States, 1837–38*, I, 59. A consonant estimate is given in *Historical Statistics of the United States* (U.S. Department of Commerce, 1949), p. 237, citing C. J. Bullock, J. H. Williams and R. S. Tucker, "The Balance of Trade of the United States," *Review of Economic Statistics*, 1: 215–266 (July 1919), where the average for those entering the United States from 1838 to 1849, including non-British, is put at $50.00 per head *on arrival*.

[26] "Fifth Report of the Select Committee of the House of Lords on the Operation of the Irish Poor Laws," *Parl. Pap.*, 1849, XVI, 977.

[27] *Ibid.*, p. 977.

[28] "Thirty-Second General Report of the Emigration Commissioners," *Parl. Pap.*, 1872 [562], App. 17, p. 71.

THE BALANCE ON OTHER CURRENT ITEMS: H. TOURIST EXPENDITURES, SMUG-
GLING AND UNRECORDED IMPORTS

In each of these accounts the balance was almost certainly unfavorable to the United Kingdom in this century, and some allowance must be made. But the amounts involved are almost purely conjectural. By the very nature of the case, there are no relevant records and the estimates which are needed must be posited on assumptions which can scarcely be confirmed.

The interrelating impressions and suppositions on which this series was constructed may be summarized as follows:

(1) *Smuggling.* There is ample testimony that smuggling into Britain was very heavy in the early protectionist years of the century. The only uncertainty is with respect to the amounts involved. A large part of it was in spirits and tobacco, laces and silks. The value of these may well have run to as much as £ 4 millions in some years, though much smaller balances are assumed in these estimates in order to allow for unrecorded exports. The scale of smuggling probably diminished after duties were reduced in the mid-century. Certainly it formed a declining proportion of the growing volume of legitimate trade. Yet the business of the illicit free trader never wholly died out, for some luxury goods continued to bear high duties. It was not, of course, wholly a one-way traffic, but British export articles were not generally suitable for surreptitious handling, and one may safely suppose that the balance was against Great Britain throughout the period. The trade was financed with gold by the small-scale smuggler and through banking channels by the large-scale operators who still flourished in the thirties and early forties.

(2) *Tourist expenditure.* It seems fairly clear that the British travelled abroad more throughout this century, and, on an average, spent more, than did foreigners in Britain. While the accounts with particular countries may well have been favorable to Britain — almost certainly so with the United States, for example — such bilateral balances were more than offset by British expenditures on the "grand tour," and on ordinary travel and holidaying on the continent and in the Mediterranean area. Quite early in this century steam packets made the Channel crossing swifter and surer, though hardly more comfortable. Then the swelling prosperity after the "hungry forties" broadened the base of the British travelling class. This development corresponded closely in point of time with the assumed decline in the volume of smuggling in the free-trade period.

(3) *Unrecorded imports.* These became considerable also and should be

allowed for, especially from 1855 on, when such an unrecorded export as ship sales is taken into account on the other side of the ledger. They include such articles as diamonds, entering in the ordinary way of trade but without official recording. Giffen put the value of diamonds imported from Cape Colony alone at over £ 4 millions in the 1890's,[29] though there was some offset in unrecorded exports of the same article.

To translate these impressions into a series of annual values is a more troublesome matter. The problem yields, indeed, only to rather arbitrary treatment. Taking 1816 as a starting-point, I assumed that the value of smuggled imports in that year might run to £ 1½ or 2 millions beyond that of undeclared or unrecorded exports. The balance of tourist expenditure I put at £ ½ to 1 million more. Other unrecorded imports I assumed were offset by unrecorded exports or by other items at that time. The next question was, to what to relate this figure of, say, 2½ millions in 1816 in order to construct a series running through a century. Import values seemed inappropriate, for the growing dependence on foodstuffs and raw materials would swell the figures later in the century out of relation to probable values on smuggled goods and tourist expenditures. This objection applies also to the values of total trade. Exports of British produce and manufactures may, by and large, give a better indication of the means to purchase and to travel, and in the end I used these values as the guiderail. The £ 2½ millions assumed for 1816 is 6 per cent of the value of British exports in that year, and I applied this rate to each year's export values through 1846. From 1847 to 1862, when the free-trade policy was developing, when exports more than doubled, and when the proportion of smuggling probably declined, though presumably with some compensatory rise in tourism and in the balance of unrecorded imports, I have allowed 5 per cent; and from 1863 to 1913, 4 per cent of export values.

Conjectural though this series is, it has been allowed to stand. When it became possible to put the various series together and check the end-product, the "Accumulating balance of credit abroad," with estimates made by others for various years,[30] it did not seem necessary to make any changes. If this series is not a fair approximation in itself, its errors must be balanced by those in other series or by unconsidered items in the international accounts of the United Kingdom.

I. THE BALANCE ON INTEREST AND DIVIDENDS

The growth of British income from foreign investments is one of the important facts in British economic development in the nineteenth century

---

[29] *JRSS*, 62:6 (1899).
[30] See section K below.

and by no means a minor one in world affairs. If the estimates constructed here are reasonably correct, the income from this source not only filled in whatever gaps were created by deficits on trade and services,[31] but it also supplied most of the surpluses which were available for new investment abroad. Evergrowing, it became, by the mid-seventies, the largest annual net credit item on this balance sheet, and it can be regarded thereafter as the major source of the phenomenally large amounts of capital which Britain continued to place abroad. British foreign investments, then, were a little like a revolving fund. A large part of the income was reinvested in the further development of other lands. In bad years it was useful, and almost invariably ample, as a reserve against adverse balances on trade and services. In only three years out of the ninety-eight in the series (namely, 1840, 1842, and 1847) does it appear to have been insufficient for this purpose, and in each of these by a relatively small margin. Except in the late seventies and from 1891 to 1905, this income was, in effect, drawn on rather sparingly for current expenses. In good years it was supplemented by the balances earned in trade and services.

In estimating British income from interest and dividends on foreign investments through the nineteenth century, one must again rely on more or less guided guesses of the amounts involved. Investment was a private matter and the income from abroad was not subject to distinctive report until late in the century, and then only for certain classes of such income. We cannot, therefore, do much more than assume what the average rates were in each period and apply these rates annually to the amount of credit estimated to have been accumulated abroad by the close of the preceding year. In this series, then, as in the others, the values computed can scarcely be considered to possess yearly precision. The most that can be hoped for is that quinquennial averages are fair approximations.

It has become a kind of convention to assume that the average rate of return on British foreign investment was about 5 per cent a year. This seems to be correct enough for the middle and later part of the period. At times, indeed, it went rather higher. Robert Nash's list of publicly issued foreign securities traded in Britain in the decade 1870–1879 shows an average annual yield of 5.81 per cent for the decade, apart from gain in market values.[32] The British share of the income from these securities

---

[31] By the estimates constructed here, the first deficit in the balance of trade and services after 1815 (Table 4, A–H) was in the boom year 1825. Thereafter, the quinquennial averages show deficits in 11 out of 18 periods to 1913. On the relative proportions of these deficits see Tables 15 and 24.

[32] Robert Lucas Nash, *A Short Inquiry into the Profitable Nature of Our Investments* (London, 1881), pp. 1–108. See also Jenks, *Migration of British Capital*, p. 413.

was probably a little less than this, say 5.5 per cent, since British holdings included a larger proportion of the lower yielding Indian and colonial stocks than is represented by the list as a whole. On the other hand, Nash calculated the rates of return on the basis of the fairly good market prices of 1870, and did not include mining and manufacturing stocks which generally produced higher returns than did government bonds. If increase in market value during this decade is taken into account, the yield shown for the whole list is over 6.25 per cent a year. Over longer periods, however, capital gains were probably about balanced by capital losses and may, therefore, be ignored in our calculations.

Nash throws much light on rates of yield and on capital gains in the seventies. Foreign and colonial government loans were far and away the favorite class of investment, taking more than two thirds of the total. Foreign governments yielded on an average 5.87 per cent (plus 0.27 per cent capital gain) for the decade 1870–1879; United States governments yielded 6.1 (plus 1.4) per cent; and Indians, 4.25 (plus 0.15) per cent. Railways were next in popularity, and Nash shows continental rails yielding 5.1 (plus 0.4) per cent; United States, 5.7 (plus 3.6) per cent; and South American, 5.3 (plus 3.4) per cent. The lowest rate of return was in Canadian railways, however, with 1.90 per cent for this decade (plus 0.15 per cent capital gain). The highest rate of return was in land and mortgage companies with 13.3 per cent (plus 10.0 per cent capital gain). Many of the land and mortgage companies fizzled out later with sad results for the over-eager investors.

In the boom years before 1913 also, the rate of return rose above the conventional 5 per cent. Sir George Paish has shown that, in 1907, the average rate of return on publicly issued securities was 5.2 per cent, again without allowance for capital gain. The popularity of government bonds had fallen, like the interest rate, in the interval since 1880. According to Paish's lists, loans to foreign, colonial, and municipal governments comprised just 28 per cent of the total British investment in publicly issued foreign securities in 1907. The proportion was less than half that of 1880, although the absolute amount, slightly over £ 800 millions, was almost exactly the same. Indian government loans offered the lowest yield with 3.21 per cent. Colonial government issues yielded 3.71 per cent and foreign government, 4.75 per cent. Railways were now the favorite foreign investment with about 45 per cent of the total. Indian railways yielded 3.87 per cent; colonial, 4.0 per cent; American, 4.5 per cent; and other foreign, 4.7 per cent. The highest return was for diamond mines with a spectacular 30.5 per cent for that year. Three quarters of the total estimated foreign investment in publicly issued securities produced an average return of 4.58 per cent. The other quarter, more speculative and presumably less consistent in annual earnings, produced in this year 6.95 per cent, which brought the overall return to 5.19 per cent.[33]

Paish's figure can be used with Inland Revenue returns to estimate income from 1886 on, as described below. The results indicate an average rate of return of 4.94 per cent in 1886, calculated on the amount of foreign investments constructed here for the end of the preceding year, and a range extending from a low of 4.31 per cent in 1897 to 5.30 per cent in 1913.

In the early part of the nineteenth century, actual rates of return seem to have fluctuated more from good years to bad. Interest rates on government bonds, which then constituted a major part of British foreign investment, were usually very high; but defaults were numerous in these early years. British investors were still inexperienced in foreign lending and the lure of high returns led them into mistakes which cost them heavily both in income and in capital. On a list of twenty-five foreign government loans sold between 1818 and 1830 and involving some £ 42 millions at issue prices and nearly £ 55 millions at face value,[34] contractual interest amounted to £ 2.78 millions or 6.6 per cent on issue prices. With allowance for gain to maturity, the interest would be about 8.2 per cent. In contrast to these lush prospects, by 1831 sixteen of these securities, involving some £ 19.3 millions at issue prices and £ 26.3 millions at face value, almost half the principal, were in default. On these defaulting securities the interest was £ 1.47 millions, slightly more than half the amount due each year on the whole sample. On the nine sound loans, interest of £ 1.31 millions averaged 5.8 per cent on their own issue prices, but for the sample as a whole the actual receipts in 1831 amounted to only 3.13 per cent on issue prices. Settlements were eventually made for some of these defaulting securities, but sometimes only after a long interval. Two Greek 5 per cent loans of 1824 and 1825, with a total face

---

[33] G. Paish, "Great Britain's Capital Investment in Other Lands," *JRRS*, 72:475 (1909).

[34] Listed in "Report of the Committee of Secrecy on the Bank of England Charter," *Parl. Pap.*, 1831–32, V, App., p. 98. Two thirds of these, or £ 28.2 millions at issue prices, were floated in 1823–25 at an average (weighted) issue price of 76.3 and more than half of these in turn, some £ 16.85 millions, were subscribed in 1825 at an average (weighted) issue price of 72.05. Estimated balances on current account for 1823–25 totaled about £ 24.6 millions of which only about £ 2.4 millions accrued in 1825. Accumulation of uninvested funds may, in part, explain why foreign securities taken up in certain years, as, for example, in 1825, were so much larger than is accounted for by the balance of payments for those years. Other circumstances were the practice of paying in instalments extending over a year or more, and the retention in Britain of part of the principal to cover commissions, initial interest payments, or purchase of goods exported in a later year.

value of £ 2,800,000 but issued at 59 and 56½ respectively, did not begin to pay interest until the 1870's.[35]

In the light of this evidence, it seemed appropriate to adjust from year to year the rate of return allowed prior to 1886 on the "Accumulating balance of credit abroad" (Table 4, Column K). We may ignore capital gains on successful investments as probably offset, by and large, by capital losses on others. For the early years, the sample cited above suggests 6.6 per cent on issue prices of actual investments in good years. However, since the accumulating balance includes some proportion of uninvested funds probably only partly offset by the instalment buying which was frequently practiced, 6 per cent may be sufficient to allow on the balance of credit accumulated abroad by the close of the preceding year. This rate is used uniformly for 1816 through 1825. In the ensuing depression years, the rate allowed is gradually cut to 3.5 per cent for 1830–1831, a little better average than the sample suggests because there were other investments. The allowance is stepped up to 6 per cent again by 1835–1836 and down to 4 per cent for 1841–1842; and so on through successive booms and depressions. In the decade of the 1870's, the annual rates allowed average 5.5 per cent in conformity with Nash's data. All changes in rate are specially marked in Table 4. The annual adjustments made are necessarily only roughly determined. It is scarcely possible with the limited data available to distinguish one year from another with confidence until the Inland Revenue returns begin to supply more precise guidance on annual fluctuations.

The Inland Revenue returns are considered to be fairly complete on the income of certain classes of foreign investment after the passage of the so-called "Coupon Act" in 1885. There was, however, a great deal of other income from abroad on which report was not required.[36] The estimates prepared by Paish indicate that the net balance of British income from all capital abroad was about £ 143.8 millions in 1907.[37] The Inland Revenue returns, adjusted for the calendar year,[38] show £ 83.7 millions.

[35] Jenks, *Migration of British Capital*, pp. 50–51.

[36] Reports of the Commissioners of Inland Revenue published annually in *Parl. Pap.* See also Sir Josiah Charles Stamp, *British Income and Property* (London, 1916), pp. 227, 234–236.

[37] Paish put the figure for income from publicly issued securities at £ 139.8 millions for 1907. To this must be added income from private investment abroad. In the discussion which followed Paish's paper, this was estimated at about £ 20 millions. From this total of £ 159.8 millions must be deducted, however, not less than £ 14 millions for income accruing to foreigners on publicly issued securities, and possibly as much as £ 16 millions to include income on foreign investment privately placed in Britain. To be on the safe side I have deducted the latter figure to make the net balance £ 143.8 millions. See *JRSS*, 72:466–475, 481–482, 489–491 (1909).

[38] To get values for the calendar year, I have assumed that income was evenly dis-

By applying the same ratio to the returns from 1886 to 1913 we should get fair approximations to the annual net balances of income from foreign investment, and this method is used for these years. Any large shift in the proportions of investment in the reportable and nonreportable classes of securities would, of course, reduce the accuracy of estimates made by this method; and there were certainly changes in the preferences of British investors over these twenty-eight years.[39] Nevertheless, this procedure should give a better check on annual variations than can be achieved by any other means.

J. THE BALANCE ON CURRENT ACCOUNT

The values shown in this column for each year are the sum of annual credits and debits indicated in the foregoing series and should represent the net balances earned on current account. The validity of this series, then, is entirely dependent on the adequacy of the component series. If the latter are sufficiently comprehensive, and if each is correct, or is corrected by compensating errors in other series or in proximate years, then the balances shown should be correspondingly correct. In any five-year period, say, they should represent fairly closely the amount of new credit accrued abroad. This is as high a degree of precision as can be hoped for in constructing estimates when so few strictly relevant data are available, particularly in the first half of the period. These annual balances should represent the new credits available for investment abroad or for repatriation of foreign capital from Britain. By either process the net balance of British capital abroad is increased. The accumulated results can be compared with estimates of foreign investments which have been made for various periods by other investigators using different data and procedures. These comparisons tend to confirm that the balances shown here are close approximations. They will be discussed in some detail in connection with the next series.

K. THE ACCUMULATING BALANCE OF CREDIT ABROAD

The great difficulty in beginning this series is the lack of clear light on Britain's creditor or debtor status at the close of the Napoleonic Wars.

---

tributed through the fiscal year, which ended 5 April, and have added, for example, one quarter of the amount returned for 1906–07 to three quarters of that for 1907–08 to represent the calendar year 1907.

[39] Hobson also used the Inland Revenue returns, beginning in 1875, with Paish's estimate for 1907, but he did not allow for income from capital privately placed abroad or deduct for foreign holdings in Britain: *Export of Capital*, pp. 199–204. His results for these years are, therefore, somewhat more conservative than those used here. In using the Inland Revenue returns for the years before the "Coupon Act" went into effect, he may be on somewhat dubious ground.

CHART 7. NET BALANCES OF THE UNITED KINGDOM ON INTEREST AND DIVIDENDS
AND ON CURRENT ACCOUNT BY QUINQUENNIAL AVERAGES, 1816–1913
(Shaded areas between bands represent deficits on trade, business
services, and other current items covered by interest and dividends.)

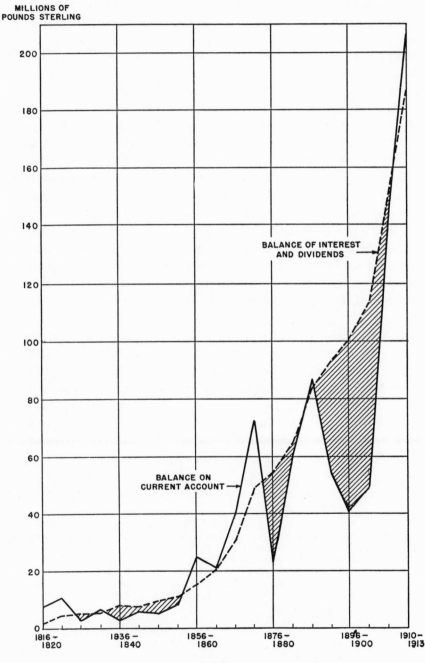

Undoubtedly there were substantial British investments abroad at that time. If the war had brought the loss or liquidation of most of the British business establishments and other investments on the Continent — as well as large military expenditures abroad — there was expansion in other foreign and colonial lands. But the total value of British holdings abroad in 1815 is quite uncertain.[40] Even if it were known, there would still be the question of the amount of foreign capital placed in Britain which must be deducted to give us Britain's net creditor position.

Undoubtedly, foreign holdings in Britain were relatively large at this time. Before the Revolutionary and Napoleonic Wars the British were accustomed to draw on continental capital, although this does not necessarily mean that, on balance, Britain was in a debtor status.[41] During these wars, concern for security of property led Europeans who could do so to place funds in Britain where, with the vast agricultural and industrial expansion which was going forward and with the heavy borrowings of the government, there were attractive opportunities for relatively safe and profitable investment either directly or through banking agencies. Reports given to the House of Commons on the claims of foreigners for income tax exemption show holdings in government stocks of £ 20 millions of principal, with £ 691,000 in dividends, in 1812, and £ 17 millions of principal, with £ 627,000 in dividends, in 1814–1815.[42] Foreigners held other equities also. Hobson notes the belief that, as late as 1817, one tenth of the proprietors of the Bank of England were aliens. Although contemporary opinion may have exaggerated the magnitude of these interests in areas which were not subject to exact reporting, there can be little doubt that the sums invested in Britain were substantial for that day. John Marshall calculated that £ 17 millions of foreign funds were withdrawn from Britain between 1817 and 1824.[43] All in all, the foreign capital placed in Britain may have equalled the gross amount of British investment abroad in 1815.

If there was a net balance in British favor at the close of the war it

[40] Hobson cites a contemporary estimate that $80,000,000 of "American National Debt" was held in Britain in 1807: *Export of Capital*, p. 96. Taken literally, this is an impossible figure, rather typical of the exaggeration which then tended to mark contemporary estimates. The gross debt of the federal government of the United States was only $65,196,000 on January 1, 1808: *Historical Statistics of the United States*, p. 306.

[41] Professor Thomas S. Ashton informs me that in each political and economic crisis from 1701 to 1797 the exchange rates moved sharply in favor of Britain. As he points out, this suggests a strong British position with respect to short-term credits abroad.

[42] *Parl. Pap.*, 1814–15 (259), X. In 1807–08 the principal so held in various government stocks was £ 18 millions with dividends of £ 600,000; *Parl. Pap.*, 1808 (320).

[43] Hobson, *Export of Capital*, p. 96; and John Marshall, *Digest of All the Accounts . . . of the United Kingdom* (London, 1833), p. 120b.

must, then, have been a modest one. I have assumed, as a guess, that the net balance at the close of the year 1815 was about £ 10 millions. If, as is not altogether unlikely, the figure should be smaller, the error is probably offset in the course of the ensuing five or six years by slightly larger foreign trade profits and insurance earnings than are shown by these estimates. Rates of profit may have been slower to subside from wartime levels than was assumed in constructing these series.

Once this initial figure was reached, it was a simple matter to construct the series on the "Accumulating balance of credit abroad." Each year's balance on current account is added to the balance of credit abroad at the close of the preceding year.

It will be noticed that no allowance is made in this series or elsewhere for capital gains, or for repayments of capital. It is assumed that the former were offset, by and large, by capital losses. With respect to re-patriation of capital, the evidence indicates that, throughout this period from 1816 to 1913, British capital credits as a whole, that is, apart from the actions of individual investors, were not brought home and that maturing issues were reinvested somewhere abroad. (See Table 4, p. 70)

With the year 1830 we can make our first comparison of these estimates with the findings of other investigators. At this point two sets of figures are available, both of them concerned solely with the amount of new capital placed abroad after the war. One, a contemporary estimate pre-pared by John Marshall but constructed in a balance sheet which is not very clear, sets the total credit balances accumulated for the years 1817–1830 at £ 100 millions.[44] This sum is 16 per cent larger than the total balances on current account of £ 86.1 millions as constructed here. If Marshall is correct, British international earnings in these years were appreciably larger than those shown in the table. But Marshall's figure is disputed by Jenks, who made the other estimate to be considered.

Jenks's estimate is more limited in content but is firmer and more clear-ly defined. His data indicate that British investment in publicly issued securities of governments and mining companies "between 1815 and 1830" was not less than 75 or 76 million pounds sterling. It may have approached 83 millions.[45] To compare these values with the estimates of the aggregate

[44] *Digest of All the Accounts*, p. 120 *g–h*. Marshall also estimated that £ 81.2 millions of the £ 100 millions were invested in Europe, a figure which Jenks considers much too high (*Migration of British Capital*, pp. 356–357) and, in view of the considerable with-drawal of foreign funds from Britain cited by Marshall, this does seem to be a large sum for new investment, though not necessarily for the balance of credits earned through trade and services.

[45] Jenks accounted for a "net investment" of £ 57 millions in European stocks alone by the end of 1825 (*Migration of British Capital*, p. 356) but counted only "at least 50

amount of net income available for foreign investment as constructed here for these years, we must first add something to Jenks's estimate to cover new capital privately placed in plantations, business establishments and other enterprises, and for securities issued in foreign currencies and purchased abroad in this interval. The question is, how much? Paish estimated the capital privately placed abroad in 1907, when there was a much broader range of publicly issued securities available to the investor, at a sum equal to about 18½ per cent of that placed in publicly issued securities. This is an estimate only, but Paish was extremely well-informed. In this period, before the development of the limited liability company, the proportion could scarcely have been lower, and may well have been higher. It should, therefore, be quite conservative to add one fifth to Jenks's estimate. This would give us at least £ 90 millions and possibly, on the basis of Jenks's higher figure of £ 83 millions for new issues of securities by 1830, as much as £ 99.5 millions of new foreign investment of all sorts between 1815 and 1830, without counting credits earned but not yet invested. The aggregate of the annual balances on current account shown by our reckoning between 1815 and the end of 1829 is £ 100.1 millions and to the end of 1830 £ 100.7 millions.

The next check point is 1854 with three estimates of British foreign investments. Far and away the most reliable is that by Jenks, who places British holdings in publicly issued securities at 195 to 235 millions sterling.[46] Adding again a conservative one fifth for British capital privately placed abroad, we may raise these figures to £ 234 and £ 282 millions, respectively, for gross investment, without considering uninvested funds. If we knew the value of the foreign offset holdings at this time we could, by deducting them, get the balance of British capital abroad — the net

---

millions" in 1830 (p. 64), apparently in order to allow for repatriation of European securities which he considered possible from the fact that poor harvests in Britain resulted in large imports of grain from, and an adverse balance of trade with, Eastern Europe in 1828 and 1829 (*ibid.* 61–62). But adverse balances with this section of Europe could not have been more than £ 2 millions in these years. Even if they were not wholly covered by the gold shipments which seem to have occurred, there is little doubt that credit balances on current account were earned in relations with the rest of the world. For these reasons Jenks's higher figure of £ 83 millions for new investment from 1815 to 1830 in the world at large may be considered to be nearer the mark.

[46] *Migration of British Capital*, p. 413. Jenks distributed these approximately as follows:

	£ millions
United States	50 to 60
French, Belgian, Dutch, and Russian government securities	45 to 55
Spain and Portugal	35 to 45
Latin America	35 to 40
French railways	25 to 30
Belgian railways	5
Total	195 to 235

creditor position — to compare with the accumulated balance of credits abroad shown in the table. In 1907 these seem to have been about 10 per cent of the value of all British foreign investment. This may be somewhat too generous an allowance to make for 1854. Using this proportion, however, we may derive from Jenks's estimate a balance somewhere between £ 211 and £ 254 millions, again without counting credits awaiting investment, to compare with the sums of £ 228.9 and £ 234.7 millions shown in the table for the end of 1853 and 1854 respectively.

The two other estimates for 1854 are both for very much larger amounts. One is Arthur L. Bowley's figure of £ 550 millions.[47] Bowley does not indicate his source or his method of computing this extremely high value. He may have been influenced by the other work to be considered, that of Ernest Seyd, although the fact that Bowley's estimate of £ 1400 millions for 1875 differs materially from Seyd's findings suggests an independent judgment. Seyd, in a paper advocating bimetallism,[48] states that, after making "careful estimates . . . following every one of the factors through the series of years" and drawing on his business experience, he had reached the conclusion that the "international wealth" of the United Kingdom in 1872 (he states later, 1874) was £ 1100 millions. In this he included, however, the value of British ships and cargoes afloat or in foreign ports. Deduct his allowance for these, and the value of British foreign investment, properly so-called, would be £ 940 millions. Deduct also 10 per cent for foreign holdings in Britain, and the balance which can be compared with the sum of £ 861.6 millions shown in the table for the end of 1872 is £ 846 millions. Seyd's figure for 1854, namely, £ 600 millions, would reduce to between £ 500 and £ 550 millions of true foreign investment. He apparently reached this by estimating the net income earned by Britain in the interval and deducting it from his base figure for 1872 (or 1874).[49] The explanation of his very high value for 1854 is found in these calculations, for he certainly underestimated British balances on current account throughout his series, which runs from 1854 through 1877. He shows, for example, deficits aggregating £ 95 millions for the years 1875–1877. Deficits of this magnitude should have required

[47] Arthur Lyon Bowley, *England's Foreign Trade in the Nineteenth Century* (London, 1905), p. 76. Bowley also gives £ 750 millions for 1860, £ 1400 millions for 1875, and £ 2000 millions for 1890 with the comment that the total can hardly be estimated accurately within 25 per cent (p. 77).

[48] Presented to the Society of Arts in 1878 and separately published under the title: *The Wealth and Commerce of Nations* (London, 1878).

[49] The sum of the annual balances which Seyd shows for the years 1855–73 inclusive is £ 400 millions which, deducted from his base figure and adjusted for ships and cargoes afloat, yields approximately the £ 600 millions which he cited for 1854. This fact suggests that his base figure may be for the end of 1873.

TABLE 4. THE BALANCE OF PAYMENTS AND EXPORT OF CAPITAL OF THE UNITED KINGDOM ANNUAL VALUES AND QUINQUENNIAL AVERAGES, 1816–1913

(All values in millions of pounds)

| Year | Balance on visible trade | | | Balance on business services | | | Balance on other current items | | A-H Net balance on trade and services | I Balance on interest and dividends | J Balance on current account | K Accumulating balance of credit abroad |
	A Merchandise	B Gold and silver bullion and specie	C Ship sales	D Profits on foreign trade and services	E Insurance, brokerage, commissions, etc.	F Net credits from shipping	G Emigrant funds	H Tourists, smuggling and unrecorded imports				
1815..	—	—	—	—	—	—	—	—	—	—	—	circa 10.0?
1816..	+ 4.1	− 5.0	—	+ 5.7	+ 2.9	+ 9.0	− 0.2	− 2.5	+14.0	+ 0.6	+14.6	24.6
1817..	− 9.1	− 2.9	—	+ 6.2	+ 3.1	+10.3	− 0.3	− 2.5	+ 4.8	+ 1.5	+ 6.3	30.9
1818..	−21.9	+ 3.9	—	+ 7.7	+ 3.8	+12.5	− 0.4	− 2.8	+ 2.8	+ 1.9	+ 4.7	35.6
1819..	−10.6	+ 1.4	—	+ 5.1ᵃ	+ 2.5ᵃ	+ 9.4	− 0.5	− 2.1	+ 5.2	+ 2.1	+ 7.3	42.9
1820..	− 7.4	− 5.4	—	+ 5.1	+ 2.5	+ 8.4	− 0.4	− 2.2	+ 0.6	+ 2.6	+ 3.2	46.1
Av.	− 8.98	− 1.60	—	+ 5.96	+ 2.96	+ 9.92	− 0.36	− 2.42	+ 5.48	+ 1.74	+ 7.22	
1821..	+ 0.6	− 2.2	—	+ 4.6	+ 2.3	+ 8.2	− 0.3	− 2.2	+11.0	+ 2.8	+13.8	59.9
1822..	+ 0.2	− 2.8	—	+ 4.5	+ 2.2	+ 8.1	− 0.3	− 2.2	+ 9.7	+ 3.6	+13.3	73.2
1823..	− 9.4	− 2.5	—	+ 4.7	+ 2.4	+ 8.6	− 0.2	− 2.1	+ 1.5	+ 4.4	+ 5.9	79.1
1824..	− 5.3	+ 3.5	—	+ 4.9	+ 2.4	+ 8.6	− 0.2	− 2.3	+11.6	+ 4.7	+16.3	95.4
1825..	−26.5	+ 5.4	—	+ 6.0	+ 3.0	+11.3	− 0.2	− 2.3	− 3.3	+ 5.7	+ 2.4	97.8
Av.	− 8.08	+ 0.28	—	+ 4.94	+ 2.46	+ 8.96	− 0.24	− 2.22	+ 6.10	+ 4.24	+10.34	
1826..	−11.6	− 4.0	—	+ 4.5	+ 2.2	+ 8.1	− 0.3	− 1.9	− 3.0	+ 5.4ᵃ	+ 2.4	100.2
1827..	−14.8	− 3.6	—	+ 5.1	+ 2.6	+ 8.3	− 0.4	− 2.2	− 5.0	+ 5.0ᵃ	+ 0.0	100.2
1828..	−14.0	+ 0.3	—	+ 5.0	+ 2.5	+ 8.1	− 0.4	− 2.2	− 0.7	+ 4.5ᵃ	+ 3.8	104.0
1829..	−11.7	+ 1.1	—	+ 4.8	+ 2.4	+ 7.9	− 0.5	− 2.1	+ 1.9	+ 4.2ᵃ	+ 6.1	110.1
1830..	−12.0	− 3.5	—	+ 5.0	+ 2.5	+ 7.9	− 0.9	− 2.3	− 3.3	+ 3.9ᵃ	+ 0.6	110.7
Av.	−12.82	− 1.94	—	+ 4.88	+ 2.44	+ 8.06	− 0.50	− 2.14	− 2.02	+ 4.60	+ 2.58	

Year											
1831..	− 18.1	+ 3.5	—	+ 5.3	+ 2.6	+ 8.6	− 1.2	− 2.2	− 1.5	+ 3.9	+ 2.4	113.1
1832..	− 8.7	− 1.2	—	+ 4.8	+ 2.4	+ 8.2	− 1.5	− 2.2	+ 1.8	+ 4.3[a]	+ 6.1	119.2
1833..	− 12.3	− 2.4	—	+ 5.3	+ 2.6	+ 8.9	− 0.9	− 2.4	− 1.2	+ 4.8[a]	+ 3.6	122.8
1834..	− 15.1	+ 2.3	—	+ 5.7	+ 2.9	+ 8.8	− 1.1	− 2.5	+ 1.0	+ 6.1[a]	+ 7.1	129.9
1835..	− 11.4	+ 0.8	—	+ 6.2	+ 3.1	+ 9.7	− 0.7	− 2.8	+ 4.9	+ 7.8[a]	+ 12.7	142.6
Av.	− 13.12	+ 0.60	—	+ 5.46	+ 2.72	+ 8.84	− 1.08	− 2.42	+ 1.00	+ 5.38	+ 6.38	
1836..	− 21.8	+ 1.5	—	+ 7.4	+ 3.7	+10.4	− 1.1	− 3.2	− 3.1	+ 8.6	+ 5.5	148.1
1837..	− 19.0	− 2.0	—	+ 6.1	+ 3.0	+ 9.4	− 1.1	− 2.5	− 6.1	+ 8.4[a]	+ 2.3	150.4
1838..	− 20.8	0.0	—	+ 7.0	+ 3.5	+10.2	− 0.5	− 3.0	− 3.6	+ 8.1[a]	+ 4.5	154.9
1839..	− 28.4	+ 4.4	—	+ 7.7	+ 3.8	+11.9	− 0.9	− 3.1	− 4.6	+ 7.7[a]	+ 3.1	158.0
1840..	− 29.8	+ 0.9	—	+ 7.6	+ 3.8	+12.6	− 1.4	− 3.1	− 9.4	+ 7.1[a]	− 2.3	155.7
Av.	− 23.96	+ 0.96	—	+ 7.16	+ 3.56	+10.90	− 1.00	− 2.98	− 5.36	+ 7.98	+ 2.62	
1841..	− 22.4	− 1.0	—	+ 7.3	+ 3.6	+12.3	− 1.8	− 3.1	− 5.1	+ 6.2[a]	+ 1.1	156.8
1842..	− 20.6	− 2.9	—	+ 6.6	+ 3.3	+11.4	− 1.9	− 2.8	− 6.9	+ 6.3	− 0.6	156.2
1843..	− 10.9	− 3.6	—	+ 6.6	+ 3.3	+10.9	− 0.9	− 3.1	+ 2.3	+ 7.0[a]	+ 9.3	165.5
1844..	− 12.3	− 3.0	—	+ 7.3	+ 3.6	+11.1	− 1.1	− 3.5	+ 2.1	+ 8.3[a]	+ 10.4	175.9
1845..	− 19.0	− 1.0	—	+ 7.9	+ 3.9	+12.8	− 1.4	− 3.6	− 0.4	+ 9.7[a]	+ 9.3	185.2
Av.	− 17.04	− 2.30	—	+ 7.14	+ 3.54	+11.70	− 1.42	− 3.22	− 1.60	+ 7.50	+ 5.90	
1846..	− 20.3	− 1.4	—	+ 7.7	+ 3.9	+13.3	− 1.9	− 3.5	− 2.2	+ 10.2	+ 8.0	193.2
1847..	− 41.6	+ 5.3	—	+ 9.1	+ 4.6	+16.9	− 3.1[a]	− 2.9[a]	− 11.7	+ 10.6	− 1.1	192.1
1848..	− 26.9	+ 1.0	—	+ 7.5	+ 3.7	+13.4	− 3.0	− 2.6	− 6.9	+ 9.0[a]	+ 2.1	194.2
1849..	− 25.7	+ 1.0	—	+ 8.9	+ 4.4	+13.9	− 3.6	− 3.2	− 4.3	+ 8.2[a]	+ 3.9	198.1
1850..	− 19.6	− 1.0	—	+ 9.3	+ 4.7	+14.2	− 2.8[a]	− 3.6	+ 1.2	+ 9.4[a]	+ 10.6	208.7
Av.	− 26.82	+ 0.98	—	+ 8.50	+ 4.26	+14.34	− 2.88	− 3.16	− 4.78	+ 9.48	+ 4.70	

[a] Beginning year of change in the content, in the method, or in the rate allowed. See text.

TABLE 4. (Continued)

Year	Visible trade			Business services			Other current items				Balance on current account	Accumulating credit abroad
	Merchandise	Bullion and specie	Ship sales	Foreign trade and services	Insurance, etc.	Shipping credits	Emigrant funds	Tourists, etc.	Sum of trade and services	Interest and dividends		
1851..	− 22.6	− 1.2	—	+ 9.8	+ 4.9	+15.0	−3.4	− 3.7	− 1.2	+ 10.4[a]	+ 9.2[a]	217.9
1852..	− 18.9	− 7.8	—	+10.1	+ 5.0	+16.0	−3.7	− 3.9	− 3.2	+ 10.9	+ 7.7	225.6
1853..	− 32.8	− 6.5	—	+13.2	+ 6.6	+19.2	−3.3	− 4.9	− 8.5	+ 11.8[a]	+ 3.3	228.9
1854..	− 36.6[a]	− 3.6	—	+13.4	+ 6.7	+21.4	−3.2	− 4.9	− 6.8	+ 12.6[a]	+ 5.8[a]	234.7
1855..	− 26.8	− 7.8	+0.9	+13.0	+ 6.5	+21.8	−1.8	− 4.8	+ 1.0	+ 12.9	+ 13.9	248.6
Av.	− 27.54	− 5.38	+0.18	+11.90	+ 5.94	+18.68	−3.08	− 4.44	− 3.74	+ 11.72	+ 7.98	
1856..	− 33.3	− 1.9	+1.2	+15.6	+ 7.8	+25.1	−1.8	− 5.8	+ 6.9	+ 14.9[a]	+ 21.8	270.4
1857..	− 41.6	+ 6.5	+1.2	+16.7	+ 8.4	+27.7	−1.9	− 6.1	+10.9	+ 16.2	+ 27.1	297.5
1858..	− 24.8	− 9.9[a]	+1.0	+15.2	+ 7.6	+24.2	−1.0	− 5.8	+ 6.5	+ 15.9[a]	+ 22.4	319.9
1859..	− 23.5	− 1.4	+0.9	+16.7	+ 8.4	+25.6	−1.0	− 6.5	+19.2	+ 16.9[a]	+ 36.1	356.0
1860..	− 46.0	+ 2.5	+0.5	+18.8	+ 9.4	+27.7	−1.0	− 6.9	+ 5.0	+ 18.7[a]	+ 23.7	379.7
Av.	− 33.84	− 0.84	+0.96	+16.60	+ 8.32	+26.06	−1.34	− 6.22	+ 9.70	+ 16.52	+ 26.22	
1861..	− 57.9	+ 2.1	+0.3	+18.9	+ 9.4	+28.7	−0.7	− 6.3	− 5.5	+ 19.9	+ 14.4	394.1
1862..	− 59.5	− 2.3	+0.7	+19.6	+ 9.8	+29.7	−1.0	− 6.2	− 9.2	+ 20.7	+ 11.5	405.6
1863..	− 52.0	− 3.5	+0.6	+22.3	+11.1	+34.5	−1.9	− 5.9[a]	+ 5.2	+ 21.3	+ 26.5	432.1
1864..	− 62.4	− 4.6	+0.9	+24.4	+12.2	+37.7	−1.9	− 6.4	− 0.1	+ 22.9[a]	+ 22.8	454.9
1865..	− 52.3	− 6.4	+1.1	+24.5	+12.2	+40.0	−1.7	− 6.6	+10.8	+ 24.1	+ 34.9	489.8
Av.	− 56.82	− 2.94	+0.72	+21.94	+10.94	+34.12	−1.44	− 6.28	+ 0.24	+ 21.78	+ 22.02	
1866..	− 56.4	−12.7	+1.2	+26.7	+13.4	+43.7	−1.7	− 7.6	+ 6.6	+ 26.4[a]	+ 33.0	522.8
1867..	− 49.7	− 9.5	+1.1	+25.0	+12.5	+43.4	−1.6	− 7.2	+14.0	+ 28.2	+ 42.2	565.0
1868..	− 66.9	− 4.6	+1.4	+26.1	+13.1	+44.9	−1.4	− 7.2	+ 5.4	+ 31.1[a]	+ 36.5	601.5
1869..	− 58.4	− 4.1	+0.9	+26.6	+13.3	+44.8	−1.9	− 7.6	+13.6	+ 33.1	+ 46.7	648.2
1870..	− 59.2	−10.5	+1.7	+27.4	+13.7	+45.7	−2.0	− 8.0	+ 8.8	+ 35.3[a]	+ 44.1	692.3
Av.	− 58.12	− 8.28	+1.26	+26.36	+13.20	+44.50	−1.72	− 7.52	+ 9.68	+ 30.82	+ 40.50	

1871..	− 47.4	− 4.4	+ 1.4	+30.7	+15.4	+47.1	−1.9	− 8.9	+31.8	+ 39.5[a]	+ 71.3	763.6
1872..	− 40.1	+ 0.7	+ 3.3	+33.5	+16.7	+52.0	−2.1	−10.3	+53.7	+ 44.3[a]	+ 98.0	861.6
1873..	− 60.3	− 4.7	+ 4.0	+34.1	+17.0	+52.0	−2.3	−10.2	+29.6	+ 51.7[a]	+ 81.3	942.9
1874..	− 72.4	− 7.5	+ 3.3	+33.4	+16.7	+52.4	−2.0	− 9.6	+14.3	+ 56.6	+ 70.9	1013.8
1875..	− 92.3	− 5.6	+ 1.8	+32.8	+16.4	+50.7	−1.4	− 8.9	− 6.5	+ 57.8[a]	+ 51.3	1065.1
Av.	− 62.50	− 4.30	+ 2.76	+32.90	+16.44	+50.84	−1.94	− 9.58	+24.58	+ 49.98	+ 74.56	
1876..	−118.4	− 7.6	+ 0.6	+31.6	+15.8	+52.1	−0.4	− 8.0	−34.3	+ 57.5[a]	+ 23.2	1088.3
1877..	−142.1	+ 2.6	+ 0.6	+32.3	+16.2	+56.3	−0.3	− 8.0	−42.4	+ 55.5[a]	+ 13.1	1101.4
1878..	−123.3	− 5.7	+ 1.5	+30.7	+15.4	+51.3	−0.6	− 7.7	−38.2	+ 55.1[a]	+ 16.9	1118.3
1879..	−114.2	+ 4.4	+ 2.4	+30.6	+15.3	+51.1	−1.3	− 7.7	−20.4	+ 55.9	+ 35.5	1153.8
1880..	−124.8	+ 2.6	+ 3.7[a]	+31.4[a]	+15.7[a]	+60.0	−1.8	− 8.9	−22.1	+ 57.7	+ 35.6	1189.4
Av.	−124.56	− 0.94	+ 1.76	+31.32	+15.68	+54.16	−0.88	− 8.06	−31.48	+ 56.34	+ 24.86	
1881..	− 99.9	+ 5.6	+ 5.4	+31.2	+15.6	+59.6	−1.9	− 9.4	+ 6.2	+ 59.5	+ 65.7	1255.1
1882..	−106.4	+ 2.6	+ 6.4	+32.4	+16.2	+60.8	−2.2	− 9.7	− 4.1	+ 62.8	+ 58.7	1313.8
1883..	−121.5	− 0.8	+ 4.6	+33.0	+16.5	+64.7	−2.5	− 9.6	−15.6	+ 64.4[a]	+ 48.8	1362.6
1884..	− 94.1	+ 1.6	+ 3.0	+30.9	+15.4	+59.5	−1.5	− 9.3	+ 5.5	+ 66.8	+ 72.3	1434.9
1885..	− 99.5	− 0.2	+ 1.0	+28.9	+14.5	+57.0	−1.2	− 8.5	− 8.0	+ 70.3	+ 62.3	1497.2
Av.	−104.28	+ 0.72	+ 4.08	+31.28	+15.64	+60.32	−1.86	− 9.30	− 3.20	+ 64.76	+ 61.56	
1886..	− 80.9	+ 0.6	+ 1.4[a]	+27.8	+13.9	+52.1	−1.5	− 8.5	+ 4.9	+ 74.0[a]	+ 78.9	1576.1
1887..	− 81.0	− 0.6	+ 2.5	+29.0	+14.5	+54.7	−2.0	− 8.9	+ 8.2	+ 79.5	+ 87.7	1663.8
1888..	− 89.0	+ 0.6	+ 3.2	+30.9	+15.4	+57.7	−1.9	− 9.4	+ 7.4	+ 84.5	+ 91.9	1755.7
1889..	−112.1	− 2.0	+ 7.1	+33.4	+16.7	+60.5	−1.5	−10.0	− 7.9	+ 88.8	+ 80.9	1836.6
1890..	− 92.4	− 8.8	+ 6.1	+33.7	+16.9	+60.6	−1.1	−10.5	+ 4.5	+ 94.0	+ 98.5	1935.1
Av.	− 91.10	− 2.04	+ 4.06	+30.96	+15.48	+57.12	−1.60	− 9.46	+ 3.42	+ 84.16	+ 87.58	

[a] Beginning year of change in the content, in the method or in the rate allowed. See text.

[73]

TABLE 4. (Continued)

Year	Visible trade			Business services			Other current items		Sum of trade and services	Interest and dividends	Balance on current account	Accumulating credit abroad
	Merchandise	Bullion and specie	Ship sales	Foreign trade and services	Insurance, etc.	Shipping credits	Emigrant funds	Tourists, etc.				
1891..	−126.3	− 2.4	+4.2	+33.5	+16.8	+60.4	−1.2	− 9.9	−24.9	+ 94.3	+ 69.4	2004.5
1892..	−132.2	− 3.4	+3.3	+32.2	+16.1	+58.6	−1.1	− 9.1	−35.6	+ 94.7	+ 59.1	2063.6
1893..	−127.5	− 3.7	+2.9	+27.3ª	+13.6ª	+55.5	−1.1	− 8.7	−41.7	+ 94.7	+ 53.0	2116.6
1894..	−134.6	−10.8	+3.1	+27.3	+13.6	+56.5	−0.4	− 8.6	−53.9	+ 92.6	+ 38.7	2155.3
1895..	−130.9	−14.9	+4.4	+28.1	+14.1	+55.4	−0.8	− 9.0	−53.6	+ 93.6	+ 40.0	2195.3
Av.	−130.30	− 7.04	+3.58	+29.68	+14.84	+57.28	−0.92	− 9.06	−41.94	+ 93.98	+ 52.04	
1896..	−145.4	+ 6.4	+7.5	+29.5	+14.8	+58.2	−0.6	− 9.6	−39.2	+ 96.0	+ 56.8	2252.1
1897..	−156.9	+ 0.8	+6.0	+29.8	+14.9	+59.9	−0.5	− 9.4	−55.4	+ 97.0	+ 41.6	2293.7
1898..	−176.5	− 6.2	+7.6	+30.6	+15.3	+60.7	−0.5	− 9.3	−78.3	+101.2	+ 22.9	2316.6
1899..	−155.5ª	− 9.8	+1.8ª	+32.6	+16.3	+64.9	−0.5	−10.6	−60.8	+103.2	+ 42.4	2359.0
1900..	−168.7	− 7.5	+1.7	+35.1	+17.5	+68.5	−0.7	−11.6	−65.7	+103.6	+ 37.9	2396.9
Av.	−160.60	− 3.26	+4.92	+31.52	+15.76	+62.44	−0.56	−10.10	−59.88	+100.20	+ 40.32	
1901..	−174.1	− 6.2	+1.0	+34.8	+17.4	+66.4	−0.7	−11.2	−72.6	+106.5	+ 33.9	2430.8
1902..	−179.2	− 5.3	+0.8	+35.1	+17.6	+67.5	−1.0	−11.3	−75.8	+109.1	+ 33.3	2464.1
1903..	−182.2	+ 0.3	+0.9	+36.1	+18.1	+72.5	−1.5	−11.6	−67.4	+112.2	+ 44.8	2508.9
1904..	−180.0	+ 0.7	+0.9	+36.9	+18.4	+73.5	−1.3	−12.0	−61.7	+113.4	+ 51.7	2560.6
1905..	−157.4	− 6.2	+1.5	+38.9	+19.5	+76.3	−1.4	−13.2	−42.0	+123.5	+ 81.5	2642.1
Av.	−174.58	− 3.34	+1.02	+36.36	+18.20	+71.24	−1.18	−11.86	−63.90	+112.94	+ 49.04	

1906..	−147.2	− 1.8	+1.2	+42.7	+21.4	+ 83.9	−2.0	−15.0	−16.8	+134.3	+117.5	2759.6
1907..	−127.8	− 5.3	+1.0	+46.6	+23.3	+ 91.9	−2.4	−17.0	+10.3	+143.8	+154.1	2913.7
1908..	−136.2	+ 6.8	+0.6	+42.0	+21.0	+ 85.5	−0.9	−15.1	+ 3.7	+151.0	+154.7	3068.4
1909..	−155.2	− 6.5	+1.0	+43.8	+21.9	+ 89.1	−1.4	−15.1	−22.4	+158.0	+135.6	3204.0
1910..	−144.1	− 6.7	+1.4	+48.5	+24.2	+ 93.5	−2.3	−17.2	− 2.7	+170.0	+167.3	3371.3
Av.	−142.10	− 2.70	+1.04	+44.72	+22.36	+ 88.78	−1.80	−15.88	− 5.58	+151.42	+145.84	
1911..	−123.3	− 6.0	+2.1	+49.5	+24.7	+ 93.4	−2.6	−18.2	+19.6	+177.3	+196.9	3568.2
1912..	−145.7	− 4.6	+1.9	+53.7	+26.9	+100.2	−2.7	−19.5	+10.2	+186.9	+197.1	3765.3
1913..	−133.9	−11.9	+2.3	+56.1	+28.1	+107.4	−2.4	−21.0	+24.7	+199.6	+224.3	3989.6
Av.	−134.30	− 7.50	+2.10	+53.10	+26.57	+100.33	−2.57	−19.57	+18.17	+187.93	+206.10	

ᵃ Beginning year of change in the content, in the method, or in the rate allowed. See text.

large export of gold and the sale of foreign securities or the calling in of short-term credits, but, as was pointed out in the discussion which followed the reading of his paper, there was no evidence that these steps were taken. There was, it is true, a small balance of gold and silver export in 1877, but for the three years 1875–1877 bullion and specie imports exceeded exports by £ 10.6 millions. We may, therefore, dismiss Seyd's estimate, and Bowley's also, for 1854.

Bowley's other estimates appear to be equally untenable. His figure of £ 1400 millions for 1875 exceeds Seyd's estimate for 1872 (or 1874) by a much larger margin than can be accounted for by the difference in dates, and it surpasses by a substantial amount Giffen's calculated estimate for 1874–1875, which will be discussed later. On the other hand, Hobson, in his work on *The Export of Capital*, cites Bowley's estimates with apparent approval. Furthermore, some support is lent by Hobson's annual values of British "export of capital" [50] — which, over the whole course of his series from 1870 to 1912, total some 24 per cent less than those for the comparable "balance on current account" constructed here. Hobson's figures for the years 1878–1907 rather neatly fill in the difference between Bowley's high estimate for 1875 and Paish's careful estimate of the total value of British foreign investments in 1907.[51] Thus, if Hobson's values are correct, Bowley's estimate for 1875 may be correct. In that case, the estimates constructed here would be too far from the mark to be useful as a measure of British development in these matters in this part of the century. The question, then, is this: can credence be given to Hobson's findings?

Part of the answer can be found by comparing Hobson's components with the ones used here. References have already been made to his series on commissions, insurance, and banking charges, on ship earnings, and on interest and dividends.[52] His results in each of these three series are lower

[50] Hobson's annual estimates of the net balance of British exports of capital for 1870–1912 aggregate £ 2332.8 millions (*Export of Capital*, p. 204) as against £ 3073.0 millions constructed here. It should also be noted that estimates made by Alexander Kirkland Cairncross in the 1930's, and since then frequently cited, produce a still lower aggregate — £ 2220 millions — for the same period. These estimates have now been published with descriptive detail and cautionary comment by the author: *Home and Foreign Investment, 1870–1913* (New York, 1953), pp. 170–186. They are a revision of Hobson's findings with respect only to earnings of shipping and of investments abroad. As Cairncross points out, his revised total leaves a very large gap between the better estimates of British investments abroad for the earlier and later years of the series. He suggests that Britain had either a larger net balance of capital abroad at the beginning or a smaller net balance at the end.

[51] Curiously, Hobson does not refer to this estimate, although he used Paish's figure for British income from foreign investments in 1907, given in the same place, and presumably, therefore, was familiar with it.

[52] See above, notes 14, 20 and 39.

through most of the sequence, although these differences are partly offset by the debits entered here for emigrant funds and for smuggling. But what chiefly accounts for the very large divergence between the annual balances constructed by Hobson and those presented here is that Hobson makes no allowance for profits on foreign trade, as distinguished from the other items included here under the general heading "Profits on foreign trade and services." In view of the nature and extent of British business enterprise overseas, this is a grave omission.

Other circumstances also argue that Hobson's estimates of Britain's international income are too low. Hobson shows deficits for the years 1876 to 1878 inclusive, although the net import of gold and silver in those three years should suggest favorable balances. Further, Hobson's approval of Bowley's estimate of a foreign investment of £ 1400 millions as approximately correct for 1875 is scarcely consistent with his estimate of only £ 49.5 millions for interest and dividend income in that year, a mere 3.5 per cent. If Hobson's interest allowance for 1875 were capitalized on the assumption of an average return of 5 per cent, it would mean an investment of only £ 990 millions; at 5½ per cent, which is more consonant with Nash's data, it would mean only £ 900 millions. In either case, Hobson's estimates of income would then fall several hundred millions short of reaching Paish's figure on British foreign investments by 1907. At the end of his series, when his estimates of the annual amounts of capital exports are more adequate, indeed excessive in 1912, as he notes, they still fall short of what was required to account for the increase in foreign investment which Paish shows to have been made after 1907. All in all, these considerations leave little doubt that Hobson's estimates of capital export are much too low. Britain's creditor position in the 1870's was, almost certainly, much less substantial than he assumes, and it developed thereafter much more rapidly than his estimates indicate.

This conclusion is supported by the estimates made by Giffen for three different years in this period and by those of Paish, already referred to, for 1907 and 1913. In the first case, Giffen calculated, on the basis of income tax returns and other evidence, that income from British investments abroad (without deduction for foreign income from capital placed in Britain) was not less than £ 65.5 millions in the fiscal year 1874–1875. Capitalizing this by classes at appropriate rates, he placed the total value of investments at £ 1048.3 millions.[53] In this he included some private

---

[53] "On Recent Accumulations of Capital in the United Kingdom," *JSS*, 41:1–39, esp. 4–7, 31 (1878). Reduced by £ 6.5 millions to allow for income on foreign investment placed in Britain, Giffen's figure on income for 1874–75 would be about £ 2.1 millions

investment so that, in adjusting the figure for comparison with the balance shown here, we should not add more than one tenth, say, for other capital privately placed abroad before deducting one tenth of the new total for foreign holdings in Britain. The balance derived in this way from his estimate for 1874–1875 is £ 1038 millions, or 2.5 per cent more than the figure of £ 1013.8 millions shown in this table for the close of 1874.[54]

Giffen supplies two further calculated estimates which can be adjusted roughly for comparison with the values built up here. The first is for the year 1881. Including private investment, he put the value at "not less than 1500 million pounds sterling" at the year end. He seems to have reached this estimate by adding to his figure for 1874–1875 the recorded value of new issues of securities wholly placed in Britain (£ 209.5 millions), plus an extremely substantial allowance (about £ 242.5 millions) for the British share in new issues partly placed in Britain. It may be safer to use only the more exact value,[55] that for the new issues placed wholly in Britain; then we may add 18½ per cent for private investment and deduct one tenth of the new total for foreign share in this financing. By this process we can add £ 224 millions to the modified figure for 1874–1875, and get £ 1262 millions to compare with our £ 1255.1 millions for the end of 1881.

In his next published estimate Giffen brought his record for new issues wholly placed in Britain up to the end of 1885, showing further additions of £ 253.7 millions.[56] This sum, when adjusted in the same way and added to the previous adjusted estimate, indicates a balance of British capital abroad of approximately £ 1532 millions to compare with the £ 1497.2 millions built up in Table 4 by the end of 1885.

With Paish's carefully prepared estimates for 1907 and 1913 we get to

---

more than the net balance of interest and dividends allowed in Table 4 and adjusted for the fiscal year.

[54] It is scarcely possible to construct a close estimate for 1880 from the lists presented by Nash without more data than he supplies. Nash gives the total amount of each issue of the stocks listed without indicating how much of each was owned or traded in Britain.

[55] *JSS*, 45:223, 271–282 (1882). If we take Giffen's £ 1500 millions and deduct one-tenth for foreign holdings, the balance is £ 1350 millions, or 7.3 per cent above the figure constructed here for the end of 1881. If Giffen's allowance for the British share of issues only partly placed in Britain is correct, however, British balance-of-payments credits for the years 1876–1881 must have been incredibly large, nearly twice the amounts constructed here.

[56] *The Growth of Capital* (London, 1889), p. 162. In 1899 Giffen supposed, without preparing lists, that more than £ 800 millions of securities had been added from 1882 to 1897 inclusive. This would mean, after adjustments, a net balance of not less than £ 2115 millions for the end of 1897. It is 7.8 per cent below the value constructed in the table, but it is manifestly not a very firm or studied estimate. *JRSS*, 62:7–8 (1899).

still more solid ground. Using various kinds of data, Paish put the amount of capital placed abroad in publicly issued securities at a minimum of £ 2693.7 millions at the end of 1907. Funds privately placed abroad, such as deposits in foreign and colonial banks and investment in unincorporated enterprises, are not included in this sum. These would, he thought, amount to another £ 500 millions at that time. Foreign holdings in British foreign securities and in Britain itself should be deducted to get the net balance of Britain's creditor status. Paish put the foreign share of ownership in the publicly issued foreign securities at 10 per cent, this being the proportion of the interest and dividends assessed to income tax which was received by foreigners in 1906–1907.[57] It seems probable, although Paish did not say so, that at least an equal proportion of the value of British private investments abroad should also be deducted to cover other foreign holdings in Britain itself. With these allowances, the net balance, to compare with the £ 2913.7 millions accumulated in the table by the end of 1907, would be at least £ 2874 millions. In view of the very different methods used in constructing the two sets of estimates, the correspondence is surprisingly close.

When Paish brought his estimates up to the end of 1913 he found that capital placed abroad in publicly issued securities alone had risen in these six years by more than a billion pounds sterling. He put the new total at £ 3714.7 millions,[58] a figure which Herbert Feis has raised even higher, to £ 3763.3 millions, to correct the low estimates which Paish placed on Russian and Turkish loans.[59] Paish himself regarded his estimates for 1907 and 1913 as understatements. By 1913, according to the Feis amendments, investment within the Empire accounted for 47 per cent of publicly issued securities, but 73 per cent of this was in the dominions, which enjoyed fiscal autonomy. Some 20 per cent of the total was placed in the United States. Railways, foreign and colonial, were, as in 1907, the favorite investment with 41 per cent of the total, a slightly smaller share than in 1907. Railway investment in the United States alone ran to £ 616 millions, or 16.4 per cent of the total of £ 3763 millions. Other foreign railways received 12.4 per cent; Indian railways 3.7 per cent, and dominion and colonial railways 8.2 per cent. Government and municipal loans continued to hold second place with 30 per cent of the total; and of these more than half, i.e., 18 per cent of the total, were in bonds of dominion, provincial, and colonial governments.

[57] JRSS, 72:456–480, and discussion, 481–495 (1909).
[58] The Statist, Supplement, 79: v–vi (14 February 1914).
[59] Herbert Feis, Europe: The World's Banker, 1870–1914 (New Haven, 1930), pp. 23–24. To compare with 1880 and 1907 see above pp. 61–62.

Paish did not give a specific estimate for capital privately invested abroad in 1913, or for the deduction to be made for foreign holdings. But he did state that an inclusive figure would not be less than £ 4000 millions. Adjusting Paish's conservative estimate in the same proportions as for 1907, we get a net balance of £ 3963.7 millions to compare with the final figure of £ 3989.6 millions accumulated in this series by the end of 1913. Applying the same adjustments to the slightly higher figure proposed by Feis, we get £ 4014 millions. The divergence from our accumulated balance of credit abroad is but o.6 per cent in each case.

CHART 8. THE ACCUMULATING BALANCE OF CREDIT ABROAD, 1816–1913
SEMI-LOGARITHMIC SCALE

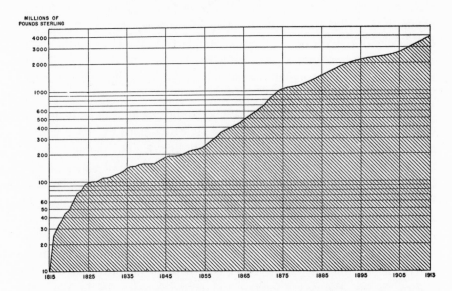

The very close correspondence with the more studied and credible estimates of the value of British foreign investments at so many points along the way invites a measure of confidence in the validity of this series on British credits accumulated abroad. Since the latter is the product of the component series, this congruence tends generally to corroborate the amounts shown in the series on trade and services and dividends also. This is not to say, however, that any of these series can be regarded as anything more than fairly close approximations. The limitations imposed by the nature of the data and by the methods which can be used clearly rule out any pretension to absolute precision. But it does seem reasonably safe to conclude that errors in the estimates of the various components are either quite small or else tend to cancel out among themselves or with unconsidered items within each year or within five-year periods. These series should, therefore, be fairly dependable in marking the relative proportions of the major elements in the British balance of payments, and in measuring the rate and the magnitude of British development in these matters during the century.

IV

THE TERMS OF TRADE OF THE UNITED KINGDOM 1796-1913

Concepts of the terms of trade as a means of measuring a country's gain or loss from exchange of goods have been discussed by students of economic theory for a hundred years or more.[1] Until comparatively recently they have remained little more than concepts, without substantive application; but interest in the subject has been strongly stimulated in the last four decades by the tremendous disturbances in prices, in international payments, in rates of exchange, and in the structure of world trade. More recently, the planning and the study of programs of economic development, in advanced as well as in underdeveloped areas, have drawn still more attention to them. The various formulas devised for the measurement of relative movements of prices and quantities of exports and imports are now used with increasing frequency for the study of relatively current situations. They have not been applied much as yet to illuminate — let alone tested against — earlier trading history, perhaps largely because of the labor involved in gathering and organizing the limited data available. Apart from this difficulty there seems to be no very strong reason why their usefulness should not be tried out in areas of economic history where the data are reasonably adequate.

For no country is systematic measurement of trade relations more valuable, or more feasible, than for the United Kingdom through the nineteenth century. Here was a great and complex commercial community traversing several periods of profound economic change and preserving a considerable body of records with respect to her foreign trade. In the first part of the century, during the period of most rapid mechanization and expansion of her textile industries, she faced the severe readjustments consequent on the Napoleonic Wars with their accompaniments of economic warfare and inflation and their aftermaths of deflation and of high and more or less haphazard protectionism. In the middle of the century she abandoned the system of high duties and restrictive regulations for a

---

[1] See Jacob Viner, *Studies in the Theory of International Trade* (New York, 1937), chaps. viii and ix. Specific applications and formulas are discussed, pp. 558–563.

free trade policy more complete than has yet been embraced by any other great state, and experienced a period of extraordinarily rapid industrial and commercial expansion. The later part of the century was marked by the rise of industrial competitors, both large and small, each with protected home markets. British trade continued to grow, but at the relatively slower tempo of the mature economic community.

Index series on Britain's terms of trade can be constructed with a fair degree of reliability throughout this century. For the earliest years, the nature of the data available imposes some limitations, but these are probably not serious enough to outweigh the advantage of having continuous series constructed with as much precision as possible and covering the whole of this important period in British trading history.[2] Such series should permit more exact and revealing comparisons than have formerly been possible. They should also throw some light on the central subject of these studies. Moreover, because the series can be checked against the facts of British economic life through a long and well-known period, they should serve to illustrate very tangibly the caution that is needed in interpreting the economic significance of measurements of this type. Since the constructions may be useful to others in following various lines of investigation, the data, the methods, and the limitations — of the net barter series particularly — will be discussed in some detail.

THE DATA AND PROCEDURES

The basic data required for constructing indexes on the terms of trade are two sets of figures recording in different ways aggregate values for exports, f.o.b., and for net or retained imports,[3] c.i.f. (cost, insurance,

[2] Two series already existed when this study was begun. First, Frank W. Taussig's well-known index numbers on net and gross barter terms of trade, based on two volume series prepared by the Board of Trade, covered the period from 1880 to 1913 but with imprecise treatment of re-exports from 1880 to 1899: Frank William Taussig, *International Trade* (New York, 1929), pp. 411–419. Second, Werner Schlote prepared a series entitled "terms of trade" running from 1814 through 1933 but using special components which are changed in 1854 so that the series itself is rather special and is not continuous: *British Overseas Trade*, Appendix Table 17. On Schlote's volume series, see also below, and Appendix.

More recently, Alexander Kirkland Cairncross, *Home and Foreign Investment, 1870–1913* (New York, 1953), p. 206, published a series prepared some years earlier by Sir Piers K. Debenham for the years 1870 to 1913. See also Appendix.

[3] Strictly, what should be used is the value of imports actually drawn into the home market. The values for net or retained imports, *i.e.* general imports less re-exports, will vary a little from these since there was usually some time lag — varying with commodities and with years — between importation and re-export, and also between importation and entry through the customhouse for domestic use. Moreover, especially from 1870 on, warehousing and merchandising charges added something to the valuations placed on re-exported goods. The net import values of any given calendar year, therefore, may not

and freight), but without customs duties, for each year of the series. One set is simply the market value as computed for each year by the quantity and the current market price of each article taken ($\Sigma q_1 p_1$). The other set, called a volume series, is constructed in terms of "absolute" values. Here the purpose is to measure quantity change in the aggregate. To accomplish this purpose amid the variety of weights and measures applicable to trade goods, a price weighting is given to each commodity, but the factor of market price fluctuation is eliminated by applying each year the same price — that prevailing in a base year — to the quantity of each commodity traded ($\Sigma q_1 p_0$). The results, although stated in monetary terms, are aggregated measures of volume movement through the series.

These absolute values are used in two ways. Divide the aggregated current market values of exports and of net imports by the corresponding absolute values for each year $\left(\dfrac{\Sigma q_1 p_1}{\Sigma q_1 p_0} \right)$ and the results constitute, in effect, index numbers of average prices of exports and of net imports respectively. However, it should be noted that, unlike the usual price index constructed with fixed quantity weights for each item in the aggregation $\left(\dfrac{\Sigma q_0 p_1}{\Sigma q_0 p_0} \right)$ these are reweighted annually according to the changing quantities of the goods actually traded. The relative movements in these index numbers, that is to say, the ratio of weighted export to weighted net import prices, represent the *net barter or commodity terms of trade*. The second purpose served by the absolute values is to measure quantity movements of exports and net imports. Because the absolute values reduce the variety of weights and measures of the goods traded to a common standard expressed in money terms according to the prices of the base year, they provide a convenient indication of over-all quantity changes in the flow of goods and for this reason are called volume series. Divide the annual absolute values in the volume series for exports or net imports by the corresponding value for the base year $\left(\dfrac{\Sigma q_1 p_0}{\Sigma q_0 p_0} \right)$ and the resulting relatives constitute, in effect, index numbers for the volume of exports or net imports. By means of these indexes, the gross barter index can be constructed, since by *gross barter terms of trade* is meant the ratio

---

exactly correspond with the total taken for the home market. However, the accepted use of net import values, which are infinitely easier to calculate for aggregates, should have only a small effect on the terms of trade indexes except in time of rapid change in price levels accompanied by long warehousing of re-exports, such, perhaps, as during the Napoleonic War period.

of the physical quantity of exports to the physical quantity of net imports.

The first requirement, then, is to establish reliable series on the market values of British trade throughout the period to be covered. For exports of home products, the series of values declared by exporters, beginning in 1798, is adequate. With the aid of Irving's and Marshall's calculations referred to in Chapter II, it is possible to establish values which are probably reasonably valid back to 1796. For import values, and for re-exports which must be deducted in order to establish net import values, there are comparable series beginning in 1854. For the interval from 1796 to 1853, the constructed values presented in Chapter II will be used. To maintain continuity, all series have been adjusted in the earlier years to cover overseas trade of the United Kingdom only, that is, Irish overseas trade with foreign and colonial parts has been included and purely Anglo-Irish trade has been excluded.

Much more difficult, but no less significant, are the volume series of absolute values. They supply, as indicated above, the sole basis for computing the gross barter terms of trade, and they are as important as the current values in determining the price relatives by which the net barter terms are calculated. Since different methods in the use of data yield appreciably different results even over a short span of years, one must approach this formidable matter with some circumspection. Although absolute precision is hardly attainable in this kind of project, even for recent times when the data are more adequate, it should be possible to harness the materials to the logic of the measurements to be made and to achieve quite close approximations.

The differences which may accrue from variant use of the basic data in preparing the volume series can be indicated by a brief comparison of price relatives derived from three separate constructions. The first are average export and average net import prices derived from the volume series prepared by Werner Schlote.[4] In order to limit the comparison to differences in the volume series, these will be used here with the same market values [5] applied in the other two constructions. The second set is from the series which I prepared some years ago, using, to 1865 and with modifications, the old "official" values which have several defects for this

[4] *British Overseas Trade*, pp. 15–30 and Appendix Tables 3, 8, 9, 17, 26. On Schlote's volume series in comparison with my own and the Board of Trade series from 1880 to 1913, see Appendix.

[5] Schlote calculated his price relatives prior to 1854 by means of his own constructed market values. Since the latter were themselves computed from his volume series simply by applying Jevons' general price index, his import price movements in these years are no more and no less than those of Jevons' general index.

purpose, and the two Board of Trade series from 1880 to 1913.[6] The third is from the new volume series to 1900, described in detail below, used with the second series of the Board of Trade for 1900–1913. The price relatives shown in Table 5 for decennial and terminal years will indicate sufficiently the range of the divergence existing between the three series.

TABLE 5. DIVERGENCES IN PRICE RELATIVES AS CONSTRUCTED FROM THREE VOLUME SERIES: AVERAGE EXPORT AND NET IMPORT PRICES OF THE UNITED KINGDOM IN SELECTED YEARS, 1814–1913

(1880 = 100)

	Average export prices			Average net import prices		
	Schlote	Imlah old	Imlah revised	Schlote adjusted	Imlah old	Imlah revised
1814...	301.1	339.1	329.7	265.2	227.6	254.5
1815...	273.9	312.9	300.0	213.7	201.5	217.1
1820...	228.4	242.0	234.8	143.4	150.5	150.0
1830...	146.6	159.6	158.2	97.4	109.6	107.0
1840...	123.9	127.8	128.5	113.6	120.5	122.3
1850...	97.7	102.2	100.8	88.2	91.0	90.7
1860...	105.7	109.6	110.6	107.5	114.3	116.0
1870...	118.2	118.7	118.5	111.6	115.5	115.8
1880...	100.0	100.0	100.0	100.0	100.0	100.0
1890...	93.2	86.6	88.3	82.8	79.1	80.9
1900...	101.1	91.4	91.7	79.1	72.5	76.4
1910...	104.5	89.9	90.2	89.7	79.4	83.4
1912...	109.1	93.1	93.4	89.3	78.8	83.0
1913...	113.6	96.8	96.9	91.0	79.2	83.4

The net barter terms of trade (average export price divided by average net import price, and multiplied by 100 for index purposes) derived from these three constructions also differ. However, when average export and net import price relatives diverge in the same direction, the net barter terms will differ less, hence the somewhat closer correspondence at times in the series shown in Table 6.

Much depends, then, on the construction of the volume series. The methods and data used here will, accordingly, be described in some detail. The main effort was directed towards developing coordinate series on exports, general imports and re-exports so that the biases that are not

[6] *The Journal of Economic History*, 10:170–194 (1950). The prime defect of the "official" values as volume series for this purpose in the 19th century is the bias introduced by the price weighting. The price base is too remote from the period and is therefore too unrealistic and takes too little account of structural changes in trade. While the results show the general trends, they are imprecise especially with respect to annual change.

wholly avoidable in this sort of long-term measurement would be as consistent in tendency as possible for each series and thus minimize bias in
the various measures on the terms of trade. Three main procedures were
followed: 1. The long span from 1796 through 1913 was divided into nine
price base periods in all, as shown in Table 7. These periods vary in length
in some relation to the rate of change in the structure of British trade.
For the period 1900–1913, the two sets of volume series prepared by the
Board of Trade were used. They appear to have been carefully constructed
with extremely comprehensive coverage of commodities.[7] For the new
construction for the years 1796 through 1899, seven price base periods
were used, with a two-year overlap for each in order to link the several

TABLE 6. DIVERGENCES IN THREE SERIES ON NET BARTER TERMS OF TRADE
AS CONSTRUCTED FROM THREE SETS OF PRICE RELATIVES
(1880 = 100)

	Schlote adjusted	*Imlah old*	*Imlah revised*		*Schlote adjusted*	*Imlah old*	*Imlah revised*
1814...	114	149	130	1870...	106	103	103
1815...	128	155	138	1880...	100	100	100
1820...	159	161	157	1890...	113	110	109
1830...	151	146	150	1900...	128	126	120
1840...	109	106	105	1910...	105	113	108
1850...	111	112	111	1912...	122	118	113
1860...	98	96	95	1913...	125	122	116

period series on this basis. 2. In each period, the quantities of each
enumerated commodity were weighted according to the prices of each in
a base year. In order to minimize bias deriving from this price weighting,
a median year was chosen for each period (see Table 7), namely, one in
which the prices for the major commodities of trade were reasonably close
to the average of the period. This procedure cannot safely be counted on
to eliminate all bias, however. The volume series for the years following
the median price base year in each period may be expected to have the
tendency to upward bias characteristic of beginning year weighting and,
conversely, the earlier years will have the tendency to downward bias
characteristic of end year weighting. These biases are attributable to the
tendency of prices of products of most rapid growth in trade to rise less
rapidly or fall more rapidly than prices in general, with the result that
these products are overweighted or underweighted according as beginning
or end year weights are applied. They will vary in degree according to the

[7] See discussion in Appendix.

rate of change in the structure of trade and the length of the period covered by the price weighting. While in any one of the price base periods used here the effect is probably within the limits of tolerance for this kind of measurement, over the long span of the linked periods it takes on more significance because the ratios at each link will tend to transmit and extend these biases. It is probable, then, that the linked volume series have an upward bias, that is to say, they tend to magnify a little the growth in volume that occurred during the century. This, in turn, will mean a corresponding tendency to downward bias in the price relatives derived from the volume series. However, since the series on exports, general imports, and re-exports are coordinate, the biases should be more or less parallel and should largely cancel out in the comparison of export-import price or volume movements. In other words, the various measures for terms of trade should not be much affected. 3. The lists of commodities whose absolute values were to be individually calculated were made as complete as the data permitted in each period (see Table 7) in order to reduce to a minimum the residue of unenumerated goods whose prices or flow may not have moved with the average of the enumerated list.[8]

Attention should be drawn also to various limitations in the data available. As one works backward in the century the number of enumerated articles declines. Insofar as this is attributable to a smaller variety in the goods of trade, or to trivial proportions of some articles in the earlier years, it does no appreciable harm, but when it is caused by the grouping of important articles into fewer classifications it results in some loss of precision even after appropriate adjustment for the re-classification has been made on the basis of the proportions at the time of the change. In 1892, the classifications of goods separately calculated in the series presented here totaled 178 for exports, 217 for general imports, and 75 for re-exports. In 1880, the totals were 102 for exports, 143 for imports, and 72 for re-exports. For the earlier years the numbers were smaller. By 1814, the export classifications used totaled 31, imports were 38, and re-exports 28. In 1798, the exports enumerated were down to 24, imports to 34, and re-exports to 21. Only in the period before 1805, however, was this decline in the number of classifications used accompanied by any appreciable falling off in the very high proportions of total value represented by these samples, and there was none at all for re-exports which in those days were limited to a small number of commodities. The respective percentages of total value are shown below for the price base year of each period. (Table 7)

[8] See also Appendix.

Another factor of imprecision is the treatment of goods recorded only by value, that is, without quantity record. A varying proportion of these are here computed by price index of a closely related commodity or group of commodities, which was the practice also of the Board of Trade for the carefully constructed series used in this study for the years 1900 to 1913. This is not exact measurement, but it should be fairly safe to assume that the prices of cotton lace and net, for example, or of woolen rugs and small wares, moved more closely in harmony with the prices of other cotton and woolen manufactures, respectively, than with the average of the aggregate of all enumerated goods.[9]

The difficulties with the data are greater in the earlier years of the century and various expedients had to be employed to surmount them. In the case of imports and re-exports, for which there were no market values recorded before 1854, the prices used in constructing the real values presented in Chapter II did service in weighting the enumerated commodities in the base years. The "official" value of each enumerated commodity was recorded for the purpose of calculating the residue of un-enumerated commodities. The period prior to 1814 is particularly trouble-some. Quantity records were not systematically published and, although quantity records on many of the principal commodities were found, un-indexed, by turning the pages of the *Parliamentary Papers*, it was neces-sary to use the "official" values in some cases in order to fill in the gaps. For these war and immediate postwar years, a time of large, swift, and erratic changes in prices and in the composition of trade, it was considered prudent to shorten the base periods. In the first and second periods, be-ginning and end years are used respectively for price bases because declared values of exports are not available commodity by commodity between 1798 and 1814. The biases commonly produced by such beginning and end year weightings in time of rapid change should be limited by the shortening of the price base periods and by the linking. In the years be-fore 1814, also, it was necessary occasionally to use interpolations and estimates for particular commodities in order to eliminate inter-kingdom trade and to represent the international trade of the United Kingdom. The hazards here are more or less controlled, however, by the published records for aggregate exports, imports, and re-exports available for the

[9] The proportions so calculated were rather substantial for exports but were very small for imports and re-exports. In 1892, for example, the value of exports covered by price index of related articles was 22.5 per cent of total exports as compared to 73.9 per cent computed by quantity record with specific base year prices. For general imports the percentage was 7.6 as compared to 80.1; and for re-exports 3.3 against 81.5.

United Kingdom back to 1798.[10] If some error has been made in such estimates for a particular commodity it is likely to have been small and should be partly balanced in the calculation of the residue of unenumerated commodities.

The method used in calculating the residue of unenumerated goods also requires a brief explanation. The easy course would be to assume that, on an average, prices of the leftover group of unenumerated items moved in harmony with the average of the large enumerated list and to calculate the aggregate volumes by means of a price index based on the latter. This assumption is not a reasonable one, however. In British trade, the average of the enumerated list was powerfully influenced by the gargantuan proportions of cottons and woolens and their raw materials. It could hardly have been quite typical of the miscellany of unenumerated goods. Accordingly, in calculating the volumes of the residues by means of a price index based on the enumerated aggregates, the weights of these fibres and their products were reduced. In the cases of imports and re-exports before 1854, however, and of exports before 1814, when it was necessary to compute the amount of the residue by means of the old volume series, the "official" values, this difficulty disappeared. It was sufficient to prorate the annual balance shown by the "official" values according to the relationship to market values in the price base year of each period.

The period data for the construction of the volume series, and the proportions of the commodities of export, import, and re-export enumerated for individual treatment, are shown in Table 7.

TABLE 7. THE PRICE BASE PERIODS AND THE PROPORTIONS OF ENUMERATED COMMODITIES USED TO CONSTRUCT THE VOLUME SERIES FOR THE TRADE OF THE UNITED KINGDOM, 1796–1913

Price base periods	Base years	Link years (with next period)	Proportions enumerated (as percentage of total value in the base year)		
			Exports %	Imports %	Re-exports %
1796–1804	1798	1804–1805	72.9	71.1	85.5
1805–1814	1814	1814–1815	89.3	84.5	88.4
1815–1822	1817	1821–1822	90.7	87.7	86.3
1823–1841	1830	1840–1841	93.7	86.9	74.1
1842–1864	1854	1863–1864	85.9	91.3	78.2
1865–1886	1880	1887–1888	95.3	94.4	84.9
1887–1899	1892	1900–1901	96.4	87.7	84.8
1900–1908 (B. of T.)	1900	——	c.88.0	c.94.0	c.93.0
1909–1913 (B. of T.)	"step by step" (1913)	c.92.0	c.95.0	c.92.0

[10] *Parl. Pap.*, 1831–32 (315), XXXIV, 2.

The export and net import price relatives constructed from the volume series and presented below in Table 8 are virtually indexes of the average prices of each. Since they are derived by dividing the current market value for each year by the corresponding absolute value, they are essentially weighted averages, but the weightings change annually with the changes in the quantities of the various goods actually traded. It will be apparent that the movements of these indexes cannot be expected to correspond closely with those of other indexes constructed with fixed weights or with other components.

THE CHARACTERISTICS OF THE TERMS OF TRADE SERIES

Each of the five series on terms of trade presented below in Table 8 (columns J to N) measures, according to its composition, a different set of characteristics of merchandise or "visible" trade. The first two express the chief established concepts capable of practical application. The index showing *net barter* or *commodity terms of trade* (column J) is a measure of the movement of the prices of exports and net imports in relation to each other. Since it is constructed here by dividing the index numbers in the export price series by the corresponding numbers in the net import price series, rising numbers indicate "favorable" movement,[11] that is to say, weighted average prices of exports of domestic products rose more rapidly or fell more slowly than weighted average prices of net imports. Conversely, falling numbers mean "unfavorable" movement, that is, the prices of British goods exported fell more rapidly or rose more slowly than the prices of net imports.

The concept of *gross barter terms of trade* was introduced by Taussig thirty years ago.[12] It is simply and solely a measure of changes in the quantity relationships of exports and net imports relative to the quantities of each in the base year.[13] Again, as constructed here, rising numbers represent "favorable" movement in the sense consonant with that of the net barter ratio, namely, that a larger quantity of exports is supplied in relation to the quantity of net imports received.[14]

[11] This reverses the older procedure, still sometimes followed, by which a rise in the index numbers indicated "unfavorable" movement. The ratio used here was suggested by Jacob Viner and is much less confusing, permits easier comparison with other indexes, and, as Viner has pointed out, does not involve any question of principle: *Theory of International Trade*, p. 558 n.

[12] F. W. Taussig, "The Change in Great Britain's Foreign Trade Terms after 1900," *The Economic Journal*, 35:1–10 (1925).

[13] For brief discussion of gross barter, see Gottfried von Haberler, *The Theory of International Trade* (New York, 1936), pp. 163–166; and Viner, *Theory of International Trade*, pp. 562–563.

[14] This ratio reverses Taussig's formula. However, the movements of the index as constructed here should be easier to compare with those for other series.

Both these indexes deal with gain from a unit of trade. They do not take into account changes in the total volume or, therefore, measure the total gain from trade in relation to the base year. To correct this limitation, Jacob Viner has proposed another index which he calls, descriptively, *"total gain from trade."* [15] It ties the relative movements of export and net import prices (net barter terms) to an index of the total volume of exports and net imports. Thus a rise in the total volume, whether the rise is of exports or net imports or both, may be sufficient to convert an unfavorable movement in the net barter terms into a favorable movement in the total gain index. This index recognizes the fact, which the first two indexes rather obscure, that actual gain from trade may be quite consistent with unfavorable movement in the net barter terms when, as with Britain almost throughout this period, and especially after 1842, there is growth in the volume of trade.[16]

This useful purpose can be met with more precision with respect to the relative roles of exports and net imports in the changes in total volume which occur. In a sense, all that is needed is simply to tie in both the net and gross barter indexes with the total volume of trade. This can be done in two steps, each producing another series. First, using the indexes already constructed, multiply the net barter index numbers by those in the gross barter index. This new series should measure, as units, the relative movements of export and net import prices *and* volumes so that favorable or unfavorable relative movements in unit prices may be counteracted or augmented by relative movements of the unit volumes. Actually, then, this initial series measures the relative movements of the current market values (*i.e.* relative movements of both prices and quantities) of exports and net imports, which is to say, the balance of merchandise trade. It may, therefore, be called simply *"market or trade balance."* [17] The second step and series, designed to allow for change in the

---

[15] Viner, *Theory of International Trade*, pp. 563–564.

[16] Another index, apparently suggested with the present day export problems of Britain in mind, has been proposed by G. S. Dorrance with the title *"income terms of trade."* *Review of Economic Studies*, 16:50–56 (1948–1949). It uses an export volume index with the net barter terms and might also be called "export gain from trade." It eliminates the doubt which is left in Viner's index as to whether the change in volume is for exports or net imports, but in doing so it ignores net import volumes which are clearly relevant also.

[17] The meaning of this step may be shown a little more directly if the relative is calculated, as it may be, without benefit of net and gross barter indexes. In this construction, simply compare the respective movements of current market values of exports and net imports to the values of the two in a base year. Thus, the values to be divided and the resulting market or trade balance relative for 1815 (1880 = 100) would be:

$$\text{Exports} \left(\frac{51.6}{223.1} \right) \div \text{Net imports} \left(\frac{54.5}{347.9} \right) = \frac{23.13}{15.67} \times 100 = 148$$

volume of total trade, that is change in the number of units traded, is to multiply the numbers in this market terms index by those in the total volume index in accordance with Viner's suggestion for the "total gain" series. This new series may be called *"market gain from trade."* The better precision can be seen by comparing (Table 8 and Chart 15) the numbers with those in the total gain series. Allowance for the relative movements of market values (*i.e.* relative movements of both prices and quantities) of exports and net imports appropriately moderates the comparatively large rise shown in the total gain series in years like 1818, 1825, or in the nineties, when the rise in total trade volume was more largely attributable to imports than to exports, and it effectively steps up the gain shown in 1815, for example, when export values rose and net import values fell.

The basic values and the various indexes are placed together in Table 8. This arrangement will permit easy reference to the movements in the basic series which produced the index results in any year, and any series can readily be followed through the years. The fact that the numbers in the more basic series are carried to the first decimal point should not be taken to imply that the measurements are infallibly precise. As the preceding account will have made clear, they can better be regarded as close approximations. The innumerable arithmetical operations and the transcriptions have been carefully checked in the effort to eliminate clerical errors.

THE NET BARTER MOVEMENTS

The most striking trend indicated by the net barter index is the great deterioration, as it is called, in Britain's export-import price relationships in the first half of this long period. It is true that in the first seven years of this series, when average export prices rose more than net import prices, the terms of trade improved, reaching the highest point in the series in 1802, the year of the brief peace of Amiens. But from that date on, through war and peace, the trend of average export prices was steeply downward for half a century. In the last year of the war, 1814, average export prices were almost down to the level of 1796, and in 1815 they fell appreciably below. Meanwhile average net import prices had advanced, however erratically, to a peak in 1814, approximately 45 per cent above the average in 1796 and in 1802. Accordingly, the net barter number, which was 184 in 1796 and 228 in 1802, was only 129.5 in 1814. Measured by quinquennial averages, the net barter terms in 1811–1815 at 159 were some 17 per cent below the average of 193 for 1796–1800.

TABLE 8. THE TERMS OF TRADE OF THE UNITED KINGDOM, WITH VALUES, VOLUMES, AND AVERAGE PRICES OF EXPORTS AND NET IMPORTS, 1796–1913

Year	Exports of U.K. products				Net imports				I Total volume relative $\frac{B_1+F_1}{B_0+F_0}$ 1880=100	J Net barter terms of trade $\frac{D}{H}$ 1880=100	K Gross barter terms of trade $\frac{C}{G}$ 1880=100	L Total gain from trade $I \times J$ 1880=100	M Market or trade balance $J \times K$ 1880=100	N Market gain from trade $I \times M$ 1880=100
	A Current value £ mill.	B Volume at 1880 prices £ mill.	C Volume relative $\frac{B_1}{B_0}$ 1880=100	D Price relative $\frac{A}{B}$ 1880=100	E Current value £ mill.	F Volume at 1880 prices £ mill.	G Volume relative $\frac{F_1}{F_0}$ 1880=100	H Price relative $\frac{E}{F}$ 1880=100						
1796	30.1	9.3	4.2	323.7	31.1	17.7	5.1	175.7	4.7	184.2	82.4	9	152	7
1797	27.5	7.9	3.5	348.1	25.1	14.4	4.1	174.3	3.9	199.7	85.4	8	171	7
1798	32.2	8.7	3.9	370.1	38.3	21.4	6.2	178.5	5.3	207.3	62.9	11	130	7
1799	36.8	10.4	4.7	353.8	41.5	23.0	6.6	180.4	5.8	196.1	71.2	11	140	8
1800	37.7	10.5	4.7	359.0	47.6	23.4	6.7	203.4	5.9	176.5	70.1	10	124	7
1801	40.6	11.2	5.0	362.5	55.8	26.0	7.5	214.6	6.5	168.9	66.7	11	113	7
1802	45.9	11.3	5.1	406.2	41.8	23.5	6.8	177.9	6.1	228.3	75.0	14	171	10
1803	36.9	9.5	4.3	388.4	44.8	24.2	7.0	185.1	5.9	209.8	61.4	12	129	8
1804	38.2	10.1	4.5	378.2	46.3	24.6	7.1	188.2	6.1	201.0	63.4	12	127	8
1805	38.1	10.2	4.6	373.5	51.0	26.1	7.5	195.4	6.4	191.1	61.3	12	117	7
1806	40.9	11.2	5.0	365.2	44.1	24.0	6.9	183.8	6.2	198.7	72.5	12	144	9
1807	37.2	10.0	4.5	372.0	45.5	25.2	7.2	180.6	6.2	206.0	62.5	13	129	8
1808	37.3	9.9	4.4	376.8	45.0	22.6	6.5	199.1	5.7	189.3	67.7	11	127	7
1809	47.4	13.4	6.0	353.7	59.4	25.1	7.2	236.7	6.7	149.4	83.3	10	125	8
1810	48.4	13.7	6.1	353.3	76.0	34.1	9.8	222.9	8.4	158.5	62.2	13	99	8
1811	32.9	9.1	4.1	361.5	44.0	24.4	7.0	180.3	5.9	200.5	58.6	12	117	7
1812	41.7	11.8	5.3	353.4	46.9	22.2	6.4	211.3	6.0	167.2	82.8	10	138	8
1813	—	Records destroyed by fire			—	—	—	—	—	—	—	—	—	—
1814	45.5	13.8	6.2	329.7	56.0	22.0	6.3	254.5	6.3	129.5	98.4	8	127	8
1815	51.6	17.2	7.7	300.0	54.5	25.1	7.2	217.1	7.4	138.2	106.9	10	148	11

Year														
1816	41.7	14.7	6.6	283.7	37.6	20.3	5.8	185.2	6.1	153.2	113.8	9	174	11
1817	41.8	16.1	7.2	259.4	50.9	27.3	7.8	186.4	7.6	139.2	92.3	11	128	10
1818	46.5	17.1	7.7	271.9	68.4	35.7	10.3	191.6	9.2	141.9	74.8	13	106	10
1819	35.2	13.6	6.1	258.8	45.8	28.9	8.3	158.5	7.4	163.3	73.5	12	120	9
1820	36.4	15.5	6.9	234.8	43.8	29.2	8.4	150.0	7.8	156.5	82.1	12	129	10
1821	36.7	16.4	7.3	223.8	36.1	26.4	7.6	136.7	7.5	163.7	96.1	12	157	12
1822	37.0	18.0	8.1	205.6	36.8	27.8	8.0	132.4	8.0	155.3	101.2	12	157	13
1823	35.4	17.8	8.0	198.9	44.8	33.6	9.7	133.3	9.0	149.2	82.5	13	123	11
1824	38.4	19.8	8.9	193.9	43.7	34.9	10.0	125.2	9.6	154.9	89.0	15	138	13
1825	38.9	18.5	8.3	210.3	65.4	45.7	13.1	143.1	11.2	147.0	63.4	16	93	10
1826	31.5	17.0	7.6	185.3	43.1	36.6	10.5	117.8	9.4	157.3	72.4	15	114	11
1827	37.2	21.3	9.5	174.6	52.0	43.7	12.6	119.0	11.4	146.7	75.4	17	111	13
1828	36.8	21.6	9.7	170.4	50.8	44.6	12.8	113.9	11.6	149.6	75.8	17	113	13
1829	35.8	23.2	10.4	154.3	47.5	43.4	12.5	109.4	11.7	141.0	83.2	16	117	14
1830	38.3	24.2	10.8	158.2	50.3	47.0	13.5	107.0	12.5	149.8	80.0	19	120	15
1831	37.2	24.5	11.0	151.8	55.3	50.3	14.5	109.9	13.1	138.1	75.9	18	105	14
1832	36.5	26.2	11.7	139.3	45.2	41.5	11.9	108.9	11.9	127.9	98.3	15	126	15
1833	39.7	28.0	12.6	141.8	52.0	45.2	13.0	115.0	12.8	123.3	96.9	16	119	15
1834	41.6	28.5	12.8	146.0	56.7	48.4	13.9	117.1	13.5	124.7	92.1	17	115	16
1835	47.4	31.0	13.9	152.9	58.7	47.0	13.5	124.9	13.7	122.4	103.0	16	126	17
1836	53.3	33.3	14.9	160.1	75.1	58.4	16.8	128.6	16.1	124.5	88.7	20	110	18
1837	42.1	28.6	12.8	147.2	61.1	53.4	15.3	114.4	14.4	129.6	83.7	19	108	16
1838	50.1	36.0	16.1	139.2	70.9	60.9	17.5	116.4	17.0	119.6	92.0	20	110	19
1839	52.2	37.9	17.0	137.7	80.6	65.7	18.9	122.7	18.1	111.8	89.9	20	101	18
1840	51.4	40.0	18.0	128.5	81.2	66.3	19.1	122.3	18.6	105.1	94.2	20	99	18
1841	51.6	41.5	18.6	124.3	74.0	65.3	18.8	113.3	18.7	109.7	98.9	21	109	20
1842	47.4	41.5	18.6	114.2	68.0	62.8	18.1	108.3	18.3	105.4	102.8	19	108	20
1843	52.3	46.7	20.9	112.0	63.2	63.8	18.3	99.1	19.4	113.0	114.2	22	129	25
1844	58.6	51.0	22.9	114.9	70.9	71.6	20.6	99.0	21.5	116.1	111.2	25	129	28
1845	60.1	50.8	22.8	118.3	79.1	80.0	23.0	98.9	22.9	119.6	99.1	27	119	27

TABLE 8. (Continued)

Year	Exports of U.K. products				Net imports									
	Current value £ mill.	Volume £ mill.	Volume relative 1880=100	Price relative 1880=100	Current value £ mill.	Volume £ mill.	Volume relative 1880=100	Price relative 1880=100	Total volume relative 1880=100	Net barter terms 1880=100	Gross barter terms 1880=100	Total gain 1880=100	Market or trade balance 1880=100	Market gain 1880=100
1846...	57.8	49.7	22.3	116.3	78.1	77.3	22.2	101.0	22.2	115.1	100.5	26	116	26
1847...	58.8	49.8	22.3	118.1	100.3	95.5	27.5	105.0	25.4	112.5	81.1	29	91	23
1848...	52.9	50.0	22.4	105.8	79.8	91.8	26.4	86.9	24.8	121.7	84.8	30	103	26
1849...	63.6	63.1	28.3	100.8	89.3	102.1	29.3	87.5	28.9	115.2	96.6	33	111	32
1850...	71.4	70.8	31.7	100.8	91.0	100.3	28.8	90.7	30.0	111.1	110.1	33	122	37
1851...	74.4	75.1	33.7	99.1	97.0	107.6	30.9	90.1	32.0	110.0	109.1	35	120	38
1852...	78.1	79.6	35.7	98.1	97.0	103.7	29.8	93.5	32.1	104.9	119.8	34	126	40
1853...	98.9	91.5	41.0	108.1	131.6	122.8	35.3	107.2	37.5	100.8	116.1	38	117	44
1854...	97.2	89.4	40.1	108.7	133.8	116.4	33.5	114.9	36.0	94.6	119.7	34	113	41
1855...	95.7	90.2	40.4	106.1	122.5	103.2	29.7	118.7	33.9	89.4	136.0	30	122	41
1856...	115.8	106.8	47.9	108.4	149.1	125.9	36.2	118.4	40.8	91.6	132.3	37	121	49
1857...	122.1	109.3	49.0	111.7	163.7	127.6	36.7	128.3	41.5	87.1	133.5	36	116	48
1858...	116.6	106.9	47.9	109.1	141.4	127.1	36.5	111.3	41.0	98.0	131.2	40	129	53
1859...	130.4	116.9	52.4	111.5	153.9	135.6	39.0	113.5	44.2	98.2	134.4	43	132	58
1860...	135.9	122.9	55.1	110.6	181.9	156.2	44.9	116.5	48.9	94.9	122.7	46	116	57
1861...	125.1	112.6	50.5	111.1	183.0	161.5	46.4	113.3	48.0	98.1	108.8	47	107	51
1862...	124.0	106.1	47.6	116.9	183.5	166.1	47.7	110.5	47.7	105.8	99.8	50	106	51
1863...	146.6	113.8	51.0	128.8	198.6	165.3	47.5	120.1	48.9	107.2	107.4	52	115	56
1864...	160.4	113.5	50.9	141.3	222.8	165.2	47.5	134.9	48.8	104.7	107.2	51	112	55
1865...	165.8	123.2	55.2	134.6	218.1	173.4	49.8	125.8	51.9	107.0	110.8	56	119	62
1866...	188.9	135.8	60.9	139.1	245.3	193.9	55.7	126.5	57.7	110.0	109.3	63	120	69
1867...	181.0	138.3	62.0	130.9	230.7	190.0	54.6	121.4	57.5	107.8	113.6	62	122	70
1868...	179.7	147.0	65.9	122.2	246.6	202.4	58.2	121.8	61.2	100.3	113.2	61	114	70
1869...	190.0	156.5	70.1	121.4	248.4	211.1	60.7	117.7	64.4	103.1	115.5	66	119	77
1870...	199.6	168.5	75.5	118.5	258.8	223.4	64.2	115.8	68.6	102.3	117.6	70	120	82

1871....	223.1	189.0	118.0	84.7	270.5	250.6	72.0	107.9	77.0	109.4	117.6	84	129	99
1872....	256.3	196.2	130.6	87.9	296.4	256.4	73.7	115.6	79.3	113.0	119.3	90	135	107
1873....	255.2	188.7	135.2	84.6	315.4	273.3	78.6	115.4	80.9	117.2	107.6	95	126	102
1874....	239.6	187.7	127.7	84.1	312.0	276.6	79.5	112.8	81.3	113.2	105.8	92	120	98
1875....	223.5	186.3	120.0	83.5	315.8	293.8	84.4	107.5	84.1	111.6	98.9	94	110	93
1876....	200.6	181.6	110.5	81.4	319.0	304.3	87.5	104.8	85.1	105.4	93.0	90	98	83
1877....	198.9	187.3	106.2	84.0	341.0	316.3	90.9	107.8	88.2	98.5	92.4	87	91	80
1878....	192.8	188.4	102.3	84.4	316.1	316.4	90.9	99.9	88.4	102.4	92.8	91	95	84
1879....	191.5	198.6	96.4	89.0	305.7	322.4	92.7	94.8	91.2	101.7	96.0	93	98	89
1880....	223.1	223.1	100.0	100.0	347.9	347.9	100.0	100.0	100.0	100.0	100.0	100	100	100
1881....	234.0	244.2	95.8	109.5	334.0	336.9	96.8	99.1	101.8	96.7	113.1	98	109	111
1882....	241.5	247.2	97.7	110.8	347.8	354.4	101.9	98.1	105.4	99.6	108.7	105	108	114
1883....	239.8	254.1	94.4	113.9	361.3	377.2	108.4	95.8	110.6	98.5	105.1	109	103	114
1884....	233.0	256.2	90.9	114.8	327.1	359.4	103.3	91.0	107.8	99.9	111.1	108	111	120
1885....	213.1	243.7	87.4	109.2	312.6	366.6	105.4	85.3	106.9	102.5	103.6	110	106	113
1886....	212.7	254.3	83.6	114.0	293.6	366.6	105.4	80.1	108.7	104.4	108.2	113	113	123
1887....	221.9	266.0	83.4	119.2	302.9	386.3	111.0	78.4	114.2	106.4	107.4	122	114	130
1888....	234.5	282.9	82.9	126.8	323.6	399.7	114.9	81.0	119.5	102.3	110.4	122	113	135
1889....	248.9	294.3	84.6	131.9	361.0	439.7	126.4	82.1	128.5	103.0	104.4	132	108	139
1890....	263.5	298.4	88.3	133.8	356.0	440.1	126.5	80.9	129.3	109.1	105.8	141	115	149
1891....	247.2	282.5	87.5	126.6	373.6	458.2	131.7	81.5	129.7	107.4	96.1	139	103	134
1892....	227.1	271.8	83.6	121.8	359.2	459.8	132.2	78.1	128.1	107.0	92.1	137	99	127
1893....	218.1	261.4	83.4	117.2	345.7	453.0	130.2	76.3	125.1	109.3	90.0	137	98	123
1894....	215.8	272.6	79.2	122.2	350.4	493.0	141.7	71.1	134.1	111.4	86.2	149	96	129
1895....	225.9	296.4	76.2	132.9	356.8	518.6	149.1	68.8	142.7	110.8	89.1	158	99	141
1896....	240.2	312.5	76.9	140.1	385.6	555.4	159.6	69.4	152.0	110.8	87.8	168	97	147
1897....	234.2	308.2	76.0	138.1	391.1	565.7	162.6	69.1	153.0	110.0	84.9	168	93	142
1898....	233.4	306.2	76.2	137.2	409.9	588.2	169.1	69.7	156.6	109.3	81.1	171	89	139
1899....	264.5ᵃ	331.3ᵃ	79.8	146.1	420.0	590.8	169.8	71.1	160.5ᵃ	112.2	86.0	180	97	156
1900....	291.2	317.5	91.7	140.0	459.9	602.1	173.1	76.4	160.0	120.0	80.9	192	97	156

TABLE 8. (Continued)

Year	Exports of U.K. products				Net imports									
	Current value £ mill.	Volume £ mill.	Volume relative 1880=100	Price relative 1880=100	Current value £ mill.	Volume £ mill.	Volume relative 1880=100	Price relative 1880=100	Total volume relative 1880=100	Net barter terms 1880=100	Gross barter terms 1880=100	Total gain 1880=100	Total Market or trade balance 1880=100	Market gain 1880=100
1901...	280.0	320.6	141.4	87.3	454.2	614.9	176.7	73.9	162.8	118.1	80.0	192	94	153
1902...	283.4	340.3	150.0	83.3	462.6	633.9	182.2	73.0	169.5	114.1	82.3	193	94	159
1903...	290.8	349.4	154.1	83.2	473.0	639.5	183.8	74.0	172.1	112.4	83.8	193	94	162
1904...	300.7	357.0	157.4	84.2	480.7	646.8	185.9	74.3	174.7	113.3	84.7	198	96	168
1905...	329.8	392.4	173.0	84.0	487.2	653.1	187.7	74.6	181.9	112.6	92.2	205	104	189
1906...	375.6	421.8	186.0	89.0	522.8	672.3	193.2	77.8	190.4	114.4	96.3	218	110	209
1907...	426.0	456.0	201.1	93.4	553.9	681.2	195.8	81.3	197.9	114.9	102.2	227	118	234
1908...	377.1	419.7	185.1	89.8	513.3	655.7	188.5	78.3	187.1	114.7	98.2	215	113	211
1909...	378.2	437.3	192.8	86.5	533.4	674.2	193.8	79.1	193.4	109.4	99.5	212	109	211
1910...	430.4	477.0	210.3	90.2	574.5	687.3	197.6	83.6	202.6	107.9	106.4	219	115	233
1911...	454.1	494.4	218.0	91.8	577.4	708.2	203.6	81.5	209.3	112.6	107.1	236	121	253
1912...	487.2	521.6	230.0	93.4	632.9	762.7	219.2	83.0	223.5	112.5	104.9	251	118	264
1913...	525.3	541.9	238.9	96.9	659.2	790.0	227.1	83.4	231.8	116.2	105.2	269	122	283

a New ships included 1899ff. For adjustment of the export volume index, the estimated value of new ships in 1880 (£ 3.7 m.) is added to the export volume cited (£ 223.1 m.) for that base year.

1880 = 100

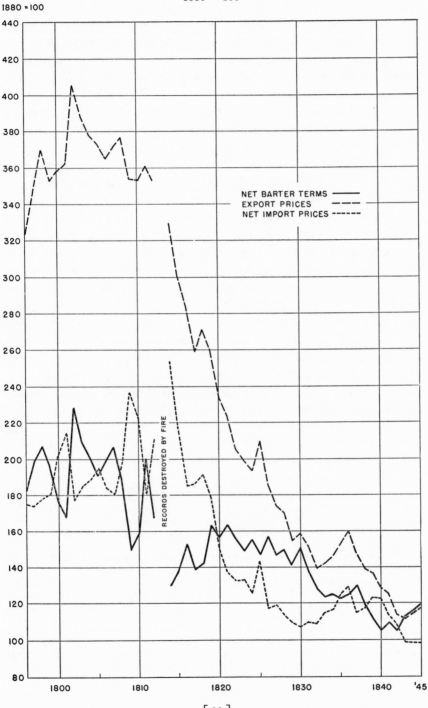

It was the decline in weighted average export prices counter to the trend of net import prices that caused this severe deterioration in British net barter terms. The economic significance of this "unfavorable" movement must be interpreted with due caution, however. What so steadily and disproportionately depressed average export prices was the phenomenal growth in the volume and fall in the prices of cotton textile exports attributable to the rapid mechanization of the industry. Since this growth is strongly suggestive of profitable business, the "unfavorable" movement in the terms of trade cannot be interpreted to signify economic adversity. The role of the textiles will be examined more closely later in this chapter.

After the war, for more than four decades, the net barter terms of the United Kingdom continued to deteriorate. However, the rate of decline in net barter terms was less rapid than in the later war years when average export and net import prices had moved in contrary courses. Although the volume of exports and of net imports doubled and redoubled and nearly redoubled again over these forty years, prices of both fell steeply in the first half of this period. By 1836–1840, average export prices had fallen almost 58 per cent from 1811–1815. Average net import prices were also severely deflated, falling nearly 44 per cent in the same interval, somewhat more rapidly than the old unweighted wholesale commodity indexes have indicated.[18] These movements brought the net barter numbers down from 159 to 118, a fall of 26 per cent over this twenty-five year period.

This decline in the net barter terms continued for two more decades. During this second part of the postwar period of deterioration, the ebbing tide of net import and export prices was checked somewhat in the 1840's, and then reversed in the fifties. Net import prices responded first, moving upward from the low point reached in 1848. Average export prices followed

[18] Silberling's unweighted index, for example, shows a decline of 38 per cent from 1811–1815 to 1836–1840, and only 22 per cent from 1816–1820, in contrast to 44 and 31 per cent respectively shown here by the weighted net import index. Jevons shows 41 and 26 per cent. Schlote's import prices are controlled by Jevons in this period and show the same rate of decline; but in export prices he shows a fall of 54 and 44 per cent, respectively (*British Overseas Trade*, pp. 176–186), as compared with 58 and 46 per cent shown here.

The new wholesale price index of 52 imported commodities constructed by Gayer, Rostow, and Schwartz — *The Growth and Fluctuation of the British Economy 1790–1850* (Oxford, 1953), p. 470 — with fixed weighting based on net import proportions in 1820, 1830, and 1840, includes customs duties and consequently is not relevant with respect to terms of trade, but near the base years it should be more nearly comparable than any of the other commodity indexes to this import price index constructed with annually changing quantities. From 1811–15 and 1816–20, respectively, to 1836–40 it shows a decline of 45 and 35 per cent. The differences from the import index constructed here are scarcely more than can be attributed to the reductions made in tariff rates in the interval for several commodities imported in rising volume. On tariff changes, see Chapter V below.

CHART IO. THE NET BARTER TERMS OF TRADE OF THE UNITED KINGDOM,
SHOWING WEIGHTED AVERAGE EXPORT AND NET IMPORT PRICES, 1845–1913

1880 = 100

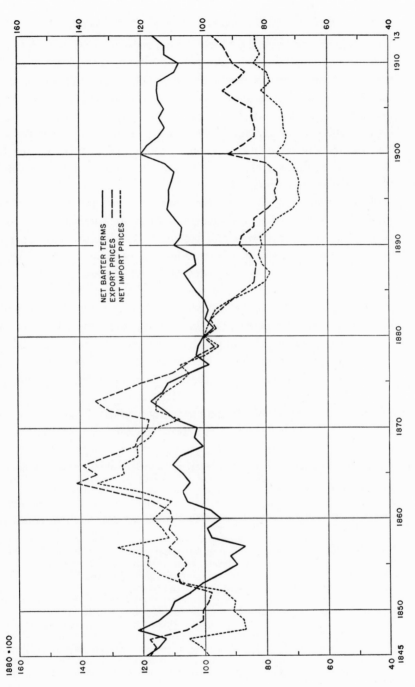

after 1852 but, through the fifties, did not recover as much as did net import prices, probably chiefly because of continuing cost-reducing improvements in production processes and in handling. By 1856–1860, the net barter numbers averaged 94, down 22 per cent over this twenty-year period. This average was less than half that of 1796–1800, and was the lowest quinquennial average in the century. Yet the fact that the 1850's were far from being a time of economic retrogression in the United Kingdom serves again as a clear warning not to attach undue significance to the net barter movements alone.

In the second half of the century average export and net import prices were somewhat steadier and changes were more consistent, so that the net barter movements were less violent.[19] Both export and net import prices recovered a good deal from their lows near the middle of the century. Although other export industries were developing cost-reducing processes and were cutting into the great preponderance which the textiles had gained in the British export trade, the export price history of the first period was not repeated. On the contrary, the trend in the net barter terms was generally, although gently, favorable. This was true from 1857 on into the "great depression" which began in the middle seventies. Then, in the first phase from 1873 to 1879, in contrast to the beginning years of each depression in the first half of the century,[20] average export prices declined a little more quickly than net import prices. From 1881 on, however, export prices held somewhat better than net import prices [21] so that

[19] On seven occasions from 1796 to 1814, net barter numbers changed by more than 10 per cent from the preceding year, and the percentages here are calculated on some very high figures. This violence of movement was perhaps to be expected in a period of general war. There were only three occasions of comparable sharpness in the century of relative peace from 1814 to 1913, namely 1816, 1819, and 1858, all of them showing favorable movement in depression years.

It is interesting also to compare the post-1814 protectionist period with post-1842 free trade with respect to frequency of large and sudden net barter change. For this we may use 8 per cent, say, as a measure. From 1815 to 1842 there were seven occasions when the numbers changed as much as 8 per cent from the preceding year, in contrast to only four in the much longer span from 1842 to 1913.

[20] Almost every business recession in the earlier period was marked by a rise in the net barter terms because net import prices fell off more, initially, than export prices. The converse was also true in boom periods. From 1810 to 1842, each upswing in the business cycle was accompanied by some downward movement in the terms of trade caused by a larger rise in import than in export prices. Beginning with 1843, there were several occasions when upswings were accompanied by favorable net barter movement.

[21] As Professor R. E. Baldwin has pointed out — American Economic Review, 45:259–269 (May 1955) — a large part of this decline in net import prices in the last quarter of the century may be attributed to the rapid fall in water-borne freight rates; and, no doubt, railway building and other improvements in handling facilities also played a part. It did not, therefore, mean equally lower prices at points of origin. In the same interval British exports, which were valued f.o.b. in Britain, presumably also declined in price

net barter movement was generally favorable. By 1909–1913, the index average was 112. This was only 26 per cent below 1816–1820, and it was 19 per cent above the low quinquennium 1856–1860 which included also the lowest year of the century. The great intervening development in cost-reducing techniques of manufacture and in the volume and composition of the British export trade had, with surprising rapidity, been followed by an almost equally significant cost-reducing revolution in the production and supply of British import commodities.

THE INFLUENCE OF COTTONS AND WOOLENS ON THE NET BARTER TERMS OF TRADE

The extraordinarily rapid deterioration in the British net barter terms in the first half of the century has special interest. The profound change which the use of machinery wrought in the export status of cotton textiles was by far the most important factor in this deterioration. A massive rise in volume, both absolute and relative to total British exports, and a precipitate fall in price in the course of a few decades, exerted together a powerful influence on the weighted average of export prices. A closer examination of the role of cotton and woolen goods and other exports after 1814, when price movements can be followed year by year with some precision, will serve a double purpose. First, it will mark out the average price changes in these groups of commodities, and their prime raw material imports, as they entered into the weighted average of the aggregates. Second, it will demonstrate quite tangibly the need for caution in interpreting the economic significance of over-all movements in net barter terms.

The rise of cottons in the British export trade was a machine-age phenomenon. It was mass production which initially made it possible, after conveying the raw cotton from distant shores, to manufacture and to sell the finished products abroad in huge quantities at prices which defied competition sometimes even in the area of origin of the raw material. Cottons began to edge out woolens as the foremost British export around 1800, and they soon assumed a preponderance which was never closely challenged by any other cognate group of commodities through the ensuing century.

The following table (Table 9), showing cottons as percentages of total exports by volume and by value at decennial intervals to 1880, that is, during the period of their rise and the beginning of their relative decline,

---

more at points of destination than at British ports for the same reasons. Improvement in British net barter terms was thus quite compatible with rising terms for Britain's trading partners.

will indicate the degree and the timing of this important change in the composition of British exports. The proportions which net imports of raw cotton, wholly imported, bore to all net imports are also shown in Table 9 in order to contrast the lesser influence that they exerted on weighted average net import prices.[22]

TABLE 9. PROPORTIONS OF COTTONS AND OF RAW COTTON IN THE TRADE OF THE UNITED KINGDOM IN SELECTED YEARS, 1796–1880

	By volume at 1880 prices				By value			
	Exports			Net imports of raw cotton %	Exports			Net imports of raw cotton %
	Manu-factures %	Twist & yarn %	Total %		Manu-factures %	Twist & yarn %	Total %	
1796–98	c. 6.0	a	c. 6.0	3.4	c.13.7	a	c.13.7	7.5
1814	19.6	5.1	24.7	6.3	38.0	6.1	44.1	9.1
1820	22.5	8.2	30.7	12.7	37.7	7.8	45.5	17.5
1830	27.0	14.8	41.8	13.8	39.9	10.8	50.7	13.6
1840	28.9	16.4	45.3	21.3	34.2	13.8	48.0	18.2
1850	27.6	10.2	37.8	14.5	30.6	8.9	39.5	18.3
1860	30.8	8.9	39.7	19.1	31.0	7.3	38.3	16.7
1870	26.2	6.1	32.3	13.2	28.4	7.3	35.7	17.5
1880	28.5	5.3	33.8	10.7	28.5	5.3	33.8	10.7

a Negligible at this time except in export from Great Britain to Ireland.

It will be obvious that increases of such magnitude in the volume proportions were bound to have a correspondingly large effect on weighted average prices. We cannot trace the export price history of particular commodities year by year prior to the destruction of records in the customhouse fire of 1813, but over the interval from 1798 to 1814, average prices of exports of cotton manufactures, already lower in price than other major exports such as woolens and moving counter to the average net import prices of the raw material, fell about 30 per cent. In the same interval, their weight in determining over-all average export prices became more than three times as large since their volume proportion to the total more than trebled. Meanwhile, too, exports of cotton yarn rose from negligible amounts to more than 5 per cent of the volume of total exports. Export prices of this commodity, which required little labor, followed those of the imported raw material upwards but, since it was a relatively low-cost product, the great growth in volume acted further to depress weighted average prices of aggregate exports.

[22] For annual values, volumes, and average prices of cotton and cotton manufactures, see Appendix Table II.

In the deflation period after 1814, average prices of exports of cotton manufactures continued to fall much more rapidly than the general export average for two more decades. By 1833, which was a low point marking off the period of most rapid decline for the cottons, they had dropped 71 per cent below those of 1814. In the same interval, average export prices of other goods omitting cottons and woolens dropped 51 per cent.

CHART II. WEIGHTED AVERAGE PRICES OF EXPORTS OF COTTON MANUFACTURES
AND YARN AND OF NET IMPORTS OF RAW COTTON, 1814–1880
1880 = 100

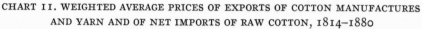
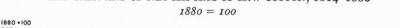

Source: Appendix Table II.

By 1843, another low point, average prices of exports of cotton manufactures had fallen 80 per cent below 1814 levels,[23] in contrast to 55 per cent for other exports. While this rapid decline in price of cotton manufactures was taking place, the volume of their exports continued to rise more rapidly than that of other exports. By 1843, their share of the volume of total exports, and their influence on average export prices, was nearly 50 per cent greater than in 1814. Cotton twist and yarn also exerted a larger depressing influence on average export prices. Here, average prices fell 70 per cent from 1814 to 1833 and 77 per cent by 1843. Their volume share in total exports more than trebled by the latter date and the in-

[23] Changes in rate of flow and in prices within the cotton group also affected the weighted averages. For example, a small part of the decline in average export prices of cotton manufactures is attributable to growing proportions of white or plain piece goods whose average export price fell 84 per cent from 1814 to 1843.

fluence of these low-priced products on weighted average prices of general exports was correspondingly magnified.

Average prices of net imports of raw cotton followed much the same course in this postwar period. By 1843 they were 79 per cent below the swollen prices of 1814 in spite of, or, if it was demand that evoked investment and supply, because of the massive increase in the volume of consumption. Actually, then, the fall in average export prices of cotton yarn and of cotton manufactures was very closely matched by that in the net import prices of the chief raw material of this industry over this period. The net barter terms of trade of these commodities did not deteriorate seriously from 1814 to 1843, and, indeed, at times they were more favorable than in the former year.

Woolen exports are of some interest also in interpreting the meaning of the deterioration shown in the net barter series. Prices were higher than in the cotton group and, with somewhat slower mechanization, fell less quickly. Woolen goods went more largely to better income classes so that the market, if somewhat steadier, was also less readily expansible especially in the face of the competition offered by cheaper and cheaper cottons. In any case, while woolen exports grew a little in volume in this period, their growth did not begin to keep pace with the cottons, or with British exports generally, and their share of the total fell off radically. Pre-eminent among British exports in 1796–1798 at more than one quarter of the total value, they had fallen to one seventh by 1814, and were only one ninth by 1840. Such was the decline in the weight of this group of goods on British export price averages. On the other hand, woolen yarn, a lower priced commodity which was negligible in export in the earlier years, had risen to nearly 1 per cent of the value of all exports by 1840.

The following table (Table 10) shows the proportions of exports of woolen manufactures and yarn to total exports, by volume at 1880 prices and by market value, in selected years.[24] The proportions which net imports of wool bore to net imports in aggregate are also shown, but it should be noted that domestic production furnished by far the major part of the raw material in the first half of this period.

Export prices of woolens fell much less than those of cottons both during the period of wartime inflation and after. From 1796–1798 to 1814 they seem to have declined only about 9 per cent in average export price. There may, however, have been some deterioration in quality consequent

---

[24] For annual values, volumes, and average prices of wool and woolen manufactures, see Appendix Table III.

on short supply and high cost of the raw material which would make this figure an overstatement. The rise in average export prices in 1815 and 1816 counter to the movement of other prices, including those of raw wool, is suggestive of something of this sort. By the 1820's, with the better grades of foreign wool again in fair supply and with prices of domestic wools much below those of 1814–1815, the qualities of the finished products were probably stabilized. From 1821 to 1842, a low year for woolens, average export prices fell 37 per cent. Looked at for

TABLE 10. PROPORTIONS OF WOOLENS AND OF RAW WOOL IN THE TRADE OF THE UNITED KINGDOM IN SELECTED YEARS, 1796–1880

	By volume at 1880 prices				By value			
	Exports			Net imports of raw wool %	Exports			Net imports of raw wool %
	Manu-factures %	Yarn %	Total %		Manu-factures %	Yarn %	Total %	
1796–98	c.35.0	a	c.35.0	1.3	c.26.0	a	c.26.0	2.0
1814	21.2	a	21.2	3.9	14.0	a	14.0	6.9
1820	19.4	a	19.4	1.8	15.3	a	15.3	3.0
1830	13.6	0.5	14.1	3.7	12.3	0.3	12.6	6.3
1840	9.9	1.2	11.2	4.0	10.4	0.9	11.3	4.3
1850	12.7	2.4	15.1	3.3	12.0	2.0	14.0	3.8
1860	9.0	2.8	11.8	4.1	8.8	2.8	11.7	4.8
1870	9.6	2.7	12.3	4.2	10.9	2.5	13.4	4.0
1880	7.7	1.5	9.2	3.4	7.7	1.5	9.2	3.4

a negligible

this more limited period, average prices of net imports of wool, already beginning to feel the pressure of cheaper Australian wool which grew rather rapidly in supply from the mid-thirties, dropped 45 per cent. Thus the net barter terms for this industry moved favorably over this shorter interval, but the diminishing share of the products in total exports reduced the weight in the over-all averages.

With cottons and woolens removed from the account, the net barter terms of the balance of other British exports and net imports show less serious deterioration over this postwar deflation period. Weighted average prices of this balance of exports fell 57.3 per cent from the high of 1814 to the low of 1842, and those of net imports fell 52.4 per cent. The net barter index for this balance dropped just 12 points, or 11 per cent,[25] whereas the over-all index dropped 24 points, or 19 per cent. Comparable figures for the quinquenniums 1814–1818 and 1838–1842 are less striking

[25] See Appendix Table IV.

than those from peak to trough years, but they bring out the same point. Whereas a net barter index of exports omitting cottons and woolens dropped from an average of 125 in 1814–1818 to 104 in 1838–1842, or nearly 17 per cent, the over-all index dropped from 140 to 110, or slightly over 21 per cent.

CHART 12. WEIGHTED AVERAGE PRICES OF EXPORTS AND NET IMPORTS AND THE
NET BARTER TERMS OMITTING COTTON AND WOOL, 1814–1880

1880 = 100

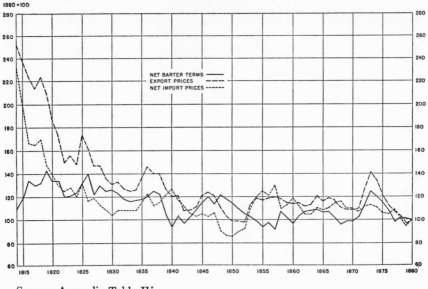

Source: Appendix Table IV.

Yet this balance of goods after omitting cottons and woolens is not by any means free from other weighting influences tending, in this period, to maximize the price decline shown for the average of total exports and to minimize that for net imports. Within this large group, exports of other low-priced goods also increased in relative proportions. For example, exports of linen yarn rose, with a very considerable reduction in price, from negligible amounts to more than 2 per cent of the value of this balance of exports by 1842. On the other hand, in the balance of other net imports, the very large increase in the amounts of grain taken after 1836 at relatively high prices tended to check decline in weighted average net import prices over this particular period. In general, the import prices of staples with fairly steady flow, such as fibres, dyestuffs, timber, and tropical products, fell more than the weighted averages indicate, while import prices of commodities with irregular and sudden demand, such as grain, fell less.

These circumstances point up the need for caution in interpreting the economic significance of net barter movements of aggregates. The weighted over-all price ratios are useful as statistical summaries; but, taken alone or apart from their intrinsic elements, they are not decisive indicators of commercial welfare. The dynamic growth of the cotton industry tended to depress Britain's over-all net barter terms of trade, while the more static woolens tended to improve them. Obviously economic success depends on the factors of growth and profit in the production and sale of the articles of trade rather than on the movements of aggregate price ratios.

CHART 13. THE GROSS BARTER TERMS OF TRADE OF THE UNITED KINGDOM, 1796–1913

Computed $\dfrac{\text{Export volume}}{\text{Import volume}}$

1880 = 100

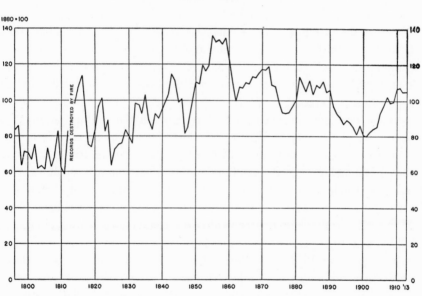

THE GROSS BARTER TERMS

The trends in British gross barter terms of trade, that is, in the quantity relationship between exports and net imports, are interesting in several respects. In the first place, this series tends to refute the notion that the developing dependence of the United Kingdom on raw materials and foodstuffs through this century brought with it a great growth in the quantitative preponderance of net imports over exports. In fact, the numbers are lowest in the earliest years, and low numbers represent, as this series is constructed, a relatively larger volume of net imports than of exports. The first two decades may be passed over as exceptional in this respect. They were war years when there were heavy strains on the economy and wild fluctuations in the volume indexes. But it is also true that during the first two postwar decades the numbers sometimes went lower (for example, in 1818–1819, 1825–1828, and 1831) than at any time thereafter to 1913. From 1816–1820 to 1836–1840, through the high protectionist period, the trend was only slightly "favorable." Amid very sharp fluctuations, the index rose from 87.3 to 89.7. In this interval, the lower numbers, signifying relatively larger net imports, occur in years of boom such as 1818 and 1825, or of poor crops such as 1819 and 1826. Indeed, each boom time, excepting only the single year 1835 when a bumper harvest reduced the need for foodstuffs from abroad, was, in some contrast to the later free-trade part of the century, either preceded or accompanied by a momentary rise in the relative proportions of net imports. The market or trade balance series (Chart 14, below), taking values into account, shows the same phenomenon in the first half of the century.

Again, the trends are particularly interesting in the free-trade period. Through the initial years of the new policy, an upward movement in the gross barter numbers is strongly marked. Neither the large reductions in import duties which began in 1842 nor the repeal of the Corn Laws in 1846 seriously deterred a relatively greater rise in export than in import volumes. The index reached its highest point in the century in 1855, in the middle of the very limited war in the Crimea. The average for 1856–1860 was 130.8, 50 per cent above 1816–1820 and 46 per cent above 1836–1840, higher, indeed, than in any other quinquennium — higher even than any single year in the rest of the series excepting only 1855. The movements in the index are also rather less sharp and extreme after 1842. In only three periods thereafter to 1913 did the relative volume of exports fall below the proportions of 1836–1840, namely in 1847–1848, which can be accounted for by crop failures, and in 1894–1904, a period of cheap foodstuffs and possibly a little heavier capital investment in Britain itself. In 1909–1913, the index averaged 104.6, that is, 20 per cent above the average of 1816–1820 and almost 17 per cent above that of 1836–1840.[26]

[26] One of the beneficiaries of the "favorable" trend in the relationship between export and net import volumes through the middle years of the century was the merchant marine. While the basic volume series from which the gross barter terms are constructed are not, of course, measures of freight tonnage or space requirements, since they are weighted by price, not by weight or size, they do offer some approximation of freight movements. They indicate clearly enough the massive quantitative growth of trade through this century. Moreover, the improvement in export-import volume proportions through the middle years of the century is rather confirmed by the records of ships entering and clearing in cargo and in ballast, though these measure ship, not cargo tonnage. Outgoing and incoming tonnage in cargo came into better balance than at the beginning of the century

TRADE BALANCE

The series entitled "market or trade balance" is based on market value relationships of exports and net imports. Numbers above 100 indicate more favorable export-net import proportions than in the base year 1880. Because it combines the movements of prices and of volumes, the fluctuations, shown in Chart 14, are sharper than those in the net or gross barter

CHART 14. MARKET OR TRADE BALANCE OF THE UNITED KINGDOM, 1796–1913
1880 = 100

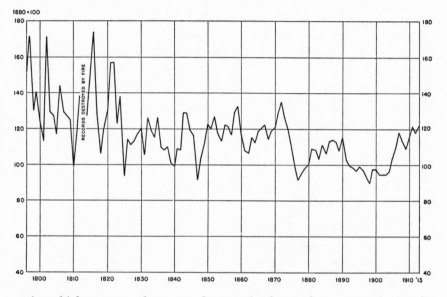

series which measure these two elements in the market separately. In the war years to 1815, the movements are particularly violent, reaching 171 in 1797 and again in 1802 — except for 1816 the highest number in the series — and dropping down to 99 in 1810. After the war the trend was downward; and it continued in this direction generally, although still with sharp swings, until 1847 when the index dipped to 91. From that year of heavy grain imports on to 1873 the line moves generally and somewhat less erratically upward. Then followed two successive troughs, the bottom of the first reached in 1877, at the same level as in 1847, and the second in 1898 at 89, by a very slight margin the lowest point in the series. Thereafter, the numbers rose, almost steadily, to 122 in 1913. In

and there was continued reduction in the tonnage clearing in ballast until about 1870. Later, however, near the end of the century, tonnage entering in ballast rose relatively high. For data on selected years, see pp. 172–173.

1816–1820, which included the highest number in the whole series — 174 in 1816, a depression year when net import volume and price fell sharply — the average was 131; in 1836–1840 it was 106; and in 1909–1913 it was 117. If that extraordinary year 1816 is omitted from the first peacetime quinquennium, the average was 121. The decline, then, in the market value of exports relative to net imports was 12 per cent to 1836–1840; while over the century as a whole, from 1816–1820 to 1909–1913 it was only a shade more than 3 per cent.

Clearly the great growth in the British trade deficit in the nineteenth century, which has attracted so much attention, was more absolute than relative. There was actually little over-all growth in the deficit when measured in proportion to the rising value of British trade. Even the free-trade program after 1842 did not produce any clear long-term rise in the value of net imports relative to the value of exports of British products. In far the greater part of this period the balance was rather improved. Only in 1847–1848, 1876–1879, 1883, and 1891–1905, in all just twenty-two years out of the seventy-one from 1842 to 1913, were these trade balance relatives less favorable than the average (105) in 1838–1842; and in the final quinquennium the average (117) was 10 per cent higher.

GAIN FROM TRADE

The two series on gain from trade measure, in their respective ways, the effects of rising volumes on the unit relationships of exports and net imports. The series on "total gain" is the product of the net barter and total volume relatives; whereas that on "market gain" is the product of the trade balance and total volume relatives and therefore takes into account relative movements of market values of exports and net imports as well as the growth in the volume of total trade. The numbers in the total gain series will be higher than those in market gain in years when it is a high relative volume of net imports rather than of exports that boosts the total volume relative. Total gain numbers are consistently higher than those of market gain from 1796 through 1812, from 1818 with only a few breaks through 1841, again in 1847–1849, in 1875–1879, and from 1891 through 1909 excepting only 1907. Market gain shows higher numbers when exports rose more or fell less than net imports as in 1815–1816, 1822, 1835, 1842–1844, then continuously, and in most years rather strongly, from 1850 through 1874. This larger role of exports in terms of market values relative to the proportions of the base year, 1880, appears again in 1881–1890, in 1907, and in 1910–1913.

Yet much more striking than these differences in the two gain series over the years from 1796 to 1913 is the phenomenal rise which they shared in lusty measure. To hold the graph lines to a single page it is necessary to resort to logarithmic scale. Both indexes indicate something of the extent and the timing of the tremendous gains in trade through the century. Even in the early decades, when the net barter terms deteriorated so much, the rise in volumes was sufficient to double the numbers in both the total

CHART 15. TOTAL GAIN AND MARKET GAIN FROM TRADE, UNITED KINGDOM, 1796–1913, SEMI-LOGARITHMIC SCALE

1880 = 100

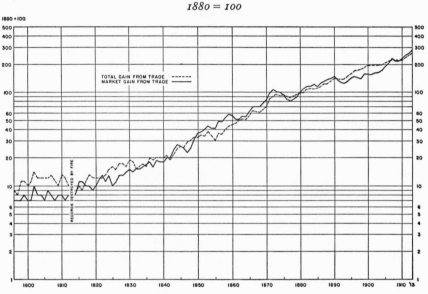

gain and the market gain series by 1830. By 1842, the index number in the market gain series was nearly trebled. In the next thirty years, when net barter movements were more favorable and rate of growth in volume accelerated also, the numbers mounted much more swiftly. Both total gain and market gain more than doubled from 1842 to 1858, doubled a lin by 1866, and yet again by 1871. After 1873 the tempo relaxed somewhat; yet the rate of growth was a bit more rapid than in the first part of the century. By 1900, total gain had doubled its 1873 figure, and had nearly trebled it by 1913, while by 1906 market gain doubled from its higher number of 1873 and was well on the way to trebling it by 1913. At the end of the series in 1913, total gain reached nearly thirty times the 1796 figure. Thanks to the relatively greater growth of exports over this long span, market gain had risen more than forty-fold.

V

THE FAILURE OF THE BRITISH PROTECTIONIST SYSTEM

Early in 1842, in the depths of a world-wide depression, Sir Robert Peel introduced, and Parliament passed, the first British budget distinctively designed as a trial approach to the practice of free trade. His cautiously calculated experiment was successful from the outset and, step by step, Britain opened her markets to the products of the world. The new policy proved wonderfully suited to her national needs and interests. Industries thrived and multiplied, commerce expanded at a rate beyond past precedent, and her people enjoyed a period of unwonted prosperity and social peace. Moreover, the fact that the markets of this giant among the trading nations of the day were opened freely to the products of other lands promoted economic development throughout the world and eased international tensions.

The circumstances leading to this epoch-making reversal of British commercial policy have been much misunderstood. It is commonly supposed, for example, that the system of high tariffs abandoned by Britain at this time was, with the exception of the Corn Law policy added in 1815, essentially the same system under which, towards the end of the eighteenth century, she had gained her head start in the industrial age. From this misconception it was easy to assume that protection had been the life-giving impulse for her young industries. It seemed to follow easily, too, that Britain threw protectionism aside only when her industries were maturely established. In the words Bismarck used in 1879, when he sought to exploit for his own protectionist purposes the influence that Britain's astounding prosperity under free trade exerted over men's minds, "the mighty athlete" stepped into the open market only after hardening her sinews under high tariffs.

The system of "official" trade valuations used by Britain prior to 1854 may have been chiefly responsible for such confused or distorted interpretations of the British tariff history through these significant transition years. The word "official," used without quotation marks, inspired confidence, and its special meaning as a volume measurement was rarely explained. As we have seen in Chapter II, the only usefulness of the "official" values was to show aggregate change in quantity from year to year by means of a kind of common measure expressed in pounds sterling. Constructed with the prices of earlier times, they had long ceased to represent the market values of the goods of trade and had become essentially fictitious values; but, for imports and re-exports, they were the only values available. To judge by them, Britain employed extremely high protectionist practice indeed through the early years of her industrial development, and with great commercial success. In the aggregate, duties on imports averaged 50 per cent of the much too low "official" value of net imports of Great Britain in 1790, and they were about 57 per cent of the United Kingdom values in 1796. This would certainly have been high protection; but it was not the pinnacle. Stiff increases during the long war period brought the average rate, measured against these "official" valuations that took no account of the great rise in the market prices of imported goods, up to 165 per cent by 1814. By 1841, on the eve of Peel's first free-trade budget, customs duties still computed to the very high rate of 46.5 per cent on "official" values of net imports. Meanwhile, on exports of British products the "official" values were also grossly deceptive but in the other direction. They took no account whatever of the reduction of costs and prices effected by machine processes in this period. These oppositely errant valuations showed trade surpluses growing handsomely throughout — from £ 4.4 millions in 1796, to £ 19.8 millions in 1814 and £ 52.5 millions in 1841. Bismarck's argument seemed amply validated.

The true sequence was quite different. In the first place, measured against actual market values, British customs rates were much more moderate throughout than the "official" values suggest. In the earlier stages of industrialism in the late eighteenth century, they had been reshaped by Pitt with an eye to revenue and, since market values of imports were actually about double what was shown by the "official" returns, had amounted to less than half the average rate calculated by the "official" values (see Chart 17). British customs rates assumed high protectionist force during and after the long French wars. They reached their highest percentage on the market value of net imports at 64 per cent in 1822, just before Huskisson's reforms. They became so much more severe in weight and effect after the war that they constituted virtually a new system. In the second place, market values show a very different trade record from that of the "official" values. Instead of the large trade surpluses shown by the "official" values, trade deficits were chronic throughout this period. Although export volumes multiplied, export values grew far less rapidly than net import values, so that the trade deficits increased in size. There is a good deal of reason to believe that, in its rigorous postwar form, protectionism hindered rather than helped Britain in developing her industrial advantages and opportunities, that it aggravated her postwar problems of employment and food supply for her rapidly growing population and intensified domestic distress and social unrest in each successive business depression. Certainly, the British abandoned protectionism in dissatisfaction, more because they found it to be seriously inadequate to their economic and social needs than from any feeling that they had acquired fitness for free competition under it.

BRITISH CUSTOMS DUTIES AND REVENUE IN WAR AND PEACE

During the twenty-two years of participation in the French Wars from 1793 to 1815, British taxation took on something of the rigors of recent times. The compelling problem was revenue. Where less than 20 millions sterling had covered all the costs of government, including the sinking funds for redemption of debt, in 1792, the last year of peace, 56 millions did not quite suffice in 1800 without sinking funds, and 106 millions was barely enough in 1813–1814. The national debt more than trebled, and by 1815 interest charges were nearly 70 per cent larger than the whole outlay of government in 1792. Additional revenue had to be found, and the search for it prompted increases in all the old taxes as well as the discovery of many new ones.[1] Even an income tax was imposed in 1799 and, after being prematurely dropped at the Peace of Amiens in 1802, was reimposed when war was renewed in the next year.

Customs rates were raised with the rest and the yield more than quadrupled between 1790 and 1815. But the share of the total tax burden borne by the duties on imported goods held remarkably steady in these war years. In 1790 these duties,[2] as closely as can be estimated on a comparable basis with later years after deducting overpayments and draw-

[1] As Sydney Smith wrote in 1820 when the country was still groaning under the load, the consequences of the war were "TAXES upon every article which enters into the mouth, or covers the back, or is placed under the foot; taxes upon everything which is pleasant to see, hear, feel, smell, or taste; taxes upon warmth, light, and locomotion; taxes on everything on the earth, and the waters under the earth, on everything that comes from abroad or is grown at home; taxes on the raw material, taxes on every fresh value that is added to it by the industry of man; taxes on the sauce which pampers man's appetite, and the drug which restores him to health, on the ermine which decorates the judge, and the rope which hangs the criminal; on the poor man's salt, and the rich man's spice, on the brass nails of the coffin, and the ribband of the bride; at bed or board, couchant or levant, we must pay." Quoted by Sidney Buxton, *Finance and Politics* (London, 1888), II, 19–20.

[2] The duties on imported goods which were assigned to excise are included here and elsewhere in this chapter. See below.

backs but not costs of collection, contributed about 34 per cent of total tax revenue, excluding Post Office, and in 1815 they were still 34 per cent (Chart 16). The proportion supplied by excises on domestic products fell off, however, from about 34 per cent in 1790 to only 17 per cent in 1815. The contribution of land taxes declined also, from about 19 per cent to 14 per cent, while stamp taxes rose from about 7 per cent to 10 per cent. The new income tax made up for the relative decline in excise and land taxes and supplied 22 per cent of the total tax revenue in 1815.

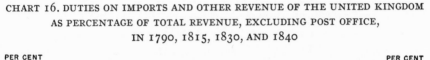

CHART 16. DUTIES ON IMPORTS AND OTHER REVENUE OF THE UNITED KINGDOM AS PERCENTAGE OF TOTAL REVENUE, EXCLUDING POST OFFICE, IN 1790, 1815, 1830, AND 1840

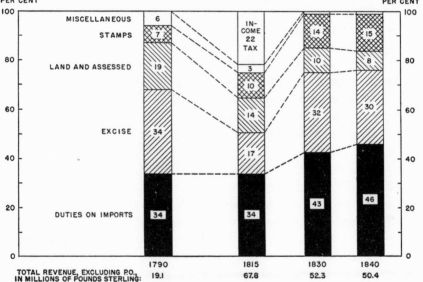

Source: Calculated from data on gross revenue before costs of collection in *Parliamentary Papers*, 1868–69 [366] XXXV, with adjustment of duties on imports assigned to excise before 1836. See pp. 120–121.

This relatively equitable distribution of tax burdens was abruptly upset when the war ended. Early in 1816, Parliament revolted against the recommendation of the Government that the income tax be retained at a lower rate in order to permit some reduction in other taxes. The majority decreed immediate and total abandonment of this hated impost even to the burning of the records.[3] Under these circumstances it was scarcely possible to give any comparable relief with respect to indirect taxes.

[3] Halévy, *A History of the English People, 1815–1830* (New York, n.d.), pp. 6–8; Arthur Hope-Jones, *The Income Tax in the Napoleonic Wars* (Cambridge, England, 1939), pp. 1–4, 110–125.

Revenue from import duties was held as closely as possible to the yield of 1815. Indeed, when collections fell off with trade in 1819, many of the imposts were increased. Only when they rose above that level in the early twenties were any substantial reductions made. The consequence was that the share of the total revenue borne by the customs at once jumped above the prewar and wartime proportions, and they continued to climb for the next twenty-five years. By 1830, they contributed 43 per cent of total tax receipts. In 1840, they supplied 46 per cent so that their share was a little over 43 per cent greater than in 1790. Excise returned to almost the prewar proportion with 32 per cent in 1830 and 30 per cent in 1840. Stamp duties rose to 14 per cent of total revenue by 1830 and nearly 15 per cent in 1840. Land taxes, in contrast, although agricultural products were highly protected after 1815, now bore a lighter load relatively (and absolutely from the 1815 yield),[4] supplying only 10 per cent of total tax revenue in 1830, and only 8 per cent in 1840, well under half the share borne in 1790 and only a little more than half that in 1815. Such were the fiscal results of the emotional and shortsighted reactions of the majority that threw out the income tax in 1816. The economic and social consequences are less easily computed.

Yet there was more than the animus against the income tax behind this postwar reliance on indirect forms of revenue raising. The great expansion in agriculture and industry had brought habits and commitments attuned to high profits and price levels. Faced with difficult and unpleasant economic readjustments and with reviving European competition, the vested interests, new and old alike, felt that they needed stiff duties and prohibitions to keep afloat. Furthermore, the stringent Corn Law of 1815, presented and passed as a security measure against recurrence of the dangerous food shortages of several of the war years, thereafter aligned the predominant political power of the landed classes rather solidly on the side of high protectionism. Protesting voices were unheeded. In 1817 the President of the Board of Trade, Frederick Robinson, lamented that many of the burdens on imports operated to hurt British exports by depriving foreigners of the means of paying for British goods. But he felt he could do nothing. Whenever he proposed to reduce restrictions he had half the manufacturers in the country in arms against him. Each claimed it would ruin him.[5]

William Huskisson, who became President of the Board of Trade

---

[4] In 1790 they supplied, in millions, £ 3.0; in 1815, £ 9.5; in 1830, £ 5.4; and in 1840, £ 4.6.

[5] Hansard, *Parl. Deb.*, XXXV (13 March 1817), 1046–51.

in 1823, was able to do much better than Robinson. Well-informed, and a determined advocate of more rational commercial policies to suit Britain's national as well as international interests, he was also a much more skillful manager of men than Robinson, who is better known to history as Lord Goderich, the "transient and embarrassed phantom" of the brief Goderich ministry of 1827. Circumstances, too, favored Huskisson. He began with prosperous years in which the protectionist interests were more amenable to reason. Revenue, too, was easier. In 1822, when the duties averaged 64 per cent on net import values, the highest percentage of the war or postwar period, the tariff yielded £ 2 millions more revenue than in the tight year 1820. This circumstance, combined with economies gradually effected in the costs of government, afforded Huskisson a margin for more liberal fiscal measures. In 1824–1825, he persuaded Parliament to allow reductions in duties calculated to cost the Exchequer some £ 4.1 millions net a year.[6] So well did he manage matters that the *Annual Register* could report that these and the other commercial reforms which he carried through at this time [7] were "extremely acceptable both to Parliament and to the country." [8] In 1826 he got further cuts totaling another half million.

These were, however, far and away the largest downward revisions of the rates made until 1842. They did not greatly reduce the total yield of the duties because growth in the volume of imports made up most of the calculated loss in revenue. A few other reductions were made for particular commodities from time to time but these were offset, unfortunately, by some increases which were made also. In all, during the twenty-seven protectionist years after Waterloo, reduction or repeal of duties cost the Exchequer some £ 8.8 millions a year, as calculated on the volumes current at the time of each action, but against this must be counted various increases totaling some £ 5.3 millions, of which £ 1.6 millions were added in 1815–1819 and another million by a general 5 per cent increase tacked on in 1840 when revenue was short. The net reduction over the

[6] Huskisson's changes in the duties on cotton goods brought rates formerly ranging from 50 to 75 per cent down to about 10 per cent when calculated ad valorem on market values at that time, and on woolen goods from 50 down to 15 per cent. Both were efficient export industries with little need to fear foreign competition, but specialty items could now more easily be imported. In the cases of industries which demanded protection, he reduced rates which had ranged, for example, from 40 to 180 per cent in the case of linens, and explicit prohibition of most finished silks, down to 30 and 25 per cent respectively, rates which he thought should be enough to protect without promoting inefficiency and mediocrity and without placing a profitable premium on smuggling.

[7] See Chapter I.

[8] 1825, p. [113].

period was, then, by this method of calculation, £ 3.5 millions,[9] over a million less than that effected by the measures Huskisson put through in 1824–1826.

The burden that the duties imposed on trade increased with the postwar deflation of prices. British customs schedules consisted mainly of specific duties — so much on each pound of wool or gallon of wine — and the reductions of these specific duties did not keep pace with the sharp fall in prices which followed the war. The net import price series presented in Chapter IV as weighted averages of actual net imports before duties shows a drop of 57 per cent from 1814 to 1842.[10] The specific duties were not reduced with anything like comparable rapidity. In consequence, the relative burden of the tariffs, that is, the percentage taken on market values, rose even higher after the war.

In measuring the over-all weight of British tariffs on import values in the war and early postwar years, it is necessary to allow for the practice of allocating part of the duties on certain high-yielding luxury imports to excise revenue. Portions of the duties on foreign and colonial brandy, gin, rum, wines, and tobacco were allotted to excise until 1825 when all were assigned to customs. On tea imports, also, the duties paid by the East India Company monopoly were divided between customs and excise until, in 1819 and 1828, respectively, British and Irish duties were thrown entirely into excise. In 1834, just after the Company lost its monopoly on the China trade, the whole revenue from tea was reassigned to customs. All of these articles were substantial producers of revenue, and in the general raising of taxes during the war period the greater part of the additional duties laid on them was credited to excise. On tea, the most striking case, the tariff in 1790, after Pitt's reforms, had been 12½ per cent ad valorem on auction prices, 7½ per cent being assigned to customs and 5 per cent to excise. By 1806 the rate was up to 96 per cent on the better grades and in 1819 it was raised to 100, leaving 96 per cent on the cheaper grades. About 80 per cent of the yield was assigned to excise.[11] Altogether, these duties that were allocated to excise amounted to 51 per cent of the revenue officially classified as customs in 1790, 44 per cent in 1796, 59 per cent in 1814, and 83 per cent in 1824 just before the beginning of their transfer or return to customs. Obviously these duties must be taken into account if the weight of the tariffs on British imports is to be measured with any accuracy for these years or compared with that of later years when they were credited wholly to customs. In all the figures

[9] Parl. Pap., 1857–58 (511), XXXIII.
[10] See also Chart 18 below.
[11] Parl. Pap., 1898 [8706], LXXXV, 200, 203.

presented here on customs and on excise, adjustment has been made as closely as is possible from the printed returns.[12]

Table 11 and Charts 17 and 18 show the percentage relationship between total duties on imports and the estimated market values of net imports. In Table 11, two series of percentages are given. The first, showing

TABLE 11. NET IMPORT VALUES AND AVERAGE DUTY RATES OF THE UNITED KINGDOM, ANNUAL AVERAGES IN QUINQUENNIAL PERIODS, 1796–1845 [a]

	Estimated market value of net imports	Duties on imports				Average rate omitting corn
		Assigned to customs	Assigned to excise	Total		
				Amount	Average rate on net imports	
	£ mill.	£ mill.	£. mill.	£ mill.	%	%
1796–1800 ...	36.6	c. 7.4 [b]	c.3.4 [b]	c.10.8 [b]	29.5	—
1801–1805 ...	47.9	c.10.7 [b]	c.5.7 [b]	c.16.4 [b]	34.2	—
1806–1810 ...	54.0	c.13.4 [b]	c.8.6 [b]	c.22.0 [b]	40.7	—
1811–1815 ...	50.3	14.1	8.6	22.7	45.1	—
1816–1820 ...	49.3	12.8	8.8	21.6	43.8	47.0
1821–1825 ...	45.4	14.4	9.7	24.1	53.1	53.6
1826–1830 ...	48.7	19.5	3.5	23.0	47.2	50.1
1831–1835 ...	53.6	19.3	2.4	21.7	40.5	41.4
1836–1840 ...	73.8	22.8	—	22.8	30.9	32.3
1841–1845 ...	71.0	22.9	—	22.9	32.3	33.5

[a] For average customs rates in the free-trade era, see Table 19.
[b] Estimated for the United Kingdom from British and Irish returns, 1796–1806.

over-all averages, indicates fairly well the upward trend in the percentage taken on goods actually traded during and immediately following the war. But the decline in the over-all percentages after 1825, when the last substantial reductions were made in the rates of duty, was probably caused almost wholly by rise in the rate of flow of goods bearing lower duties. The second percentage series is calculated omitting the net import values and the duties on corn in order to indicate the downward bias in the over-all measurements caused by the fluctuations of this peculiarly taxed commodity. Under the Corn Laws after 1815, imports of grain were negligible except when domestic prices were high enough to render the duties nominal. That fluctuations in the volume of a single commodity could affect the over-all average so much suggests the limitations of measurement by the aggregate and supplies a clue to the influence exerted by changes in the volume proportions of other commodities of high or low duty.

[12] From the annual "Financial Reports" in *Parl. Pap.* Since there may have been other cases with yields too small for separate listing in these reports, the figures presented here may slightly understate customs and overstate excise.

The percentages shown as five-year averages in Table 11 and graph-
ically for each year in Charts 17 and 18 are weighted values and considerably understate the gravity of the case. A large part of the decline in the
over-all customs rates after 1825 must be attributed to a much more
rapid increase in the flow of commodities with low duties than for those
of high duties. Some very great changes of this sort occurred in the postwar period. For example, the quantities of wheat and wheat flour — im-

CHART 17. AVERAGE CUSTOMS RATES OF THE UNITED KINGDOM: ANNUAL NET
CUSTOMS REVENUE AS PERCENTAGE OF NET IMPORT VALUES, 1796–1845

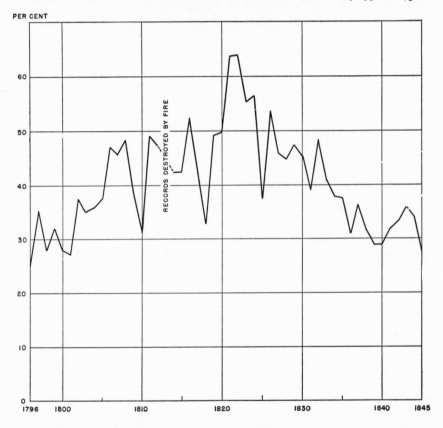

ported in times of high prices at low specific duties — had risen 251 per
cent above 1816–1820 in the last protectionist quinquennium 1838–1842.
Net imports of cotton and wool, with very low average duties, increased
by 195 and 269 per cent respectively, and in every boom period net imports
of these and other low duty commodities spurted ahead so that the over-
all customs rate dipped on each such occasion (see Chart 17). Over the

same interval, all other net imports increased by about 83 per cent in volume. Where these three commodities together made up 21 per cent of all net imports by volume in 1816–1820, they were 37 per cent in 1838–1842.[13] Net imports of commodities bearing high duties diminished very significantly in relative importance. Notable instances were tea, tobacco, sugar, molasses, and wines. On tea, the duty was made specific in 1836 at 25*d*. per pound and averaged 106 per cent on import prices in 1838–1842 — shades of Pitt the Younger! Net imports of these five commodities constituted about 30 per cent of the volume of all net imports in 1816–1820 and were just 15.5 per cent in 1838–1842.[14] The drop in the proportions of these high-duty articles accounts for a considerable part of the decline in the over-all tariff rates shown above. Moreover, many miscellaneous articles with high duties were virtually driven out of trade. The gain in average rate of duty shown in Table 11 and Chart 17 for the quinquennium 1841–1845, which included three full years under Peel's first free-trade budget, is explained largely by the beginnings of a trend back to former proportions in trade of goods of this sort.

EXPORT-IMPORT TRENDS UNDER HIGH PROTECTIONISM

In many respects the first half of the nineteenth century should have been bonanza times for British trade. The technical efficiency of her increasingly mechanized industries, the possibilities of developing demand at home and abroad for her coal and for her machinery, both more freely exportable after 1825, the potentialities of her merchant marine and business services, and the demand for her capital, created an opportunity with few parallels in economic history.

The opportunity was not fully realized under the high protectionism of the postwar years. The various elements in Britain's complex international economy did not always work together in the total national interest and each part suffered a little in consequence. There are a good many signs that Britain's high protectionism fostered economic discord, and that it aggravated her problems of postwar readjustment, which were bound to have been grave enough without being further complicated. It should throw some light on the central theme of this chapter, the development of British dissatisfaction with protectionism, to review the symptoms of injury to balanced economic growth particularly as manifested in foreign trade relations.

---

[13] These volume calculations, involving disparate measures, are made from the absolute values prepared for the volume series presented in Chapter IV.

[14] See also note on high-yield sample for 1839, p. 148, n. 49.

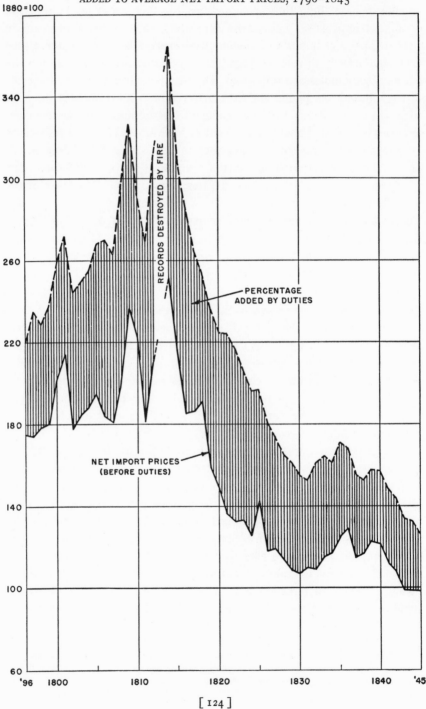

CHART 18. AVERAGE CUSTOMS RATES OF THE UNITED KINGDOM IN RELATION TO
NET IMPORT PRICES: ANNUAL NET CUSTOMS REVENUE AS PERCENTAGE
ADDED TO AVERAGE NET IMPORT PRICES, 1796–1845

1880=100

340

300

260

220

180

140

100

60

RECORDS DESTROYED BY FIRE

PERCENTAGE
ADDED BY DUTIES

NET IMPORT PRICES
(BEFORE DUTIES)

'96 1800   1810   1820   1830   1840   '45

The various textile industries were rapidly mechanizing and already supplied more than half the British export business by the end of the Napoleonic Wars. Machine methods are mass production methods. Because the pressures of overhead are steady and insistent, they require large and steady markets for successful operation. The home market itself, though by far the largest single outlet for British textiles, was much too small to support very intensive use of machinery; and one may, indeed, doubt if machine methods could have been developed as swiftly as they were in Britain from the 1780's on without the supplement of extensive foreign demand. In the cottons, the least expensive of the British export textiles, the home market commonly took 40 per cent or more of the estimated domestic production in this period, and only in such depression years as 1839 and 1840 did it take less.[15] With the population growth that occurred — close to 40 per cent from 1816 to 1841 — and with the possibilities for general rise in living standards which machine methods offered, the home market itself should have been an expanding one for the whole range of textile products. No doubt it was, but, unlike population growth, the expansion came in spurts with sharp relapses.[16] For one thing, the Corn Laws held up food prices without equally arresting deflation in other sectors of the economy and at times the high price of wheat laid heavy hands on the means of the British population to buy other goods. Every poor harvest meant high prices of bread. So inelastic was the demand for this basic food that rise in price, unless accompanied by some approach to good employment as in 1818 and 1824–1825, brought a marked slackening of demand for all other goods whether produced at home or brought from abroad. Indeed, on such occasions, only the basic foodstuffs were in strong demand in Britain.

The large increases in the volume of exports of cotton yarn, requiring little fabrication, and the sharp reductions all along the line in prices of cotton goods in depression years, are suggestive of the marketing difficulties faced by the cotton industry. In 1819–1820, in 1826–1832, and in 1837–1842, the sharp cuts in export prices, and the marked expansions in export volume of both yarn and manufactures, rather strongly suggest that the slump in the home market impelled the industry to expand exports in order to keep factories operating.[17] Inevitably, wages felt the pressure, too, particularly those of the less skilled workers in abundant

---

[15] Robert Charles O. Matthews, *A Study in Trade-Cycle History: Economic Fluctuations in Great Britain, 1833–1842* (Cambridge, Eng., 1954), pp. 128, 151.

[16] *Ibid.*

[17] See Appendix Table II; see also Matthews, *Study in Trade-Cycle History*, pp. 128–144.

supply. Wage reductions and unemployment could only further depress demand in the home market.

Because of Britain's own tariffs, British industries probably found less compensation abroad for the deficiencies of the home market in depression times than might have been the case had trade been freer. The duties tended to fall on the seller in such times of slack demand and so forced prices down, further reducing foreign purchasing power along the usual channels of trade. This tendency may be part of the explanation why the net import prices shown in Table 8 fluctuated so much more violently in the protectionist period. The matter was the more serious because it most sharply affected established British markets. It is true that the poor harvests in depression years led to large imports of grain into Britain[18] and that these British takings provided the main areas of supply, mainly North Europe at this time, with considerable gains in sterling purchasing power. But the gains of this area were offset by the losses in other areas. Moreover, this was a spasmodic, an emergency trade, and the further purchasing power that it supplied did not bring quick or equivalent response in the taking of British exports. Neither the habits of using British goods, nor British marketing facilities, were quite like water faucets to be turned on at will. At such times, some British export of gold was generally needed to balance accounts with the areas of supply. In any case, the gain in foreign sterling earnings was not at all commensurate with the cost to the British nation because, under the operation of the Corn Laws, speculators' profits (and losses) and other extra expense of this irregular trade made up a high proportion of the cost of the imports. It could not balance the losses in foreign sterling earnings elsewhere brought about by the contraction of British takings of other foreign and colonial goods and by the fall in the prices of these goods. Credit, too, was tighter in these depression periods. There was less supplementing of foreign purchasing power with British loans.

Thanks mainly to the cheaper textiles, British exports did expand over the twenty-six years of high protectionism in this postwar period. Quantitatively, the increase was indeed large. By the volume series constructed in Table 8, it amounted to over 150 per cent from 1816–1820 to 1838–1842. But the increase in market values was very modest. The fall in prices, which protection may have aggravated, limited it to a mere £ 10.2 millions, a gain of only 25 per cent, with the cheaper textiles contributing much

[18] Net imports of grain averaged about £ 4.3 millions a year in value in 1816–20 £ 4.9 millions in 1827–31, and £ 8.2 millions in 1838–42. In 1839 they amounted to about £ 11.4 millions and accounted for the rise in the weighted average net import prices counter to the trend of other prices.

the greater part. Cottons altogether accounted for £ 7.4 millions, or 72 per cent of total increase in market values from 1816–1820 to 1838–1842. Moreover, of this amount, cotton twist and yarn, requiring little labor or use of machinery, accounted for £ 4.8 millions, leaving a gain of only £ 2.6 millions for the more highly fabricated cotton manufactures. Export of linens increased by nearly £ 2 millions, but linen yarn accounted for nearly half this gain. Exports of woolen manufactures declined in annual value by £ 1.5 million, but those of woolen yarn rose from negligible amounts to £ 0.5 million a year. Together, these three yarns accounted for fully 60 per cent of the total gain in the market values of all exports of domestic products. On the other hand, exports of iron and steel goods, hardware, cutlery, and machinery, requiring much skilled labor, accounted for slightly less than 25 per cent of the increase in export values. On balance, then, the changes in the structure of British exports over this quarter century of high tariffs were not very favorable and certainly they do not suggest very profitable development of Britain's technical advantages.

Foreign demand for British goods was logically the major determinant of the market for British exports. There was generally little problem of supply of the main export goods. British manufacturers were able again and again to expand production, without much, if any, rise in price, when home and foreign demand was favorable. But demand in this broad sense was conditioned by many factors, such as usefulness and price of the article, habits and purchasing power (income) of potential consumers, marketing facilities, and the extent to which sterling cash or credit was available abroad.

Sterling was obviously a prime factor in the demand for British goods. It could be obtained in significant amounts only by the sale of goods, services, or monetary metal to Britain or to third parties who traded with Britain, or by borrowing. It set up purchasing power for British goods and services, and when such purchasing power was established and sustained, consumption habits and marketing facilities would tend to follow, conditioned, of course, by the relative usefulness and price of competing goods. In these respects, then, the quantity and the terms of British taking of foreign goods and services, as well as the credit that British bankers and merchants could extend, were logically significant conditioners of success in the British search for markets for their goods and services. Whatever promoted the steady flow of goods and services to Britain on satisfactory terms, or prompted extension of credit, tended to promote British exports of goods and services. Whatever checked the flow, or rendered the terms unsatisfactory — whether it was unequal changes in prices without compensating changes in quantities, or tariff barriers, or too rigid trade regulation, or limitations on credit — would more or less promptly bring corresponding weakening in British markets abroad.

The aggregate values presented in relation to the terms of trade and to British exports of capital tend to confirm the economic logic of the matter. As was pointed out in Chapter IV, each boom time that brought an increase in British export values in this period was preceded by a much greater rise in the value of net imports. A considerable margin of net imports was needed to balance the "invisible" exports — the earnings of British shipping, business services, and investments — which also increased in boom times. It is significant, too, that in those boom periods, with their rise in British acceptance of foreign goods, British confidence in foreign investment opportunities promoted greater lending abroad, which further fortified the export trade. In each trade recession these processes were reversed. At the outset of each depression period, except in 1839 and 1840 when grain was taken in large quantities, net import values fell off more sharply than export values. They led the decline in trade values (see Table 8 and "Market or trade balance" series). Moreover, although the depression changes in export-import relations generally produced favorable balances on current account — apparently very strong in 1816, 1819, 1821 and 1829 (see Table 4 and "Balance on current account") — British reluctance to lend at such times deprived the export trade of the stimulant of credit.

The changes in the direction of flow of British exports over this period also indicate some significant relationships in export-import fluctuations suggestive of defects in the British tariff system. It is true that correlations in export-import flow with particular areas cannot be traced with any precision in this period. The market values (f.o.b.) of British exports to each of the main outlets are known, but those of imports from the same areas are not determinable from the printed records except for a few commodities. Even if these import values were known, one would need to adjust them for the British share of freight and other charges contained in valuation c.i.f., and to make allowance for multilateral trade and for all the other elements in the balance of payments both on current and on capital account, all similarly broken down for each area considered — an impossible task. Nevertheless, the indications are clear enough that there was a remarkable degree of export-import interdependence in many areas.[19] Possibly the rigidities of tariff schedules and Navigation Acts

---

[19] Matthews has carefully examined these matters in his recent *Study in Trade-Cycle*

and regulations in this high protectionist period tended to promote bilateralism, limiting flexibility or multilateralism in Britain's trade relations.

The market values of exports to various areas [20] are shown in Table 12 as annual averages in three selected five-year periods. In the first period, 1816–1820, there were three depression years broken by 1817 and 1818 when net import volumes and values expanded strongly with some rise in the volume and value of exports (see Table 8). In the second period, 1832–1836, the year 1832 was a poor one with respect to import and export values, but it was followed by a strong and steady rise in the value of net imports c.i.f. — in all, 66 per cent by 1836 — and by a great spurt in foreign investment. Exports f.o.b. rose by 46 per cent and there was corresponding growth of activity in shipping and business services. In the

TABLE 12. EXPORT OUTLETS FOR PRODUCTS OF THE UNITED KINGDOM, BY AREAS AND AVERAGE ANNUAL MARKET VALUES IN SELECTED PERIODS, 1816–1842

(All values in millions of pounds sterling)

	1816–20	1832–36	1838–42	Per cent change from 1816–20 to 1838–42
North Europe	11.4	9.8	12.8	+ 12
South Europe	7.3	7.5	9.5	+ 30
Africa	0.4	1.1	1.7	+325
Asia	3.4	5.2	7.9	+132
U.S.A.	7.0	8.6	6.5	− 7
British North America and West Indies	7.0	5.1	5.8	− 31
Foreign West Indies	1.0	1.2	1.1	+ 10
Central and South America	2.8	5.0	5.4	+ 93
Total exports	40.3	43.7	50.5	+ 25

third period, 1838–1842, the first two years showed a considerable revival in net import and export values following the collapse of 1837, although with continuing fall in average export prices. But 1840–1842 were years of deepening depression, falling import and export values, and virtual cessation of foreign lending.

The gains in British exports to four of these areas exceeded the general

History for the 1830's (especially pp. 43–105). With respect to British trade with areas other than the United States and Northern Europe, he states that "it is clearly right to regard exports rather than imports as the dependent variable in the relation between the two" (p. 78).

[20] As prepared by Porter for his Progress of the Nation over one hundred years ago and reproduced, business cycle by business cycle, 1816–48, by Gayer, Rostow, and Schwartz, The Growth and Fluctuation of the British Economy, 1790–1850 (Oxford, 1953), I, 146, 215, 251, 282, 314.

average from 1816–1820 to 1838–1842. These areas were Africa, Asia, Central and South America, and South Europe, in that order. Africa and Central and South America constituted virtually new outlets for British goods and small absolute gains calculate to high percentages on the low initial values. For Africa, the increase of 325 per cent required only £ 1.3 millions, but this was one eighth of the net gain of £ 10.2 millions in the value of all British exports; and exports to these four areas together showed gains totalling £ 10.6 millions or a little more than the net gain in all British exports. In all of these four areas it was no doubt a factor that climate and standards of living rendered Britain's specialty of cheaper cotton goods particularly acceptable. Yet it is also probable that the gain in British exports to each area was closely equivalent to the growth in British acceptance of goods from each over this period. Fluctuations in particular years certainly point strongly to close export-import relationships. For example, the sharpest drop in Asian takings of British exports came in 1819 when the price of East Indian cotton fell 37 per cent, and prices of other commodities only less steeply, in that single year. The largest increases came in 1835–1836 and in 1838–1840 when cotton prices rose and there were substantially larger British imports from the area.

North Europe was the area of the largest taking of British goods in each of the three periods shown in Table 12. The percentage gain made in this established marketing region was only half of that made for exports generally to 1838–1842, however; and in 1832–1836, the average annual value had dipped 14 per cent below that of 1816–1820. Again the fluctuations in particular years are suggestive of the interdependence of export-import values. British exports to North Europe fell with each decline in net import prices except in 1820, 1827–1830, 1832, and 1837–1842, when, indeed, increases over immediately preceding years were recorded, sometimes counter to the trend of export values to other areas. These exceptions supply a clue to the trend and to the low takings in 1832–1836. Ten of these twelve exceptional years showed relatively large British takings of grain, which came mainly from countries in this area. The larger British exports to the area seem to have followed the rise in British grain imports. In 1832–1836, on the other hand, when British imports of grain were negligible, exports to the area dropped. With the strong revival of grain imports after 1836, British exports to the area again rose, although relatively less than the increase in grain import values (c.i.f.). After duties were reduced in 1842, including reduction of preferential advantages for colonial timber, British exports to this region showed slightly greater gain than did exports to other areas as a whole.

The over-all decline in the value of British exports to the United States and to the British American colonies is particularly interesting. The value of British net imports from both areas increased greatly from 1816 to 1842. Imports of American cotton alone multiplied six-fold and, prices falling nearly 65 per cent, values slightly more than doubled. Quantities of other imports rose much less steeply but also fell less in price and showed net gains in market value. The American merchant marine was growing also, presumably with increased earnings. One can find a few occasional signs of positive correlation between export-import fluctuations in particular years — for example, a rise in both export and import values in 1818 and a sharp fall in 1819, and again a rise in export values in 1838–1839 when British imports of grain and of American cotton increased and some credit was extended. But by and large, export response to net import growth was negative. While trade with third countries complicated matters a good deal here, by far the most important known factor was the deepening debtor position of both these areas and particularly of the United States, then, as later, the favorite country for British investment abroad. Jenks estimates that British investment in the United States had grown to about $174,000,000 by 1838.[21] Capital movements were certainly reflected in a large increase in British exports to America in 1835–1836. But rising interest and dividend accounts — which on paper must have run close to £ 9 millions a year by 1838 — claimed a substantial part of American earnings on trade goods and shipping when not reinvested. When further British lending slacked off in 1837 and 1840–1842, while British import quantities and prices dropped also, the margin for American buying of British goods, or payment of interest, was cut very thin. British exports to the United States dropped from £ 12.4 millions in 1836 to £ 4.7 millions in 1837 and to only £ 3.5 millions in 1842.

THE RE-EXPORT TRADE

The re-export trade in foreign and colonial goods was even slower to develop than the export trade for British products. During the war, Britain had controlled the overseas routes of trade and virtually all European colonial possessions. When the Continent was opened once more to British commerce in 1814–1815, the re-export business had soared to unprecedented heights in volumes and values. But it quickly subsided following the very prompt restoration of overseas territories according to treaty terms, and the quinquennium 1816–1820 is probably a fair point of comparison for later years. In spite of the great advantage Britain possessed

[21] Jenks, *The Migration of British Capital to 1875* (New York, 1938), p. 85.

in her developed facilities for large-scale handling of her own imports, the re-export trade did not thrive under high protectionism. Although re-exported commodities were exempt from British duties, the regulations involved a certain amount of expense and risk which held back development. Moreover, British trade restrictions and Navigation Laws prompted other states to set up similar regulations, whether in emulation or in retaliation. In these years, the trade developed little beyond the handling of colonial products. Volumes rose only 40 per cent from 1816–1820 to 1838–1842, much less than half as fast as British general import volume (109 per cent). Weighted average prices of the re-export goods traded fell a little further than import prices, dropping from 153 to 94 (1880 = 100), or 38.5 per cent.[22] Aggregate market value averaged 14 per cent less in 1838–1842 than in 1816–1820. By the 1840's, a smaller proportion of general imports was marketed abroad than at any other time in the nineteenth century (Table 13).

TABLE 13. THE RE-EXPORT TRADE OF THE UNITED KINGDOM IN RELATION TO GENERAL IMPORTS, ANNUAL AVERAGES IN QUINQUENNIAL PERIODS, 1796–1845 [a]

| | Market value of general imports | Re-exports | | | Market value of general imports | Re-exports | |
| | | Market value | Per cent of general imports | | | Market value | Per cent of general imports |
	£ mill.	£ mill.	%		£ mill.	£ mill.	%
1796–1800 ..	47.4	10.6	22.4	1821–1825 ..	53.4	8.0	15.0
1801–1805 ..	59.1	11.2	19.0	1826–1830 ..	55.3	6.6	11.9
1806–1810 ..	64.2	10.2	15.6	1831–1835 ..	61.2	7.6	12.4
1811–1815 ..	64.7	14.3	22.1	1836–1840 ..	83.3	9.5	11.4
1816–1820 ..	60.4	11.1	18.4	1841–1845 ..	79.7	8.7	10.9

[a] For the free-trade era, see Table 21.

GROWTH OF THE MERCHANDISE TRADE DEFICIT

British net imports rose faster than exports of home products in the period of high protectionism after the Napoleonic Wars. The system supposed to limit imports and so to effect a favorable balance of trade somehow permitted or promoted the reverse result. Net imports, already higher in value than exports in 1816–1820, rose 52 per cent by 1838–1842, more than twice as rapidly as the value of exports. In other words, the

[22] Because of different components and proportions, weighted average general import prices fell less rapidly — from 169 in 1816–20 (1880 = 100) to 114 in 1838–42, or 32.5 per cent. Net import prices, relative to 1880, were higher than those of re-exports throughout this period — compare prices in Table 8 with those in Appendix Table I where a continuous run is shown for annual values, volumes, and average price relatives of re-exports, and for value proportions to general imports, 1796–1913.

annual merchandise trade deficit grew relatively as well as absolutely. It more than doubled as a percentage of slow-rising export values and almost doubled as a percentage of the value of exports and net imports combined (Table 14). Moreover, the invisible exports of services and investment earnings, which must be considered also, did not rise in the same magnitude. Somehow, the considerable growth in the value of net imports, although this meant larger purchasing power abroad for British goods and services, was not accompanied by anything like an equivalent rise in the value of British exports of goods and services. Some of the gains in net imports were, perhaps, too spasmodic to permit developing either the habit of using British goods or efficient marketing facilities for sup-

TABLE 14. MERCHANDISE TRADE DEFICITS OF THE UNITED KINGDOM, ANNUAL AVERAGES IN QUINQUENNIAL PERIODS, 1796–1845 [a]

			Negative balance of merchandise trade			
	Net imports	Exports of British products	Amount	Per cent of net imports plus exports	Per cent of exports	Trade balance relative 1816–20 = 100
	£ mill.	£ mill.	£ mill.	%	%	
1796–1800 ..	36.6	32.9	− 3.9	− 5.6	−11.9	109
1801–1805 ..	47.9	39.9	− 8.0	− 9.1	−20.1	100
1806–1810 ..	54.0	42.2	−11.8	−12.3	−28.0	95
1811–1815 ..	50.3	42.9	− 7.4	− 7.9	−17.2	101
1816–1820 ..	49.3	40.3	− 9.0	−10.0	−22.3	100
1821–1825 ..	45.4	37.3	− 8.1	− 9.8	−21.7	102
1826–1830 ..	48.7	35.9	−12.8	−15.1	−32.9	88
1831–1835 ..	53.6	40.5	−13.1	−13.9	−32.3	90
1836–1840 ..	73.8	49.8	−24.0	−19.4	−48.2	80
1841–1845 ..	71.0	54.0	−17.0	−13.6	−31.5	90

[a] For continuation of these series in the free-trade era, see Table 20. Annual values are shown in Tables 4 and 8. See also Chart 14.

plying them. The large emergency imports of grain required when harvests were poor had to be gathered rather suddenly, mainly from northeast Europe, while the luxury or semi-luxury commodities taken in better quantities in boom years came from south and west Europe and from overseas. The violent price fluctuations, accentuated by the British tariffs, also interfered with steady trade. Although depression changes in price relations sometimes brought momentary improvement in the net barter terms of trade for the British, the reduction of foreign purchasing power reacted against British exports. British willingness, or ability, to extend credit also tended to dry up in depression times.

THE DECLINING MARGIN IN BRITISH BALANCE OF PAYMENTS

British international income from business services did not gain sufficiently through these postwar protectionist years to offset the rising
deficits in merchandise trade. Against the increase of £ 15 millions in the
size of the annual merchandise deficit from 1816–1820 to 1836–1840,
business services and other current items apart from interest and dividend
credits (as constructed in Chapter III) showed a gain of only £ 4 millions.
The average surplus of £ 5.5 millions a year in these combined accounts
in 1816–1820 was transformed into a deficit of £ 5.4 millions a year by
1836–1840, and in 1840 the indicated deficit was £ 9.4 millions. In relation
to total trading activity, the trend in trade and business services was unfavorable. Income from foreign loans provided credit to cover these
deficits in all quinquenniums — and in every single year but 1840 and 1842.
The comprehensive net balance on current accounts, therefore, remained

TABLE 15. THE BALANCE OF PAYMENTS OF THE UNITED KINGDOM, ANNUAL
AVERAGES IN QUINQUENNIAL PERIODS, 1816–1845 [a]

		Trade, services, and other current items			
		Net balance	Per cent of total trade	Interest and dividends	Net balance on current account
		£ mill.	%	£ mill.	£ mill.
1816–1820	..	+5.5	+4.7	+1.7	+ 7.2
1821–1825	..	+6.1	+6.2	+4.2	+10.3
1826–1830	..	−2.0	−2.0	+4.6	+ 2.6
1831–1835	..	+1.0	+0.9	+5.4	+ 6.4
1836–1840	..	−5.4	−3.8	+8.0	+ 2.6
1841–1845	..	−1.6	−1.1	+7.5	+ 5.9

a For continuation in the free-trade era, see Tables 24 and 26.

positive in every quinquennium, as shown in Table 15. But, although
investment income more than quadrupled, the margin of coverage was becoming less secure. In 1839, according to the estimates in Table 4, a deficit
was avoided only by large net export of gold. In 1840, a deficit of £ 2.3
millions was indicated after some net export of gold. In 1841 there appears to have been a small balance and in 1842 another small deficit, although perhaps with some replenishment of gold stocks. The marked
upturn in the net balance on current account shown in Table 15 for 1841–
1845 occurred after 1842.

THE MERCHANT MARINE

Although shipping and foreign investment income made large contributions towards balancing the deficits in British merchandise accounts, neither did as well as it should have done through this postwar period. British shipping did not quite keep up with the growth in total trade volume, and investment income did not maintain the promise suggested by the amount of investment and the contractual interest rates. Neither did relatively as well under protection as it was later to do in the free-trade era.

The great quantitative growth of British trade indicates something of the opportunity that was open to British shipping in this period. By the series constructed for Table 8, general imports increased in volume by 109 per cent from 1816–1820 to 1838–1842, while the volume of exports and re-exports together rose by 119 per cent from a relatively lower base. Total shipping activity, British and foreign, to judge by records of tonnage in cargo and ballast (since the returns do not distinguish ballast before 1827), rose in fairly close correspondence to these gains in import and export volumes. Total entries increased by 102 per cent, and clearance by 121 per cent. But, for all the protection afforded by the Navigation Acts, the British did not maintain their initial share of the business. Foreign entries and clearances rose at a faster rate. According to the estimates prepared for Chapter III, British international income from shipping, including a small proportion from foreign expenditure in British ports,[23] was just beginning to move ahead in the late 1830's. By 1838–1842, it had increased only £ 1.8 millions, or 18 per cent, over 1816–1820. While this very slow growth in earnings is mainly attributable to the great fall in freight rates — which at times went as much as 50 and 60 per cent below the first postwar years on some import goods and on some routes, and perhaps more on exports in which cargoes were scarcer through most of this period [24] — other factors also contributed to this relatively poor showing.

The British merchant marine was rather slow to respond to the swift expansion of British trade volumes in the postwar period. Net registered

[23] See Table 4.
[24] In 1827, when the records first distinguish between cargo and ballast, total British and foreign tonnage cleared in cargo was almost 40 per cent less than that entered. Thirty-seven per cent of all outbound tonnage had sailed without freight, although only 4 per cent of inbound was in ballast in that year. In 1842, tonnage cleared in cargo first moved ahead of tonnage entered and this new relationship became characteristic after the mid-fifties.

tonnage had increased perhaps 50 per cent [25] during the war and was perhaps a little overexpanded in relation to restored use of shorter continental trade routes and revived foreign competition. In poor trade years, freight rates fell very sharply. The energy and vision of the highly protected shipping interests in general found little challenge in these altered circumstances. Long accustomed to handsome, if also rigid and cumbersome, protection from the Navigation Acts, they tended to look to the government rather more than to their own enterprise for salvation. Repair, replacement, and improvements seem to have been held to a minimum; and no interest complained more of foreign competition and distress.[26] Net tonnage declined rather steadily from 1816 to 1825, and not until 1838 did it regain the position of 1816. In boom times, like 1818 and 1825, it was left to foreign shipping to pick up the extra cargoes. Foreign entries and clearances jumped from 22 per cent of the total in 1816 to 29 per cent in 1818, and from 21 per cent in 1820 to 32 per cent in 1825. The Board of Trade was not very sympathetic to the complaints of British shipowners, and it was impressed by the evident dangers of foreign retaliation for British restrictive regulations, for in this game the largest merchant marine afloat had much to lose. In 1824, Huskisson persuaded Parliament to allow relaxation of restrictions on a reciprocal basis and in the next dozen years some useful treaties were made without real harm to British shipping.

In the later 1830's, the merchant marine began to grow more rapidly. Perhaps the impulse came partly from realization that the impressive growth in the volume of exports and imports was a durable one; perhaps more largely from the energy and example of some of the shipping interests who demonstrated that with faster ships and better service they could compete successfully even on the unprotected routes. George R. Porter of the Board of Trade later showed that British tonnage on the relatively unprotected routes to foreign countries had grown almost twice as rapidly after 1824 as on the closely controlled empire routes.[27] At any rate, by 1842, seagoing net tonnage had risen perhaps as much as 27 per cent above 1816,[28] and the whole of this increase came after 1837. In these

[25] Rough deduction, on the basis of 1826–27 tonnage figures, is made for unreported (lost) ships carried on the register until 1827.

[26] Porter, *The Progress of the Nation* (London, 1838), II, 164.

[27] Testimony given to the Select Committee on the Navigation Laws, *Parl. Pap.*, 1847 (678), X, 74.

[28] It is hardly possible to establish a firm figure on the increase. Unless loss was confirmed, unreported ships were carried on the register until 1827. The above percentage is based on net registered tonnage records after adjustment of 1816 figures on the basis of 1826–27 proportions. A change in the formula for measuring net tonnage made in 1840 may also have affected the continuity of the data.

later years British shipping held its new relative position in the British carrying trade. Its share of total entries and clearances in cargo in 1842 was the same as in 1827, namely, 73.9 per cent. But, in terms of cargo and ballast records which must be used before 1827, it had shrunk nearly 6 percentage points below the British proportion of 1816–1820.

INCOME FROM FOREIGN INVESTMENT

British investments abroad ran into severe difficulties in the business depressions after 1825 and 1836. Grown into sizable sums but channeled to areas of major trade relations and into foreign government bonds, they tended as yet to lack diversity, perhaps partly because, with the peculiarities of British tariffs and regulations, British trade itself lacked the diversity it later acquired. Payment of interest was dependent essentially on good trade conditions for the debtor area, on ability to sell goods and services to Britain on satisfactory terms, or on further extension of credit which, in turn, was largely conditioned by British confidence in future capacity to pay. Each boom period brought a rise in British imports accompanied by a wave of British investment abroad; but each succeeding bust brought reduction of imports, severe drop in prices, and contraction of credit which made payment of interest more difficult and sometimes imperiled the capital itself. As was shown in Chapter III, of £ 42 millions in foreign government bonds sold in Britain from 1818 to 1830, nearly half were in default by 1831. Instead of the handsome average yield of 6.6 per cent promised on issue prices, interest actually paid in 1831 amounted to an average of only 3.1 per cent on the total investment. Again, British loans to the United States, already large, were expanded greatly during the "cotton" boom of the mid-thirties when the value of British net imports of cotton from the United States about doubled from 1832 to 1836, rising from around £ 6 millions to around £ 12 millions. As noted earlier, Jenks estimates that the total British investment in the United States was approximately $174,000,000 by 1838, which was nearly a quarter of all British capital abroad at that time, and that almost the whole was in default or repudiated by 1842. He adds: "It was highly embarrassing for an American to be in London in the winter of 1842–1843." [29]

This typical creditor reaction is humanly understandable; and it had its debtor counterpart in the United States. Yet one of the difficulties which American debtors faced in meeting their obligations at this time may be illustrated by the collapse in the price of cotton, the chief export

[29] Jenks, *Migration of British Capital*, pp. 85, 104.

to Britain. By the beginning of 1843, the price of American cotton was only 47 per cent of the average for 1835–1836 when many of the loans were placed. By 1845, when it reached the lowest point for many decades just as the duties were repealed, it was only 42 per cent of the 1835–1836 average. Now the specific duties on American cotton were very light, yielding in all a fraction over 6 per cent on net import values in 1842; but the volume had become huge. The British customs yield on cotton from the United States alone was close to £ 550,000 in that year — equivalent to the interest at 5 per cent on £ 11 millions ($55 millions) or nearly one-third of the capital placed in the United States. Earlier repeal of the duty might have modified a little the gravity of this crisis.[30] The higher rates on other goods also offered considerable opportunity to effect some remedy.[31] This is not to say that more liberal British trade policy could have prevented this crisis of overexpansion and too optimistic investment, but rather that the duties offered a good deal of scope in which to moderate the effects, and with considerable advantage to British industry, labor, and investment. As it was, investment income, and the capital itself, suffered from the same law-made forces which limited British export opportunities.

THE STANDARD OF LIVING UNDER THE POSTWAR PROTECTIONISM

Trends in the national income and in standards of living throw some further light on these postwar protectionist years. National income in Great Britain almost certainly increased over the period as a whole. The severe deflation of prices in the first few years of peace involved some setback in terms of current values from the levels attained in the last years of the war, but thereafter, growth in productivity more than offset the fall in prices. In terms of real income, that is, after adjustment for price change — though our adjustments can be only rough ones — the gains made were probably greater than the growth in population. Accord-

[30] Cancellation of the duty should proportionately have improved American credit either by raising the price of American cotton to about the same extent or, if the savings accrued to British manufacturers, by stimulating larger consumption of raw cotton until demand for it improved prices. It is interesting that import prices of American cotton did not fall quite as low in the depression of 1848, after the duties were repealed, as in 1843, and then they quickly recovered although production was very high. The lower weighted average net import price for 1848 shown in Appendix Table II was caused by somewhat larger takings of cheaper East Indian supplies in that year.

Curiously, none of the witnesses who appeared before the Select Committee on Import Duties in 1840 (see below) referred to the implications of the duties with respect to Britain's creditor status, although Thomas Tooke, in testimony given to the Select Committee on Banks of Issue in the same year, did make some reference to it. Tooke and Newmarch, *A History of Prices* (New York, 1848), V, 468–469.

[31] See list of goods of large revenue yield below, p. 148, n. 49.

ing to our calculations from the best estimates we have of national income, the trend in real income per capita seems to have been upward to 1831 and probably through 1836. By 1841, however, real income per capita had fallen below that of 1831. Moreover, the gains in the national averages were very unevenly distributed. During the economic slump at the end of the period, it is likely that the standard of living of a considerable part of the population fell about as low as — perhaps lower than — in the first hard years immediately after the war.

For the national income changes through this period we can rely on Miss Phyllis Deane's series derived, with important adjustments, from the more careful contemporary estimates that were made from time to time.[32] With the possible exception of the estimate for 1841, which will be discussed later, these should give some approximation to the development which occurred. Her adjusted estimates for population and national income in Great Britain are shown in Table 16. Real income per capita is computed from her values by means of two series. One is the Gayer-Rostow-Schwartz wholesale price index which is broadly based on monthly quotations for twenty-six domestic products and fifty-two imported commodities (after duties) and weighted in relation to consumption; and the other is Rufus S. Tucker's index of the cost of living for London artisans.[33] While neither index can be counted to be closely representative of changes in actual living costs in the nation as a whole, they offer some approximation to the trends. The results by both indexes suggest a very great rise in real income per capita from 1812 to 1831, and both show a reversal of this trend by 1841. Because it is reasonable to assume that, with improving business and the bumper crops which reduced food prices, the rise continued to 1836, we must conclude that the decline shown by the 1841 average was more sudden and sharp than these decennial averages indicate. Furthermore, William F. Spackman's allowance for agriculture in 1841 is probably exaggerated, although it may be partly compensated by a downward bias on manufactures, as Miss Deane has pointed out. If allowance were made for these biases, the figure on average real income per person in 1841 might be as little as £ 23.6, or about 14 per cent below 1831.[34]

[32] P. Deane, "Contemporary Estimates of National Income in the First Half of the Nineteenth Century," *Economic History Review*, 8:339–354 (April 1956).

[33] Gayer, Rostow, Schwartz, *Growth and Fluctuation of the British Economy*, I, 468; R. S. Tucker, "Real Wages of Artisans in London, 1792–1935," *Journal of the Statistical Association*, 31:73–84 (1936).

[34] Spackman allows £ 220 millions for agriculture, including inland transport and distribution of products, for the United Kingdom in 1841. After rough deduction for what was added by inland transport and distribution, this would represent a gain of at least

However this may be, the per capita values at best are merely statistical averages. They do not indicate the actual distribution of income within income groups, for the "average man" is only a fanciful conception placed somewhere between the well-to-do and the laboring bulk of the population. There is no ready set of answers on this aspect of the matter, but we can, perhaps, find some clues to the trends by looking at consumption of certain foodstuffs and at wage rates and employment.

TABLE 16. NATIONAL INCOME PER CAPITA IN GREAT BRITAIN, BASED ON CON-
TEMPORARY ESTIMATES OF NATIONAL INCOME IN SELECTED YEARS,
1812–1846

| | | | | Real income per capita at 1821–25 prices | |
| | Popu-lation | National income | Income per capita | By Gayer index | By Tucker index |
	mill.	£ mill.	£	£	£
1812 (after Colquhoun)	12.33	330	26.75	16.31	18.71
1822 (after Lowe)	14.45	288	19.93	22.65	20.76
1831 (after Pebrer)	16.37	424	25.90	27.26	26.26
1841 (after Spackman)	18.55	445	23.99	24.73	24.23
1846 (after Smee)	19.71	467	23.69	27.55	24.17

Critical data for this age of relatively static dietary regimen would be consumption accounts for the basic foodstuffs. Unfortunately, records on foodstuffs produced at home — the prime source of supply of the basic foods — are almost wholly lacking, and estimates which have been attempted appear to be little more than exercises in arithmetic. The case of

---

30 per cent over Pablo Pebrer's reasonable allowance of £ 150 millions for agriculture in 1831. Spackman's allowance amounts to 40 per cent of his estimate of total national income. So great a proportion is improbable. It contrasts with Patrick Colquhoun's estimate of 26 per cent (the same as manufactures) in 1812, with 28 per cent in 1831 (manufactures, 30 per cent), and with Spackman's own allowance of only £ 137 millions or 25 per cent for manufactures (here including inland transport and distribution) in 1841. Moreover, so great a gain by agriculture between 1831 and 1841 is not consistent with other data. Since changes in agricultural prices were small, it would have required an increase in production amounting to 25 or 30 per cent. Yet population in this decade increased only 11 per cent; and imports of foodstuffs in 1841 were much larger than in 1831. Unless, in defiance of the decline in per capita income, average consumption increased appreciably, a gain of anything like this magnitude is ruled out. Allowance of £ 170 to £ 180 millions for agriculture, and of £ 150 to £ 160 millions for manufactures, might be nearer the mark. With these adjustments, the national income of the United Kingdom would figure to about £ 533 millions, and that of Great Britain to about £ 425 millions in 1841. However, while this amended total for the United Kingdom is more compatible with a "derived estimate" of £ 530 millions for 1843, prepared later by Miss Deane, it is low in relation to an "implicit estimate" by Michael G. Mulhall of £ 562 millions for 1840. Mulhall allowed still less for agriculture but more for manufactures, mines, forests, and fisheries: see Deane, "Contemporary Estimates of National Income in the Second Half of the Nineteenth Century," *Economic History Review*, 9:454 (April 1957).

wheat will illustrate the deficiencies of the data. Wheat for bread was a standard necessity of British diet throughout the nineteenth century. To the north of the island, oat products were also heavily consumed; but wheat bread, garnished when possible with butter or treacle, and supplemented, again when possible, with cheese or meat, was the basic article of diet for the vast majority of the population of Britain itself. Unfortunately, no comprehensive returns on British acreage or harvest yields were collected in this part of the century, and the comments of contemporary observers on crop conditions are not very helpful and are sometimes quite contradictory. Estimates of British wheat production hazarded for this period seem to be based on the assumption, which is probably correct, that demand was extremely inelastic regardless of price so that home production should be indicated by computing per capita consumption and deducting known supplies from outside. The difficulty is that per capita consumption in this period is not known, and notions differ rather widely. Leo Drescher's projections on production seem to assume, after allowing for Irish and foreign supplies, consumption of about 5.6 bushels per head of population in Great Britain around 1838–1842.[35] Although this was about the level for the United Kingdom as a whole in the 1880's when production records were begun, it was then fully a bushel per person less than consumption in Great Britain itself. Others put consumption in the earlier part of the century as high as eight bushels per capita.[36] About all that is certain is that, although domestic production of wheat had increased very substantially in these postwar years, poor harvest seasons brought more and more dependence on foreign supplies to feed the growing population (Table 17). In good years like 1833 to 1836, home production plus Irish supply was about sufficient; but in poor years larger and larger drafts on foreign supply were imperative. In the poor years 1838–1842, the quantities required from abroad were four times what they were in the poor years 1816–1820. Moreover, the cost of this basic commodity was, for a large part of the population, a major determinant of what could be spent on other foods and on other goods. The fluctuations in costs were frequently severe, effecting large changes in income distribution which

[35] Reading from graph, in L. Drescher, "Die Entwicklung der Agrarproduktion Grossbritanniens und Irlands seit Beginn des 19 Jahrhunderts," *Weltwirtschaftliches Archiv*, 41:272 (Jena, 1935), and converting to bushels.

[36] Porter, *Progress of the Nation* (London, 1851), pp. 138–139. Schlote's estimates of purely British production of wheat, *British Overseas Trade*, p. 61, yield, with imports, nearly eight bushels per capita prior to 1854. But his estimates of purely British production are about what would be reached by applying the high per capita consumption in Britain itself in later known years to the population of the whole United Kingdom as cited in his table (*i.e.* including Irish population which was near its peak in 1841).

must have exerted multiplied influence on the national economy. Over the four years from 1835 to 1839, the *Gazette* price of wheat rose from 39.3s. to 70.7s. the quarter of 8 bushels. If consumption in Great Britain itself was only about 6 bushels per capita, the nation's wheat bill alone must have risen by no less than £ 22 millions, an amount close to 5 per cent of the national income.

TABLE 17. POPULATION GROWTH AND OUTSIDE SUPPLIES OF WHEAT AND WHEAT FLOUR IN GREAT BRITAIN, ANNUAL AVERAGES IN SELECTED PERIODS, 1816–1842

			Supplies of wheat and wheat flour		
				From foreign and colonial sources	
		Population	*From Ireland*	*Total*	*Per capita*
		mill.	*mill. bushels*	*mill. bushels*	*bushels*
1816–20	...	13.5	1.36	4.79	.35
1826–30	...	15.6	3.87	7.67	.49
1833–36	...	17.1	5.77	0.40	.02
1838–42	...	18.3	2.23	19.85	1.09

Sources: Wheat and wheat flour imports from Porter, *Progress of the Nation*, pp. 139–140, 345; population calculated as mean values for each period from decennial census returns.

For commodities wholly imported, the records on entries for home consumption make the matter of demand fairly certain. There may be some discrepancy between such entries and the actual consumption in any one year, but five-year averages should level this out effectively. Perhaps the two most significant imported commodities, indicating what national standard of living was possible under the conditions of national income and its distribution, were sugar and tea. Consumption of tobacco and foreign and colonial spirits (brandy, gin, and rum) is also suggestive with respect to amenities. From 1816–1820 to 1838–1842, prices of sugar and tea, influenced in the later quinquennium by a loss in production in the West Indies and by the "Opium War" with China, fell less before duties, and still less after duties, than the weighted average prices of net imports in general. Average import prices of sugar declined only about 15 per cent before duties and only about 10 per cent with duties added, in contrast to 33 per cent and 40 per cent respectively for all net imports.[37]

[37] As calculated in Chapter IV, weighted average prices of all net imports before duties fell from 174.3 (1880 = 100) in 1816–20 to 116.6 in 1838–42, or 33.1 per cent. Weighted average prices after duties fell more — from 238.8 to 144.2, or 39.6 per cent — mainly because of the larger relative increase in volume of low duty articles.

Average import prices of tea fell 31 per cent before duties but only 28 per cent after duties.

Altogether, the per capita figures on consumption of these commodities (Table 18) suggest that the depression years 1838–1842 were harder on the national standard of living than those immediately after the war. In the relative prosperity of 1832–1836, all but tobacco showed some small gains from 1816–1820. But by 1838–1842, only tea showed any gain, and it was extremely small. It is interesting also to compare these per capita values with those for non-boom quinquenniums twenty and forty years later.

TABLE 18. PER CAPITA CONSUMPTION OF SOME IMPORTED COMMODITIES, ANNUAL AVERAGES IN SELECTED PERIODS, 1816–1882

		Sugar lbs.	Tea lbs.	Tobacco lbs.	Spirits imp. gals.
1816–1820	....	16.8	1.24	0.87	0.16
1832–1836	....	17.4	1.48	0.84	0.20
1838–1842	....	16.2	1.31	0.59	0.14
1858–1862	....	34.8	2.64	0.90	0.17
1878–1882	....	61.8	4.64	1.42	0.25

These per capita figures are averages only. Such evidence as we have on wages and living costs makes it fairly clear that some of the population, at least those in full employment in factories and crafts, did a little better in terms of purchasing power than the averages suggest, while others lost ground.

Real wages among the well-employed seem to have improved a little over these high protectionist years. Money wages, it is true, seem to have been generally on the down grade for nearly twenty years after 1815. In the textile industries they reached their lowest point in 1831, in agriculture in 1830, and among London artisans, apparently, in 1837. By 1838–1842, money wages in all three groups were above their postwar lows, but all were down from 1816–1820 — in textiles by 8 per cent, in agriculture by 17 per cent, and among London artisans by 7 per cent.[38] What offset these losses, and apparently more than offset them for textile workers and London artisans, was the decline in living costs. How much this decline can soundly be said to have been is by no means clear, for there is no very exact guide on this point. Net import prices obviously will not serve.

[38] From the money wages series of Nikolai D. Kondratieff, Bowley, and Tucker, respectively, as shown together in Gayer, Rostow, and Schwartz, *British Economy*, I, 167, 208, 238, 273, 301.

As indicated above for sugar and tea, domestic prices on foodstuffs did not decline as much as net import prices, for the latter are calculated before the specific customs duties were added and these were not commensurately reduced. For this reason as well as others, Silberling's cost of living index, indicating a decline of 19 per cent from 1816–1820 to 1838–1842,[39] will not serve. Tucker's cost of living series for London artisans attempts to take into account other necessities and services as well as foods and indicates a decline of almost 21 per cent over this period. But it, too, uses some wholesale prices before duties and has other uncertainties and weighting problems.[40] Moreover, as Ashton has pointed out in discussing these two indexes, retail and wholesale price movements often diverged and there were large regional differences.[41] But whether the fall in the cost of living for the working class was, thanks to other unconsidered factors perhaps, Silberling's 19 per cent, or Tucker's 21 per cent for London artisans, or only about 15 per cent, say, it was probably somewhat larger than the decline in money wages for London artisans and textile workers and presumably for other well-employed groups, but perhaps not for agricultural workers.

Real wages and standard of living can be held to have improved, then, among some part of the working classes. If this conclusion is correct, it should follow that the lower averages on per capita consumption shown in Table 18 for 1838–1842 understate the losses suffered by some other sections of the population by the last quinquennium of this protectionist period.

Britain's postwar system of protection contributed to this unhappy trend in diverse ways. The absurd practice of levying duties on needed raw materials which were not produced in Britain had the effect of limiting foreign markets for the products of British industry (either by raising costs to British manufacturers or by pushing down the prices paid to foreign producers) and so tended to restrict employment and purchasing power among the British working classes. Duties on other goods were high and sometimes almost prohibitory, and they, too, restricted the capacity of Britain's trading partners to buy her products. The stiff protection of British agriculture, which was less and less able regularly to provide for growing needs, in bad years hurt virtually all classes of the

[39] Silberling, "British Prices and Business Cycles, 1779–1850," Review of Economic Statistics, 5:219–262 (1923).
[40] Tucker, "Real Wages of Artisans in London, 1729–1935," Journal of the Statistical Association, 31:73–84 (1936).
[41] T. S. Ashton, "The Standard of Life of the Workers in England, 1790 to 1831," The Journal of Economic History, Supplement IX (1949), particularly pp. 28–38.

population. The years leading up to boom times showed what was possible when food was cheap. Good harvests in 1820–1823 and in 1834–1835 brought down the price of wheat and bread — in 1823 the average *Gazette* price of wheat was lower than in any prior year since 1798, and in 1835 below any prior year since 1780. On these occasions, the greater quantities of grain produced went far, even at the lower prices, to sustain the purchasing power of the agricultural classes, and they brought fuller employment for farm labor. For the population as a whole, a fall in the cost of bread by a penny or two a loaf meant that each family gained the means for larger consumption of other goods and services. Multiplied by the millions of families, and by the hundreds of loaves each family needed in the course of a year, the sums were significant enough to explain much of the chain reaction that followed: a better home market for a variety of British products and services, better employment, larger consumption of foreign goods of the sort regularly imported, better markets abroad for British goods, and a buoyant spirit prompting British investment and promoting still more business at home and abroad. Conversely, poor harvests brought higher food prices which could contribute powerfully to reversing the chain of causation. If the income of farmers and landlords was sustained by higher prices for smaller quantities, the income of the bulk of the population was pressed and squeezed, forcing contraction throughout the rest of the national economy.

Again and again Britain was hit by poor harvests in depression times. Even if they were not a prime contributory cause of business recession, they certainly hurt most when they could do the most harm. In the depression year of 1826, average retail prices of basic diet in Manchester went up more than 8 per cent above the average in the boom year 1825, raising them 29 per cent above 1823 when the boom was generating. They remained appreciably above 1823 prices at least through 1831.[42] Again, after 1836, food prices were consistently above those at the height of the preceding boom and still further above those of the build-up years. In 1839, according to Tucker, food prices in London were 24 per cent above 1836 and 32 per cent above the good years 1834–1835. The retail price of the four-pound loaf of bread in London averaged 10*d*. throughout 1838–1840, 25 per cent above 1836 and 33 per cent above 1834–1835. Even for the well-employed, whose wages did not advance correspondingly, these differences were serious enough in reducing the margin between modest

---

[42] Ashton, *loc. cit.* Tucker's index of food prices in London, which is not distinctively based on retail price behavior, however, shows prices down 4 per cent in 1826, but above 1823 each year through 1831.

comfort and mere subsistence. For the poorly-employed or the un-employed, whose number now increased,[43] relief allowances covered only the direst necessities. British imports of sugar and tea and other regular commodities of trade fell off and, although cereals were imported in large quantities, as we have seen, this was an emergency business, improvised and expensive and bringing a good deal less compensatory market abroad for British wares than its cost.

Nor was it simply the Corn Laws which limited food supply and trade. There was prohibition of import of cattle and fresh meat which was probably as bad for trade as for diet.[44] Gladstone put the commercial aspects of the case quite simply and cogently to the House of Commons in 1842 when the government proposal to replace the prohibition by a moderate duty of £ 1 per head raised a great alarm among spokesmen for the agricultural interest.

Suppose that 50,000 head of cattle were to be annually imported, such importation would produce but a small effect upon the prices of meat, but it would create an import trade to the amount of half a million of money, a trade which, in its nature, would lead by a smooth, certain course of operation to an export trade in return, of equal amount; which would contribute — he did not say in a moment, but in the course of years — to an increased demand for employment and labour.[45]

Once a believer in protectionism, Gladstone had been converted by his work at the Board of Trade where he had been placed by Sir Robert Peel in 1841. Every day spent at the office, he wrote later, "beat like a battering ram on the unsure fabric of my official protectionism. By the end of the year I was far gone in the opposite sense."[46]

THE POLITICAL CLIMATE

After Huskisson's moderating measures in the middle twenties it took two more decades with two more major depressions before revision of trade policy again became practical politics. Institutional reform became the order of the thirties, and there was much to be done. First, the far

[43] By 1842 poor relief expenditure in nonagricultural counties was up 36 per cent from the low point of 1836, and in agricultural counties it rose about 20 per cent. The gradual application of the new Poor Law may have limited the increase. In some communities it was much greater. Poor rates in hard-hit Stockton, in the Lancashire textile district, almost trebled from 1836–1837 to 1841–1842. The *Spectator* reported in June, 1842 that more than half the master spinners were out of work there.

[44] E. J. Hobshawm in a recent and important article, "The British Standard of Living," *The Economic History Review*, 10:46–68 (August 1957) presents, among other data, evidence indicating a falling off in beef consumption.

[45] Hansard, *Parl. Deb.*, LXIII (1842), 645. This debate (pp. 617–654) rang all the changes on the theme. It is also an illustration of the care with which Peel and Gladstone had prepared their case to meet every phase of the protectionist argument.

[46] John Morley, *The Life of William Ewart Gladstone* (New York, 1903), I, 250.

reaching and hotly contested redistribution of representation in the House of Commons, then poor laws, municipal government, and many other institutions, successively absorbed political energy and public attention. In 1830, Sir Henry Parnell had published a concisely reasoned little volume, *On Financial Reform*, in which he concentrated a sharp attack on the import duties on raw materials, foodstuffs, and manufactured goods. He proposed reforms similar in all essentials to those Peel began to carry out in 1842, including an income or property tax to make up the revenue lost by reducing customs duties. Lord Althorp, the new Whig Chancellor of the Exchequer, announced in 1831 that his "general view of finance" would be based on the principles Parnell had advanced. But he grasped the nettle rather inexpertly and, lacking the margin of revenue from which to make substantial reductions in duties, he shrank from Parnell's plan for an income or property tax to make good the losses. When reviving trade later produced better revenue, domestic tax reductions were favored. What was done for the customs duties was piecemeal, without systematic overhaul, and without reducing the heavy dependence of the revenue on good trade.[47] As we have seen, customs duties supplied 43 per cent of net revenue in 1830 and 46 per cent of the deficient yield of 1840.

When business activity slumped badly in 1837, the political climate began to change very rapidly and events crowded thick and fast. Poor harvests sent up the price of food. Although some compensation was subsequently found for the hurt to the home market by increasing the volume of exports, this was accompanied or accomplished by a sharp fall in average export prices. By 1838 export prices were back to the previous low level of 1832, and in each succeeding year through 1843 they dropped still lower. The terms of trade moved very unfavorably. By 1842, average export prices had dropped 22 per cent below 1832 (nearly 30 per cent below the boom year 1836), while average import prices were only then back to the 1832 level. In 1838 the Anti-Corn Law League was organized and began its telling attack on the whole system of protectionism. The succession of poor harvests with high food prices, unemployment, and distress rendered their systematic and thoroughgoing campaign particularly appealing. Agitation multiplied, and there were revivals of riots and rick burnings reminiscent of 1816 and 1819. The Chartists published their demand for manhood suffrage and annual elections. They collected over a million and a quarter signatures in 1839 and more than three and one quarter million in 1842. The noise they made for this large and premature program of political change as a preliminary to social reform high-

[47] Halévy, *A History of the English People, 1830–1841* (New York, n.d.), pp. 89–99.

lighted the unrest in the country, alarmed the propertied classes, and made tariff reform seem moderate and practical by contrast. Beginning in 1838, also, a series of budget deficits put a stop to the small, and inadequate, tariff reductions which had been made from year to year when revenue permitted. Indeed, in 1840, customs along with excise duties were boosted 5 per cent, and the assessed taxes 10 per cent, but these higher rates failed to bring revenue into balance with expenditure.

THE SELECT COMMITTEE ON IMPORT DUTIES

In 1840, the House of Commons agreed to the appointment of a select committee to study the import duties. The more active members of the committee were very favorable to tariff reform and at the hearings the free traders made an impressive showing. Officials and former officials of the Board of Trade — James D. Hume, John MacGregor, and George R. Porter — presented their liberal views supported substantially by trade statistics, and the businessmen who were called in to testify were all critical of one phase or another of the protectionist system. Altogether, they built up an extremely strong case. The Report of the Committee itself was a succinct and straightforward charter for free trade. It pointed out the incongruous and often incompatible aims of the existing tariffs:

The duties are sometimes meant to be both productive of revenue and for protective objects, which are frequently inconsistent with each other; hence they sometimes operate to the complete exclusion of foreign produce, and in so far no revenue can of course be received; and sometimes, when the duty is inordinately high, the amount of revenue becomes in consequence trifling. . . . [The] attempt to protect a great variety of particular interests [is] at the expense of revenue, and of the commercial intercourse with other countries.[48]

Out of 1146 articles subject to duty, only 741 actually entered in 1839 and yielded a revenue of £ 22,962,610. Seventeen articles supplied 94.5 per cent of this amount.[49] At the other end of the scale, 531 articles yielded only

---

[48] *Parl. Pap.*, 1840 (601), V, iii. For a careful review of the personnel of the committee, the witnesses heard, and the influence of the Report, see L. Brown, "The Board of Trade and the Tariff Problem, 1840–42," *English Historical Review*, 68:394–421 (July 1953).

[49] The 17 were: butter, cheese, coffee, corn, cotton, currants, raisins, seeds, silk manufactures, spirits, sugar, tallow, tea, timber, tobacco, wines, and wool.

In 1839, the estimated market value of the net imports of these articles, before customs, was about £ 59.4 millions; and the revenue, after drawbacks and repayments, on the goods actually entered for home consumption, probably in that year somewhat less than net imports, was £ 21,700,630. The average rate on the market values of these net imports in that year was, therefore, approximately 36.5 per cent, and on actual entries for home consumption, somewhat more. But the estimated value of net imports of cotton, wool, and corn together was £ 27.3 millions in this particular year and, all 3 entering at low duties, produced a revenue of only £ 1.88 million, or an average of 6.9 per cent. The value of net imports of the remaining 14 commodities was £ 32.1 millions, the duties

£ 80,000, in many cases because the duties were so high as to reduce trade to a mere trickle. The Report contended that

The effect of prohibitory duties, while they are of course wholly unproductive to the revenue, is to impose an indirect tax on the consumer, often equal to the whole difference of price between the British article and the foreign article which the prohibition excludes. . . .[50] On articles of food alone . . . according to the testimony laid before the Committee the amount taken from the consumer exceeds the amount of all other taxes levied by the Government. And the witnesses concur in the opinion that the sacrifices of the community are not confined to the loss of revenue, but that they are accompanied by injurious effects upon wages and capital, they diminish greatly the productive powers of the country, and limit our active trading relations.[51]

The Committee also pointed out that "continuation of our illiberal and exclusive policy" was likely to lead to still more imposts and restrictions by foreign governments. Officials of the Board of Trade had reported a strong trend in Europe and the Americas towards customs rates and practices detrimental and even hostile to British trade. Moreover, the specific duties used by other states were also becoming more oppressive with the fall in prices. The schedules of the Prussian *Zollverein*, for example, which had been quite moderate in their ad valorem weight twenty years earlier, had grown in some cases into very stiff percentages on market values, as much as 80 per cent on the coarser grades of cotton goods.[52] The change to the Prussian standards of weights and measures in 1840 augmented the protective effect further.[53] Reduction of British tariffs, the Committee declared, would

give an example to the world at large, which, emanating from a community distinguished above all others for its capital, its enterprise, its intelligence, and the

---

were £ 19.8 millions, and the average ad valorem rate of the customs was at least 61.7 per cent. Eleven of these 14 commodities were clearly contributory to the national welfare. Only 3 had sumptuary significance.

[50] This contention was based on the fact that the duty on wheat, plus shipping and other charges, about equaled the difference between average prices of British and foreign wheat. For example, the average price in Britain in 1840 was 66s.4d. a quarter, while in Prussia it was 37s.6d. — *Parl. Pap.*, 1850 (460), LII, 2, 23. At this average British price, the duty would be 20s.8d. and this amount, plus freight and other charges, would about fill the price gap. In actual practice, speculators held off for further rise in British price since the amount of the duty dropped by 2s. or more for each shilling that the price advanced. However, after the British market was thrown practically open to foreign grain in 1846, world prices soon rose towards British levels. The British were able to absorb the surpluses available in the world for the next thirty years so that British farmers were not suddenly confronted with much lower prices. The chief gains for the British people lay in more stable supply and in better conditions of employment and of living because of steadier markets at home and abroad for British goods and services.

[51] *Parl. Pap.*, 1840 (601), V, v.
[52] *Parl. Pap.*, 1840 (601), V, 27.
[53] William Otto Henderson, *The Zollverein* (Cambridge, Eng., 1929), pp. 138–139.

extent of its trading relations, could not but exercise the happiest effects and con-
solidate the great interests of peace and commerce by associating them intimately
and permanently with the prosperity of the whole family of nations.

The Committee marshalled some very strong evidence and, not
surprisingly, found that opinion among manufacturers was swinging away
from protectionism. Some who were "supposed to be the most interested
in retaining these duties," they reported, "are quite willing that they
should be abolished, for the purpose of introducing a more liberal system
into our commercial policy." [54]

The Report exerted considerable influence on public opinion. The
Spectator gave it a special supplement, including a summary of the evidence, and sold thirty thousand copies.[55]

THE PEEL ADMINISTRATION

In the spring of 1841, the Melbourne Cabinet, already tottering,
sprang a surprise in presenting its budget. Having failed to meet the deficit
by increasing taxes in the preceding year, it now proposed to try the experiment of reducing the duties on sugar and timber to promote a larger flow
for larger receipts, but without proposing any new tax to cover the interval
before the full revenue expectations could be realized. With suspicion
strong that it was merely a pre-election maneuver hastily devised to catch
the free-trade vote, it was defeated in the Commons by 371 to 281. In the
general election which followed, the Conservatives, under the leadership
of Sir Robert Peel, won a clear majority of seventy-six seats, carrying
nearly half the urban constituencies and most of the financial centers
which by now had free-trade leanings. Peel himself had studied Parnell's
book *On Financial Reform*, though, curiously, he had not read the Report
of the Committee on Import Duties.[56] In his election speeches, as in the
debates in the Commons, he had been careful not to commit himself
against free-trade principles. It was the Whigs who were defeated, not
free trade, and Peel became Prime Minister explicitly claiming "the liberty
of proposing to Parliament those measures which I believe to be con-

---

[54] Alexander Johnston, cotton manufacturer and merchant of Glasgow and also with a
foot in the agriculturalist camp, testified comprehensively for a change in policy. "As a
landowner in the country, I should be very glad that no protective duty should exist at all;
because . . . there would be a general flow of commercial prosperity, a general increase in
traffic and trade, so that capital would be circulated, and the country generally would be
more prosperous than it is; the workingman would be more comfortable than he is, and
the produce of the land would become more valuable than it is under a system of depression and restriction, while starvation such as at present exists could scarcely occur."
Parl. Pap., 1840 (601), V, 136–137.

[55] Halévy, *History of the English People, 1830–1841*, p. 351.

[56] Morley, *Gladstone*, I, 251.

ducive to the public weal. . . . Free as the wind, I tell every man in the country that he has imposed no personal obligations upon me by having placed me in this office." [57]

Peel's bent was statesmanship, to bring tax policy into harmony with national needs and interests in an industrial and commercial age. He knew that there was no turning the clock back to the agricultural system idealized by the protectionist wing of his party, and that mere drifting was equally unthinkable. As he wrote his angry Tory friend, John W. Croker, a little later:

Something effectual must be done to revive, and revive permanently, the languishing commerce and languishing manufacturing industry of this country. . . . If you had to constitute new societies, you might on moral and social grounds prefer corn fields to cotton factories; an agricultural to a manufacturing population. But our lot is cast; we cannot change it and we cannot recede.[58]

Halévy has suggested that Peel was confronted by a choice "between the demagogies of Chartism and of the League." [59] It is a neat but a mistaken antithesis. The energetic efforts of the Anti-Corn Law League were certainly useful in developing public opinion and perhaps, like the Chartist agitation, in prompting reluctant members of the Conservative party to accept substantial tax reforms in preference to radical programs. But the reforms themselves were derived from the facts of the situation, and were designed to effect lasting improvement. At most, the two demagogies determined only how far Peel could go with his own party majority. Peel himself was emphatic in the same letter to Croker that he had not gone in any instance in his tariff of 1842 half far enough on the side of reduction of duties.

If, in the rather critical state of the country in 1842, Peel had real alternatives, they were those pointed out in a long, carefully analytical leading article published in the independent-radical *Spectator* shortly after the election. "Active evil we are not likely to get from Sir Robert Peel," it admitted. "Are we likely to get any good? Yes, if he understands his own position. . . . He is compelled to action through two circumstances — the distress of the country and the deficiency of the revenue." The choice lay between grappling "thoroughly and fairly with the great question of the import duties," or relapsing into discredited weakness with a piddling program, or attempting "the old Tory strong-hand methods of rule." If he chose the first, he could establish a strong govern-

---

[57] Hansard, *Parl. Deb.*, LIX (1841), 555.
[58] Louis John Jennings, *Croker Papers* (New York, 1884), II, 175.
[59] "Peel in 1841," *Revue d'Histoire Moderne*, 13:107 (March 1938).

ment in the best sense of the term. Pursuing either of the other courses, he would soon have a weak government, deserted by the moderates and reviled by the country.[60]

Truly, there was no real choice for an honest and intelligent statesman to make. Peel certainly could not revert to merely strong-handed methods of dealing with social unrest without estranging the support of thinking men everywhere and nullifying the clear implications of the constitutional decisions of the thirties which he had pledged himself and his party to maintain. The shape of the past, the condition of the country, the bent of his own mind, all pointed the same way. Two, at least, of his principal colleagues in the Cabinet were as sure of this as Peel's own actions soon proved him to be. The Duke of Wellington saw the editorial and drew Sir James Graham's attention to it. Cautiously conservative though he was, the Duke put tariff reforms literally at the very top of the "must" list. They "must be the first things to do," he wrote, adding that they were in accord with Tory traditions. Graham, a constant and admiring reader of the *Spectator* [61] for some years, and Peel's closest colleague, had already seen the article and had called Peel's particular attention to it. The only objection he himself had to offer to the analysis was that an income or property tax must accompany tariff reductions, not be held in abeyance for future use should the larger volume of trade expected at the lower rates fail to produce enough revenue.[62] In other words the reforms must be put on a sound basis with an eye to permanence through a balanced budget at the outset, not left to the hazards of future revenue requirements.

On this matter of an income or property tax, Peel was in agreement with Graham on fiscal grounds, but with a social purpose in mind also. In 1830, when the publication of Parnell's book had led to serious consideration of this part of his proposal in the Wellington cabinet, Peel had been "decidedly for a property tax," but "he wished to reach such men as Baring, his [Peel's] father, Rothschild, and others, as well as absentees and [from] Ireland," Lord Ellenborough recorded in his Diary, in order "to reconcile the lower with the higher classes and to diminish the burthen of taxation on the poor man." [63] However, enjoying a prospective surplus of revenue, the Cabinet had then decided to postpone the matter until another year — and fell before the year was out. Now, twelve years later, faced with a budget deficit, with class bitterness evidently rampant, and

[60] *Spectator*, XIV (31 July 1841), 731.

[61] It was under the brilliant direction of Robert Stephen Rintoul from 1828 to 1858.

[62] Sir Charles Stuart Parker, *Sir James Graham* (London, 1907), I, 307–308.

[63] Lord Colchester, ed., *A Political Diary: by Lord Ellenborough* (London, 1881), II, 213.

with the country ready for large changes, it was possible to put the central idea into practice.

FREE TRADE AND AN INCOME TAX

Free trade and an income tax was the formula adopted. The latter was presented as a temporary measure, to cover the deficit and avoid what Peel called "the miserable expedient of [continued loans]. . . . adding during peace to the burdens which posterity would be called upon to bear" [64] until revenue from the remaining duties recovered as the volume of trade rose. But the first experiments in freer trade were so successful that the income tax was retained by successive governments to finance, step by step, further application of the policy over the ensuing twenty years. Expenses in the Crimean War also compelled retention and brought some temporary additions to the import duties. By the time the free-trade program was complete, the income tax had become an accepted element in British national finance. It permitted putting an end to taxation of vital commodities, which too often meant taxation of poverty and distress, and it corrected the fiscal shame of the postwar years by placing a more substantial part of the cost of government explicitly on the shoulders of the well-to-do. Conscience, infused with more enlightened self-interest gleaned from twenty-five years of experience, had re-asserted itself, and the representatives of the propertied classes agreed to levy a direct tax upon themselves.

Peel presented his first budget early in 1842. As a beginning for a free-trade policy, it was extremely cautious. His boldness lay rather in declaring the principle of reducing old tax burdens on foreign trade in favor of a different kind of levy to meet the budget deficit than in the extent of the reductions proposed. His plan went only a few degrees beyond Huskisson's prescription of 1824–1825. Duties on raw materials should not exceed 5 per cent, on partly manufactured goods, 12 per cent, and on manufactured goods, 20 per cent, while others, such as on spirits and wines, should be reserved unchanged as subjects for reciprocity agreements. In all, his reductions cost the revenue only £ 1.3 millions, a little less than Huskisson's measures in the year 1824.[65] The income tax was to make up the loss, wipe out the deficit, and supply a small surplus. It was set at 7d. on the pound (2.9 per cent) and was applied only in Great Britain — but took in Irish absentees resident in Great Britain — and was levied only on incomes over £ 150.

[64] Hansard, *Parl. Deb.*, LXI (1842), 466.
[65] Data from report in *Parl. Pap.*, 1857–58 (511), XXXIII.

In the next four years, revival of prosperity afforded Peel the opportunity to go much further. In 1845, renewal of the income tax permitted repeal of duties on some four hundred fifty articles and commodities, including raw cotton, and the lowering of many others. In this single year, tariff reductions cost the revenue almost as much as Huskisson's total in 1824–1825. In 1846, hurried by crop failures in Britain and by the potato blight in Ireland, Peel secured repeal of the Corn Laws, leaving only a registration duty of 1s. a quarter. This action, more perhaps than any other, symbolized the triumph of free-trade principles. It meant that the agricultural interests, politically the most powerful protectionist group in the country, had been overcome, and that now the food of the masses as well as the raw materials of the factories would be untaxed. Peel was bitterly opposed by a considerable section of his own party and he was forced to resign on the very morrow of his victory. In his four years he had cut the tariffs by about 25 per cent and brought the average rate down close to that of 1790.[66]

The Whigs carried on the development of the free-trade policy. In 1849, they repealed the Navigation Acts. This not only freed the merchant marine, and its foreign competitors, from a network of regulations and restrictions, but also left the self-governing colonies free to adopt their own commercial policies, a course which was unique in European imperial practice. In 1854, foreign ships were admitted to the coasting trade of the United Kingdom. Step by step, as revenue needs permitted, duties on the staples of British life were reduced and abolished. With the budget of 1860, when duties were repealed on three hundred seventy-one articles, the free-trade policy was complete.[67] The number of articles liable to duty, which had stood at 1146 in 1840, had been reduced to forty-eight, and all but twelve of these were purely for revenue on luxury or near luxury commodities.[68] Net customs duties in 1860 averaged 12.9 per cent on net

[66] On the basis of trade at the time each cut was made, the reductions made under Peel in 1842–46 were calculated to have cost the revenue £ 6.3 millions — a little more than one quarter of total customs revenue. Comparison of percentage relations of customs duties to net import values also shows the general trend, but it is complicated by changes in the relative flow of goods of low and high duty. Over-all, the average percentage dropped from 31.4 in 1837–41 to 25.0 in 1847–48, or 21 per cent.

[67] The net value of duty reductions, calculated on the volume of imports at the date of each reduction or repeal and after allowance for increases in rates on other articles, was £ 12.3 millions from 1842 to 1860 inclusive. By the end of 1863, further reductions in the revenue duties added £ 2.3 millions net to this amount. Calculated roughly on the basis of the volume of net imports in 1863, the tax saving would be nearer £ 43 millions. Data from reports in *Parl. Pap.*, 1857–58 (511), XXXIII; and *Parl. Pap.*, 1864 [3340], LVIII, 7. See also Table 19 and Table 29.

[68] Of these 12, 10 were countervailing to excise taxes levied on home products (such as beer, cards, and dice) and 2 (cork and hats) were scheduled to go out at fixed dates.

import values, about half the rate of the late eighteenth century, and their share of total revenue was down to 35 per cent, very close to the prewar proportion. Concurrent with this release from tax burdens and restrictions on trade, the British economy demonstrated a truly phenomenal capacity for balanced and profitable growth.

VI

THE SUCCESS OF BRITISH FREE TRADE POLICY

The new British tariff policy was a success from the very beginning. It opened an era of unprecedented prosperity that soon reached into all sectors of British national life and carried the program along with comfortable majorities. The British Parliament and public accorded the principle of free trade not only the most thoroughgoing practice, but also the most long-lasting adherence yet given by an important industrial state. Among the landed interests in the Conservative party there was lingering talk of a tariff on grain, for them the sum and substance of protectionism, but the general election of 1852 proved to the leaders of the party that the issue was "not only dead but damned." They quietly discarded its "rags and tatters," [1] and free trade was not again seriously contested for over half a century. Then, after thirty years of slower trade development, rising tariffs, trade controls, and imperial rivalry through the world, Joseph Chamberlain was able to commit the Conservative party to a tariff project as part of a plan for imperial economic federation. In the elections of 1906 the Conservatives were decisively defeated. Shortly after the war of 1914–1918, when depreciated European currencies raised a new kind of threat to British industry, British free-trade policy was modified a little, yet when once again directly tested before the voters in 1923 it was again sustained. Not until the grave economic crisis of 1931, in a world segmented by still higher trade barriers and restrictions, did Parliament consent to abandon the principle, acting in this instance without prior reference to the electorate. From first to last, then, the life of this unique experiment was eighty-nine years.

The general soundness of these electoral judgments can scarcely be doubted. Free trade did not prove to be a panacea for all the ills which afflicted modern society, as some of its more enthusiastic proponents seemed to expect, but it certainly reduced the drag on British international economy and lubricated the bearings for a period of phenomenally rapid growth. Virtually every sector of the varied economic life of the country —

[1] William Flavelle Monypenny and George Earl Buckle, *The Life of Benjamin Disraeli* (New York, 1910–1920), III, 506.

even agriculture for several decades — was swept along in expanding prosperity, and social tensions were correspondingly eased.

In the course of events, many other tributary streams swelled the main current of British industrial and commercial growth. There was, for example, railway building which reached boom proportions in Britain in the forties and was soon carried abroad, with much use of British materials, contractors, and technicians. There was further mechanization of industries and more rapid steamship building. There was a rise in real wages and a considerable improvement in employment which expanded the home market by augmenting the purchasing power of the British working classes. There was the developing market for British coal along the trade routes and in other lands which further diversified British exports. Activity and prosperity drew more of both as a well-watered countryside attracts rainfall. Each ensuing development added something to the total success in the exchange of goods and services.

Other forces in the world at large also contributed to the rapid and durable expansion of the British economy during the mid-century decades. Many factors stimulated demand and supply of goods and facilitated the balancing of the two. Population grew rapidly in Europe and in the New World, while industrial development and improvements in agriculture and in transportation increased productivity, promoted trade, raised living standards and purchasing power, and generally multiplied economic opportunities and incentives. After 1849, too, new gold fields came into production and about doubled the world's stock of monetary gold by 1885.[2] Thanks to the relative freedom from the old notions and practices of mercantilist control and thanks, too, to the foreign lending of the chief creditor states, gold could flow to areas where it was useful in meeting the currency needs of rapidly expanding business activity during a period when world trade alone — that is, apart from the vastly greater commercial activity within countries — was quadrupling in value. These new supplies of gold may not have been as prime a factor in promoting price rise through the world in general — that is, outside of the areas of gold production — as has sometimes been supposed,[3] but, concurrent with the

[2] The new gold produced from 1850 to 1885 is estimated at £ 858.9 millions, of which about half went into monetary stocks. See data in Sir Walter Thomas Layton and Geoffrey Crowther, *An Introduction to the Study of Prices* (London, 1935), pp. 239–240.

[3] The drama of the new gold fields, and, perhaps, the simplicity of the explanation that the new gold supplies seem to offer for the rise in prices which occurred in the mid-century, has made it easy to exaggerate their importance and to pass over other factors such as those springing from the great growth in demand for goods through the world and especially in Europe. Quantitatively, this growth in demand for goods is impressive. Take one example of a country which produced both goods for export and gold. United States gold production, rising from less than a million dollars a year in value in 1841–45,

development of banking and credit techniques within the more advanced countries,[4] they were generally sufficient for expanding business needs. The new gold was not unduly absorbed by the chief creditor nation of the time. While a large part of the new supplies flowed into Britain, an almost equally large part also flowed out again during this significant period.[5] It was thanks largely to the distribution of monetary gold that more and more of the national currency systems could be geared to gold standards and integrated internationally through the gold flow mechanism. In these respects the new gold contributed usefully to stability of national currencies and of exchanges.

The series of localized wars in the fifties and sixties provided a certain short-term impetus to price rise by momentarily raising demand in relation to supply. In the one major war in which Britain participated — the Crimean, in 1854–1856 — revenue needs briefly interrupted tariff reductions.

Many more or less concurrent forces contributed, then, to the vast expansion of British and of world economy in the mid-century. It is scarcely possible to isolate and measure the precise degree of stimulus given by the reductions in British tariffs. The cautious gradualness of the steps taken by the British makes it the more difficult to disentangle the particular influence which they exerted from the interplay of other factors. But it is possible to indicate roughly the rate and degree of British tariff reductions and, by correlating with the trade development that followed, to find some clues to their significance.

---

averaged $51.2 millions a year for 1856–60, virtually all of it exported in this quinquennium. The value of American merchandise exports, the bulk of them to Europe with Britain taking by far the largest part, in 1856–60 exceeded those of 1841–45 by an average of $184 millions a year: *Historical Statistics of the United States*, pp. 152, 244, 245, 250. The rise in prices accounted for barely one eighth of this increase in value; volume rose by somewhere around 175 per cent.

[4] The great growth in British credit and currency needs consequent on expanding business activity seems to have been met, with some transitional strains and stresses, largely by greatly increased use of checks. Cf. Hartley Withers, *The Meaning of Money* (New York, 1930), pp. 27–33. Retained imports of gold in this period were remarkably small in relation to the growth in Britain's business activity and her creditor and banking position in the world. From 1850 to 1885, British net imports of gold totaled about £ 100 millions, or less than one eighth of world production in this period. Presumably about half went into monetary stock.

Estimates of gold in circulation in the United Kingdom are subject to a considerable margin of error, but the more reliable ones indicate that the amounts about doubled from 1844 to 1892. See Layton and Crowther, *Study of Prices*, p. 244. Paper currency was rigidly tied to gold under Peel's Bank Act of 1844.

[5] See the series on the net movements of gold and silver coin and bullion shown in Chapter III, Table 4. See also H. J. Habakkuk, "Free Trade and Commercial Expansion, 1853–1870," *The Cambridge History of the British Empire* (Cambridge, Eng., 1940), II, especially pp. 769–771.

CUSTOMS DUTIES AND REVENUE

Some general idea of the timing and extent of British tariff reductions can be indicated by the changes in the percentages which net customs revenue bore to net import values. By 1850, the average rate was down to 24 per cent, slightly below the level in the last years of the eighteenth century. By 1870 it had dropped to 8.2 per cent, and in subsequent years it fell lower. At its lowest in 1898 it was 5.2 per cent, and in 1913, 5.3 per cent. The average rates are shown in Table 19 as five-year averages and in Chart 19 on an annual basis. As was pointed out in Chapter V, this over-all method of measurement yields, at best, only a rough picture because such averages are influenced by fluctuations in the flow of goods of high and low duty which occurred. In the first few years after 1842, such fluctuations continued to be rather marked — for example, that caused by the heavy imports of grain free of duty in 1847 — but they became less and less significant as the new system took shape.

CHART 19. AVERAGE CUSTOMS RATES OF THE UNITED KINGDOM : ANNUAL NET CUSTOMS REVENUE AS PERCENTAGE OF NET IMPORT VALUES, 1841–1913

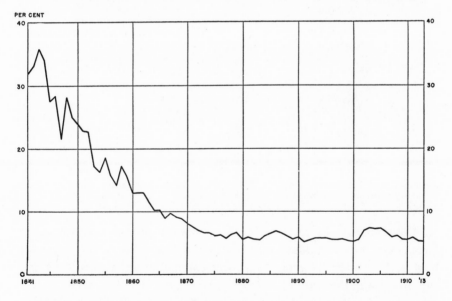

The data in Table 19 show that the net revenue from customs remained remarkably stable at the old level through the transition years. To hold it so was accepted as a main political test as to how far and how fast tariff cutting could go. However, the volume of revenue imports quickly responded to the reductions in rates and to the improvements in the economy.

In the case of two highly taxed articles, tea and sugar, per capita consumption doubled in fifteen years after 1842, four times as fast as the growth in population in Great Britain. The rate at which duties on staples, and presently on near luxuries, could be cut was, therefore, fairly rapid. Because the volume of these and other high-tax imports rose very quickly, the over-all percentages shown in Table 19 and Chart 19 understate the extent of tariff cuts on other goods in the transition years.

TABLE 19. AVERAGE CUSTOMS RATES OF THE UNITED KINGDOM: NET CUSTOMS REVENUE AS PERCENTAGE OF NET IMPORT VALUES, ANNUAL AVERAGES IN QUINQUENNIAL PERIODS, 1841–1913 [a]

		Market value of net imports	Net customs revenue after drawbacks, etc.	
			Amount [b]	Per cent on net import values
		£ mill.	£ mill.	%
1841–1845	...	71.0	22.9	32.3
1846–1850	...	87.7	22.2	25.3
1851–1855	...	116.4	22.2	19.5
1856–1860	...	158.0	23.7	15.0
1861–1865	...	201.2	23.1	11.5
1866–1870	...	246.0	22.0	8.9
1871–1875	...	301.8	20.2	6.7
1876–1880	...	325.9	19.8	6.1
1881–1885	...	336.5	19.7	5.9
1886–1890	...	327.4	20.0	6.1
1891–1895	...	357.1	19.8	5.5
1896–1900	...	413.3	22.1	5.3
1901–1905	...	471.5	32.8	7.0
1906–1910	...	539.6	31.9	5.9
1911–1913	...	623.2	33.6	5.4

[a] For corresponding data on the protectionist period see Table 11.
[b] Adjusted for calendar year from 1854, following the change in the fiscal year.

These changes in customs tariffs, combined with the revival of an income tax, brought a much more equitable distribution of the rising tax load in the United Kingdom. With free entry of essential foodstuffs and raw materials, the burden on the population was lifted where it had pressed hardest. Since customs yields were held fairly constant while other revenue collections increased, the share of total revenue supplied by customs receded from the extreme proportions of the last years of protectionism. The changes gradually effected are indicated in Chart 20. In 1840, customs had supplied 46 per cent of the total revenue (excluding

Post Office) of £ 50.4 millions. By the fiscal year 1860/1861, they yielded 35 per cent of £ 67.0 millions, about the proportion of 1790 and 1815; [6] and by 1880/1881, they were 25 per cent of £ 75.7 millions. In 1900/1901, total revenue had risen to £ 113.1 millions and the customs yield was down to 23 per cent; and in 1913/1914 it was only 21 per cent of the total tax load of £ 167.4 millions. The other great branch of indirect taxation, the excise duties on domestic products, supplied some of the new revenue

CHART 20. CUSTOMS DUTIES AND OTHER REVENUE OF THE UNITED KINGDOM AS PERCENTAGE OF TOTAL REVENUE, EXCLUDING POST OFFICE AND TELEGRAPH, IN SELECTED FISCAL YEARS, 1840–1914

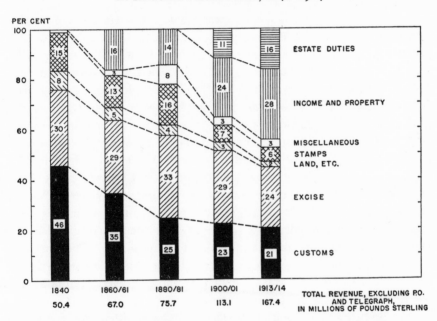

Source: Calculated from data on gross revenue (before costs of collection) in *Statistical Abstracts for the United Kingdom.*

needed after 1840. Levied on luxury and near luxury articles, excise duties produced larger amounts as national income and standard of living improved. However, their share of total revenue remained quite stable at about 30 per cent until the early years of the twentieth century when other revenue rose more steeply. It was the direct taxes that supplied by far the greater part of expanding revenue requirements. Assessed land taxes payable to the central government were reduced, to be sure, until they contributed a negligible proportion of the revenue. But other direct

[6] See Chart 16.

taxes took up the load. Income taxes contributed 16 per cent in 1860/1861, 24 per cent in 1900/1901, and, with much stiffer rates and a surtax, 28 per cent in 1913/1914. By the end of the century estate duties had also become significant, providing 11 per cent in 1900/1901 and 16 per cent in 1913/1914. Such were the great fiscal developments which followed Peel's modest steps to diminish the burden of taxation on the poor man as one means towards reconciling "the lower with the higher classes." They go far to explain the remarkable freedom from serious class bitterness or tension that Britain enjoyed through this era.

THE EXPANSION OF BRITISH FOREIGN TRADE

The timing of Peel's first mild measures for freer trade could hardly have been happier. Rapidly improving business activity eased revenue problems and promoted confidence to go forward with the experiment. Even in the first full year under his first budget there was a very promising turn in British foreign trade, although prices went down a little further. In 1843, exports rose 10 per cent in value but fell 2 per cent in average price. Net imports dropped 7 per cent in value and 8 per cent in price. By all the conventional standards, the terms of trade moved favorably.[7] The numbers in "market gain" jumped from 20 to 25 (1880 = 100), by far the largest rise in a single year since 1815 when the European market had been reopened after years under Napoleon's "Continental System." Thanks to these favorable developments, there was a credit of something like £ 9.3 millions in the balance of payments after some further replenishment of stocks of gold and silver depleted in 1839–1840.[8] These trends were sustained even through the poor harvest year 1846. There was a sharp setback in 1847, however, when the weather imposed severe crop failures; but this reversal was of very brief duration.

Yet British weather must be given the major credit in this fortunate turn in export-import relationships in the initial years of the new policy. Better harvests cut the need for foreign grain by two thirds in 1843 and this circumstance accounted for the whole of the drop in net import values and a little more. Actually, apart from grain, net imports rose a little in value. In this respect, Peel's slight easement of the tariffs may have played a part in stimulating trade in the kind of import goods which best produced responsive markets for British exports. Investment abroad, after three negative years, should also be counted as a factor in boosting the export trade. Logically, the freer trade prospects should have contributed

[7] See Table 8.
[8] See Table 4.

to revival of British confidence in foreign lending, for lower duties would mean that foreign debtors should have less difficulty in making good on their contracts.

The next few years brought still more advance in all sectors. By 1850, when over-all customs rates had been brought down below the average in the late eighteenth century, and before any of the other major stimulants to economic growth except railway building in Britain itself could have exerted much influence, prices had steadied from the sharp setback of 1848. By 1850, the value of British exports had expanded £ 24 millions, or 51 per cent, above 1842. Net imports c.i.f. had risen in almost equal amount — £ 23 millions — but smaller percentage — 34 per cent. Composed of goods of steady consumption, they were therefore conducive to steady reciprocal markets for British goods and services. The repeal of the Corn Laws in 1846 had terminated the erratic system of sliding scale duties and put grain in this category thereafter. The relatives for market gain from trade had risen 85 per cent since 1842. In these eight years, British credits on balance of payments amounted to about £ 52 millions. Investment of these credits increased the British stock of capital abroad by no less than 33 per cent [9] and contributed to the more rapid growth of exports.

In the long term, to the outbreak of the war of 1914, the record of British foreign trade under the new policy divides into three main periods. In the first, stretching through 1873, the initial spurt in exports, and in foreign investments, was remarkably well sustained. Over this period, exports expanded at a phenomenal, indeed, at an unprecedented rate. In the second, from 1873 to about 1898, development for Britain, and generally for the world, was so much slower that it has become known as the "Great Depression," and the term is certainly appropriate with respect to prices, though hardly with respect to the volume of trading or business activity. The third period, from 1898 to 1913, brought resumption of rapid growth in trade volumes and, thanks to improvement in prices, more rapid rise in trade values.

In the first period, British exports continued to grow both in value and in volume at a far faster and steadier pace than in the high protectionist years after 1815. Setbacks were few and were invariably brief. In this extended ascent from the trough of 1842 to the peak in 1873, volume rose by 355 per cent, an average rate of growth of slightly more than 11 per cent per annum in contrast to about 7 per cent per annum from 1816 to 1842. Since average export prices improved over this interval, rising from 114 in

[9] See Table 4.

1842 (1880 = 100) to 135 in 1873, export values show still more striking contrast to the protectionist period. They rose by 439 per cent, or 14 per cent per annum as compared to one half of one per cent per annum in the period of precipitous fall in average prices from 1816 to 1842, or, to take a trough-to-peak comparison, in contrast to 1½ per cent per annum from 1816 to 1836.

This rise in the weighted average export prices of British goods is partly attributable to the growing importance of metal goods and of a diversity of other higher priced products of British skills. Exports of cotton and wool yarns and manufactures, for example, while continuing to grow in value, dropped to a somewhat more modest share of total exports. Where, in 1842, they constituted together 58 per cent of total value, by 1873 they were down to 42 per cent. Moreover, exports of cotton manufactures grew much faster now than those of cotton yarn which required little labor and was low in price. Where cotton yarn made up nearly one third (31 per cent) of the value of all cotton exports in 1842, it was only one fifth in 1873. Average export prices of cotton manufactures, which had fallen so fast in the preceding period, were only a few points below the 1842 level in 1873; but raw cotton prices had not yet subsided from the scarcity levels of the American Civil War period and prices of cotton yarn were 32 per cent higher. Average export prices of woolens were slightly stronger by 1873.[10] But the significant thing was the rise in the proportions of goods other than cottons and woolens, and it was this healthy development — symptomatic of fuller utilization of British skills and resources — which lifted average prices of British exports as a whole. Although further cost-reducing improvements in methods of manufacture were made in many of the industries producing them, weighted average prices of these other goods rose 31 per cent from 1842 to 1873, nearly twice as much as for exports in general.[11]

This extraordinary rate of growth in British export volumes and values was not maintained in the second period to 1898. While business continued to expand, the rate was much slower. Export volume rose 62 per cent, on an average barely 2½ per cent per annum, from the high level attained in 1873, in contrast to 7 per cent per annum from 1816 to 1842 and 11 per cent from 1842 to 1873. Average export prices fell sharply. By 1898, they had dropped 44 per cent, a little more than average net import prices between the same dates (40 per cent) and almost two thirds as much as export prices in the quarter century after Waterloo (62 per cent). Except

[10] See Appendix Tables II and III.
[11] See Table 8 and Appendix Table IV.

in 1890, export values consistently fell short of the 1873 peak. In 1898 they were almost 9 per cent lower.

The third period, from 1898 through 1913, was marked by another strong spurt in British exports. Quantitatively, the rate of growth was twice as rapid as in the preceding period, averaging 5 per cent a year. Average prices also improved considerably. By 1913 they were 27 per cent above those of 1898. Export values, accordingly, rose by 125 per cent over these fifteen years, on an average, slightly over 8 per cent a year.

Turning to British import records, one is surprised more by the moderation than by the magnitude of their growth in the free-trade period. It is true that, in absolute amount, the increase was even greater than the huge rise in export values, but the *rate* of increase was less rapid. Net imports rose from £ 68 millions in 1842 to £ 315 millions in 1873, a gain of 364 per cent, or an average of 12 per cent a year as against an average of 14 per cent a year for exports. This meant, however, that the merchandise trade deficit grew from £ 20.6 millions to £ 60.3 millions. Yet some such increase in the trade deficit was to be expected, not simply because of the lowering of trade barriers, but because of the very great growth in British current income from goods and services and interest charges for which British acceptance of goods was far and away the chief means of foreign payment.

What is surprising is that net imports increased at a less rapid rate than British export values in the first period, and less rapidly in amount than total British income through the era as a whole. In spite of the great reductions in tariff schedules, in spite of the stimuli to consumption consequent on large capital development at home, and in spite of population growth with generally good employment and improving wages, British imports did not rise quite as much as British purchasing power abroad. Indeed, in this period, in some contrast to the preceding high protectionist interlude, imports took on a dependent quality, tending to be pulled up in the wake of a rise in the export of British goods and services. Relatively, the growing merchandise trade deficit was a shrinking one. In 1842, it was 43 per cent of export values, while in 1873, it was barely 24 per cent. We can follow the export-import value relationships more easily by reference to the trade balance relatives constructed in Table 8. In no quinquennium in this first period (Table 20) was the relative lower than the average in 1838–1842 (*i.e.*, 105) ; and, in respect to single years, only in two — 1847 and 1848, with unusually large imports of grain in the first and business recession in the second — did the relatives fall lower. The reduction of British tariff barriers, then, did not result in any flooding of the British market with foreign goods. Rather, the balance of merchandise trade improved and, since the income from invisible exports and from foreign investment grew, handsome credits accrued on the net balance of current accounts and were invested abroad. These will be discussed later, but their significance here in relation to the limited rise in import values in this period will be obvious.

TABLE 20. MERCHANDISE TRADE DEFICITS OF THE UNITED KINGDOM, ANNUAL
AVERAGES IN QUINQUENNIAL PERIODS, 1841–1913 [a]

			Negative balance of merchandise trade			
	Net imports	Exports of U.K. produce	Amount	Per cent of net imports plus exports	Per cent of exports	Trade balance relative
	£ mill.	£ mill.	£ mill.	%	%	1880 = 100
1838–1842 ...	74.9	50.5	− 22.4	−17.9	−44.6	105
1841–1845 ...	71.0	54.0	− 17.0	−13.6	−31.5	119
1846–1850 ...	87.7	60.9	− 26.8	−18.0	−44.1	109
1851–1855 ...	116.4	88.9	− 27.5	−13.4	−30.9	120
1856–1860 ...	158.0	124.2	− 33.8	−12.0	−27.2	123
1861–1865 ...	201.2	144.4	− 56.8	−16.4	−39.3	112
1866–1870 ...	246.0	187.8	− 58.2	−13.4	−30.9	119
1871–1875 ...	301.8	239.5	− 62.3	−11.5	−26.0	124
1876–1880 ...	325.9	201.4	−124.5	−23.6	−61.8	96
1881–1885 ...	336.5	232.3	−104.2	−18.4	−44.9	107
1886–1890 ...	327.4	236.3	− 91.1	−16.2	−39.0	113
1891–1895 ...	357.1	226.8	−130.3	−23.3	−57.5	99
1896–1900 ...	413.3	252.7	−160.6	−24.1	−63.6	95
1901–1905 ...	471.5	297.0	−174.5	−22.7	−58.8	96
1906–1910 ...	539.6	397.5	−142.1	−15.2	−35.7	113
1911–1913 ...	623.2	488.8	−134.4	−12.1	−27.5	120

[a] For corresponding data for 1796–1841 see Table 14.

The free-trade program undoubtedly contributed a good deal to this curious phenomenon of a favorable change in British export-import relations at this time. The reduction, step by step, of British duties narrowed the price differential between the foreign producer and the British consumer and in this way strengthened foreign purchasing power for British goods and services. All in all, as we have seen, these tariff cuts reached very large proportions. In 1843, when, with some revival of more normal composition of the import trade, the average rate went higher than since 1837, customs duties added 35.8 per cent to the cost of net imports. By 1850, the average rate was down to 24.2 per cent, by 1860 to 12.9 per cent, and by 1873 to only 6.6 per cent. In the upward movements of world prices that occurred in the period of these British tariff reductions, British net import prices *after* duties rose less than did prices *before* duties (see Chart 21). As was to be expected when the British market — and soon, too, world markets — imposed such strong pressure on supply, a considerable part of the tax savings[12] conferred by the duty reductions accrued to foreign suppliers. Moreover, British net imports, rising at an average rate of 12 per cent per annum in this period, were a truly formidable force in world trade. In 1840, they were close to 36 per cent of the value of the exports of all other countries; in 1860, they were still about 31 per cent; and in 1873, about 26 per cent (see Table 28). British demand, supplemented as it was by the concurrent — and certainly related — growth in the imports of other countries that is mirrored in this decline in the relative proportions of British takings of the world's export goods, must have pressed supply very hard indeed.

These interacting factors and circumstances account for much of the upturn in world prices, as well as for the huge growth in foreign purchasing power for British goods and the demand for capital for expansion that now so strongly attracted British investment. The readiness of the British to respond in growing volume to the investment opportunities developing abroad established the extra margin of foreign purchasing power for British goods and services above and beyond what dependable — and fairly responsive — British takings of foreign goods and services supplied. And all this was accomplished without serious cost to any party — unless we count the British income tax as the modest price. Even the customs revenue of the British Treasury remained stable, thanks to the increase in the flow of imports.

These very satisfactory export-import proportions did not hold up during the so-called "Great Depression." A series of poor harvests, beginning in 1876, brought greatly increased dependence on overseas supplies of cereals which were soon produced abroad in surging abundance at extremely low prices and which continued thereafter to be absorbed in Britain in rising volume. Prices of other goods also fell sharply and were taken in much greater quantities. From 1873 to 1898, net import volume slightly more than doubled; average prices dropped nearly 40 per cent. The net result was that import values rose 30 per cent, while export values, as we have seen, slumped off and, with the exception of the single year 1890, remained below the high level of 1873 until 1899. Foreign investment fell off in this period as prices and prospects declined and rarely

[12] See Table 29.

equalled income from capital already placed abroad. Merchandise trade deficits exceeded the high relative proportions of 1838–1842 in 1876–1880, in 1883, and again steadily from 1891 through 1905. The larger volume of imports taken through this period at lower average prices undoubtedly meant higher standards of living in the country, for British wage levels were generally rising. No doubt there was also a good deal of capital investment at home in this time when rates of return on foreign investment fell off a little and prospects abroad were less inviting. But the rate of domestic investment could hardly have been as high as in the preceding period of extraordinarily rapid economic growth.

CHART 21. AVERAGE CUSTOMS RATES OF THE UNITED KINGDOM IN RELATION TO
NET IMPORT PRICES: ANNUAL NET CUSTOMS REVENUE AS PERCENTAGE
ADDED TO AVERAGE NET IMPORT PRICES, 1840–1880

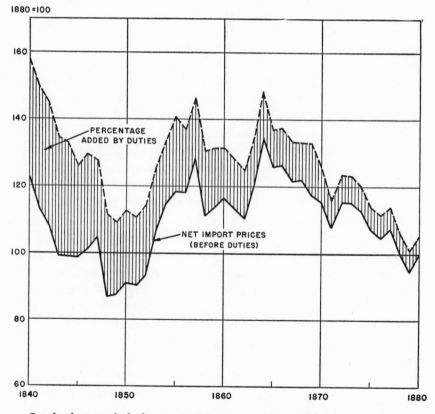

In the last period, from 1898 to 1913, more rapid advance in export values gradually restored the predominant pattern of export-import relationships of this free-trade era as a whole. Expanded production capacity in such lines as iron and steel, coal mining, and ship building came strongly into play. Foreign investment, again stimulated by rising prices and business abroad, increased rapidly from 1905 on. By 1906, the trade deficit was again relatively less than in 1838–1842, and it remained less through 1913. In that year the trade balance relative, at 122, was 16 per cent higher than in 1838–1842, and indeed, only 7 per cent below 1816–1820 which includes that phenomenal year 1816.

THE RE-EXPORT TRADE

The sequel for the British re-export trade was even more impressive in rate of growth than for exports or net imports. In certain respects, Britain was marked by nature and by her own lines of development to be a great distributing center for overseas commodities. Lying athwart the sea routes to northern Europe and importing a vast variety of products for her own consumption, many of them in massive quantities, with business establishments and merchant marine literally girdling the globe, with sorting, grading, warehousing, and brokerage facilities, Britain should have been able to supply many commodities efficiently at relatively low cost and to develop a great business to the advantage of all concerned. The postwar protectionist system, as we saw in Chapter V, had not been favorable to the development of this trade much beyond the marketing of British colonial produce.[13] It is true that goods for re-export could be warehoused in bond, and that refunds for duties paid were allowed on reshipment abroad. But the system had involved expenses and risks which limited flexibility. Moreover, imperial and protectionist restrictions invited retaliatory measures by other states.

The repeal, step by step, of duties and imperial preferences on staple commodities opened wide the great opportunity for Britain in the re-export business. The home islands became, in effect, a great free port where British merchants could more easily develop the re-export potentialities incident to large-scale supply of the home market. By 1873, the value of re-exports had risen 564 per cent over 1842, an average rate of growth of 18 per cent a year in contrast to 14 per cent for exports and 12 per cent for net imports over this interval. This much more rapid expansion in re-export values is attributable not only to greater growth in volume of business — volume increased 407 per cent from 1842 to 1873 as against 355 per cent for exports and 335 per cent for net imports — but also to changes in composition which brought much more improvement

[13] See Chapter V.

in weighted average re-export prices [14] — 30 per cent as against 18 per cent for exports and 7 per cent for net imports. The trade became more diversified, less specialized in a few relatively low-priced colonial products than in the earlier period. At least three major factors promoted this profitable growth in volume and change in structure of the re-export trade: the larger scale on which Britain herself imported a wider variety of commodities; the release from former trammels, both British and foreign; and the growth of demand in Europe thanks to more rapid economic development there.

TABLE 21. THE RE-EXPORT TRADE OF THE UNITED KINGDOM IN RELATION TO GENERAL IMPORTS, ANNUAL AVERAGES IN QUINQUENNIAL PERIODS, 1841–1913 [a]

	General Imports	Value	Re-exports Per cent of general imports		General imports	Value	Re-exports Per cent of general imports
	£ mill.	£ mill.	%		£ mill.	£ mill.	%
1841–1845 ...	79.7	8.7	10.9	1881–1885 ...	399.5	63.0	15.8
1846–1850 ...	98.4	10.7	10.9	1886–1890 ...	389.6	62.2	16.0
1851–1855 ...	132.8	16.4	12.3	1891–1895 ...	417.8	60.7	14.5
1856–1860 ...	182.9	24.9	13.6	1896–1900 ...	474.3	61.0	12.9
1861–1865 ...	247.6	46.4	19.5	1901–1905 ...	541.8	70.3	13.0
1866–1870 ...	292.8	46.8	16.0	1906–1910 ...	629.9	90.3	14.3
1871–1875 ...	360.0	58.2	16.2	1911–1913 ...	728.0	104.8	14.4
1876–1880 ...	382.5	56.6	14.8				

[a] For values and proportions in the protectionist period, see Table 13.

During the "Great Depression," the growth in re-exports was much slower. Nevertheless, although it was a period of revival in trade restrictions abroad, volume grew by 77 per cent from 1873 to 1898, and the variety developed in the preceding period was well maintained. Average prices of re-exports fell no more than those of Britsh net imports. Total value rose 9 per cent.

In the final period re-exports resumed more rapid advance. By 1913, re-export values were 81 per cent more than in 1898 while net import value had risen 61 per cent. Again, this greater increase in value is partly attributable to favorable changes in the relative proportions of the various goods traded. Weighted average re-export prices rose by 38 per cent, nearly twice the rise in weighted average net import prices which was 20 per cent. Over-all, from 1842 to 1913, re-export values had multiplied full

[14] For annual values, volumes, and weighted average prices of re-exports, and for percentages of general imports, see Appendix Table I.

thirteen times — from £ 8.4 millions to £ 109.6 millions. From 1850 on, the proportions which re-export values bore to general imports were consistently stronger than in the last years under the protectionist system. (See Table 21)

BUSINESS SERVICES: SHIPPING

Other elements in Britain's complex international economy were carried along with the expansion of British trade in the mid-century, and in closely co-ordinate measure. Merchant shipping, insurance, banking, brokerage, merchandising, and every other form of British business enterprise in foreign and colonial fields had all along been intimately linked with trade, and they appear to have flourished now with equal vigor. The estimates of net earnings presented in Chapter III were, with the exception of those for shipping, constructed on this hypothesis, and the fact that the end results correspond closely at several check-points through the period with the best estimates of British foreign investments tends to confirm their validity as annual averages.

British shipping was the most important of British services abroad throughout the century and the records permit fairly close examination of the results in the carrying trade to and from the home islands. The experience of the merchant marine under free trade is a particularly significant one. Long the most steadily protected interest, it had been one of the most demanding; and the rules and regulations developed in the Navigation Acts had been more provocative of friction with and retaliation by other maritime states than any other element in the old commercial system. The claim that the merchant marine was the bond of empire and the nursery of seamen for the navy had given it political and security roles, too, although the regulations shaped by these concepts had often been more restrictive than helpful in an economic sense. The fact that British shipping activity had grown twice as fast on "unprotected routes" since 1824, when reciprocity agreements with other maritime states began to breach the network of regulations, was an augury that the merchant marine could hold its own in open competition. By the mid-century, too, economic considerations came more generally into their own. The multiplying years of peace cleared the atmosphere, reducing the weight formerly attached to security arguments. But in any case, there was no place for Navigation Acts in the liberal philosophy of trade, of empire, or of international relations in general. Over the organized protests of the shipping interests, they were repealed in 1849. No sign of the ruin predicted appeared, and five years later the coasting trade, too, was thrown open.

The release from restrictions and penalties was certainly timely. The phenomenal growth in the volume of British trade in the mid-century decades not only eased the transition for the British merchant marine but actually seems to have provided more business than it proved able to handle. The ending of protection brought some compensatory gain in freedom, too. It meant that ships could operate more efficiently, accepting cargoes in and out on any route with much less fear that the laws would force a profitless leg in ballast. At the same time, the repeal of all flag restrictions was almost a necessity in these times of surging demand. Without larger use of foreign shipping, British exporters and importers might have been hard pressed for carriage of their goods at reasonable freight rates.

British shipping itself failed to keep up with the swift growth in British trade volumes in the first transition years of the new fiscal policy. Even before repeal, between the two depression years 1842 and 1848 when tariff reductions were just getting under way, this was true in a small degree. Total entering tonnage in cargo increased by 53 per cent and outbound tonnage by 37 per cent.[15] While the British took the greater part of this new business, the increase in the foreign share was significant. By 1848, foreign shipping had already gained nearly 3 percentage points on entries in cargo since 1842, and nearly 4 on clearances (Table 22). Meanwhile, British net tonnage expanded only 12 per cent. However, virtually the whole of this increase was employed in foreign trade and the percentage of British entries in ballast declined.[16] Over the first

[15] In interim years, however, clearances in cargo rose more than entries and began to run ahead for the first time, a relationship that became characteristic of the rest of the century.

[16] The ballast proportions of entering and clearing tonnage, British and foreign respectively, were as follows for the selected years shown later in Table 22:

	British		Foreign	
	Entered %	Cleared %	Entered %	Cleared %
1827	4.3	33.3	2.7	45.5
1842	18.5	19.2	19.8	23.2
1848	12.0	24.8	20.4	27.7
1858	18.3	8.8	20.8	17.1
1868	14.8	4.7	20.7	18.6
1873	14.2	9.7	13.5	26.5
1898	21.0	13.6	29.6	14.7
1913	30.7	14.0	52.8	23.0

1827 was the first year in which the records distinguish between cargo and ballast. Entries in ballast in that year were probably unusually low, clearances in ballast unusually high, because of abnormally large imports of grain, particularly of oats and oatmeal.

decade after repeal, from 1848 to 1858, again both depression years when freight rates dropped, total tonnage entering in cargo rose by another 58 per cent, and tonnage cleared jumped 97 per cent. British net tonnage now grew much faster, 35 per cent in all in this single decade, yet even this rate of growth was slow in relation to the growth of trade. But competition was strong; and a large part of the increase in cargoes was carried in foreign vessels. British shipping took only a little more than a third of the increase in import tonnage but, thanks to a sharp fall in ballast proportions, managed to take almost half the additional export cargoes. Measured by the tonnage records, foreign shipping carried nearly 41 per cent of the cargoes both inwards and outwards in 1858, the highest proportion in the century.

TABLE 22. SHIPPING ENTERED AND CLEARED IN CARGO IN THE FOREIGN TRADE OF THE UNITED KINGDOM, SHOWING RATES OF INCREASE AND BRITISH SHARE IN SELECTED YEARS, 1827–1913

	Entered in cargo				Cleared in cargo			
	Total British and foreign				Total British and foreign			
		Gain in period		British per cent of total tonnage		Gain in period		British per cent of total tonnage
	Total tonnage	Total	Average gain per year		Total tonnage	Total	Average gain per year	
	mill.	%	%	%	mill.	%	%	%
1827 ..	2.73	—	—	73.3	1.68	—	—	75.0
1842 ..	3.65	33.2	2.77	73.4	3.69	93.2	7.77	74.0
1848 ..	5.58	52.9	8.82	70.3	5.05	36.9	6.15	70.3
1858 ..	8.81	57.9	5.79	59.4	9.94	96.8	9.68	59.2
1868 ..	13.85	57.2	5.72	69.1	15.47	55.6	5.56	70.5
1873 ..	18.79	35.7	7.14	66.4	19.04	23.1	4.62	71.7
1898 ..	34.51	83.7	3.35	72.9	39.46	107.2	4.29	71.1
1913 ..	49.07	42.2	2.81	65.8	67.82	71.9	4.79	59.1

During the second decade after repeal British shipping got its second wind. It not only kept up with current trade development, but almost caught up with the growth in trade volume since 1848. British net registered tonnage rose by only 24 per cent in all, but there were great improvements in design and speed, and more than a third of the net increase was in steam in which Britain was to have no close rival for the rest of the century. American competition also declined during the Civil War. While total entries and clearances in cargo rose by 57 and 56 per cent respectively, British entries and clearances increased by 83 and 85 per cent and in 1868 accounted for 69 per cent of inbound and over 70 per cent of outbound tonnage in cargo. Symbolic of improved efficiency in cargo placement, but also of the great rise in export volume, clearances in ballast dropped to the lowest point in the century. In the boom year 1873, the British inbound share slipped by nearly 3 percentage points, but the increase in total inbound cargo had again been very large and British ships had taken more than half. The British share of outbound tonnage in cargo, where the percentage increase in the total was more moderate, improved a little. (See Table 22)

In the next period, from 1873 to 1898, the British merchant marine moved energetically into the age of steam and steel. Net registered tonnage increased 55 per cent, and the proportions in steam rose from 30 per cent in 1873 to 73 per cent in 1898. With the great growth in cargo carrying capacity which steam afforded over sail, and with the somewhat slower expansion of trade volumes during this "Great Depression" period, the British merchant marine recovered a little more of the home trade and was apparently in a much stronger position in the carrying trade abroad. Over these twenty-five years, British tonnage entering and clearing in cargo doubled and by 1898 took a larger share of both imports and exports than in 1848 before repeal.

Over the final period, from 1898 to 1913, the British share in the foreign trade of the home islands slipped once more. This time the decline is rather surprising for it occurred when the average annual rate of growth in cargo, measured over the period as a whole, was comparatively moderate, especially for entries, and when increase in British cargo carrying capacity was certainly more rapid than that in inbound cargoes (42 per cent) and possibly only a little less rapid than that in outbound cargoes (72 per cent). British net tonnage altogether rose 35 per cent, but steam tonnage, with at least three times the carrying capacity of sail, grew by 63 per cent. Moreover, a larger proportion of net tonnage now engaged in foreign trade. The explanation of this loss in share of cargoes by 1913 may lie in the fact that the increases in the volume of British trade came in two rather sudden spurts, one in 1906–1907 and the other in 1912–1913, and in both cases, as on similar previous occasions, the extra demand was left to foreign ships. A considerable part of the added capacity of the British merchant marine, then, seems to have been committed to the longer routes and to trade between third countries.

The British certainly took a large part of the world's carrying trade, but whether their share was now any higher than it had been in the mid-century, it is not possible to judge with any assurance on the evidence at hand. The rise in the proportions of entries and clearances in ballast after the 1860's may suggest that this business grew, since it may signify ships brought home for repair, refitting, or as scrap for replacement. But this increase in ballast proportions may also have been incident to the rise of steam and to some specialization for particular kinds of cargo. The notable growth in the British share of world tonnage which seems to have occurred after the middle years of the nineteenth century (Table 23) also suggests that British shipping took a larger part in the world's carrying trade. In sail, a high point was reached about 1870 when the British proportion of world tonnage was again almost as high as in the first years after the Napoleonic Wars although at that time, it should be added, a much smaller part was employed in foreign trade. In steam, the peak was reached in the 1890's when around 60 per cent of the world's steam tonnage was British. In 1914, British steam was still 41 per cent of world steam tonnage.

TABLE 23. SHIPPING OF THE UNITED KINGDOM IN RELATION TO WORLD SHIPPING, BY NET TONS OF SAIL AND STEAM IN SELECTED YEARS, 1820–1914

	World shipping		British shipping			
			Sail		Steam	
	Sail	Steam or motor		Per cent of world sail		Per cent of world steam or motor
	mill. net tons	mill. net tons	mill. net tons	%	mill. net tons	%
1820	5.81	.02	2.22	38.2	.003	15.0
1840	9.01	.37	2.49	27.6	.09	24.3
1860	14.89	1.71	4.20	28.2	.45	26.3
1870	12.90	3.04	4.58	35.5	1.11	36.5
1880	14.40	5.88	3.85	26.7	2.72	46.3
1890	9.17	8.30	2.94	32.1	5.04	60.7
1900	6.67	13.86	2.10	31.5	7.21	52.0
1910	4.62	23.05	1.11	24.0	10.44	45.3
1914	3.69	28.25	.79	21.4	11.62	41.1

Sources: World tonnage figures from *Encyclopaedia Britannica*, 14th ed., XX, 549, where, when necessary, gross tons are converted to net tons for continuity and comparison; British tonnage figures from *Statistical Abstract for the United Kingdom*.

The record under free competition, then, does not afford much evidence of the ruin predicted for the shipping that was so vital to this highly commercial island nation. Swept along by the expanding economy, and soon infused with its energy and fortified by its technical resources, British shipping interests had been able by 1913 to raise their net tonnage to nearly four times what it was in 1848 and to put 94 per cent of it into steam. Total British clearances had multiplied almost ten times and clearances in cargo nearly twelve times. International earnings, after expenses abroad, had risen from about £ 12.7 millions in 1848 to approximately £ 84 millions in 1913.[17] Very important also, British trade was undoubtedly much more efficiently and economically served than was possible under the old discriminatory regulations, fees, and penalties; and a long-standing source of friction with other states was eliminated.

THE BALANCE OF PAYMENTS ON TRADE AND SERVICES

The earnings from shipping and other business services were important in Britain's balance of payments. In the first nine peace years, 1816–1824, they had consistently covered the merchandise trade deficits and other minor items and had apparently supplied two thirds of the credits which had launched Britain as the foremost lending nation of the world. Thereafter in the protectionist period, the relatively faster growth of imports had brought trade deficits which frequently swallowed all of this income and more. In fourteen out of the next eighteen years from 1825 to 1842, these earnings had failed to fill in the trade gap.[18] By 1838–1842, the deficits in net balance of trade, business services and other current items combined, after some net export of gold, had averaged £ 5.9 millions a year, or 4.1 per cent on total trade, almost as high as the credit percentage in 1816–1820 (4.7 per cent) after some net import of gold.[19] Under high protectionism, the transition towards a partly *rentier* status — the balancing of international accounts by drawing on the income of foreign investment — had threatened to be a swift one.

This trend was checked, and, indeed, postponed for another generation in the free-trade era. Eighteen of the next thirty-two years through 1874 show positive balances on these combined trade and service accounts, and in rising magnitude to 1873. The exceptions were confined to the twenty years of transition to free trade, and in these the trend was rather more favorable. Relative to the rise in trade values, deficits were smaller except in 1847 when very large imports of grain (and exports of gold) were needed. The five-year averages shown in Table 24 summarize the balances constructed in Table 4 and indicate the relationship to the rapidly rising values of total trade.

In the last quarter of the nineteenth century the signs of transition toward a partly *rentier* status are unmistakable. From 1875 on, frequent deficits in the earnings of trade and business services absorbed a consider-

[17] From worksheet constructions for Table 4, excluding allowance for expenditure of foreign ships in British ports.
[18] See Table 4, Columns A–H.
[19] See Table 15.

able part of the large margin of income from British foreign investments (Table 26). In 1875–1880, and again from 1891 through 1906, the deficits were larger relative to total trade than in the last protectionist years. Yet the tide turned once more after 1905. From that year to 1913, the relative proportions of the merchandise trade deficit were strongly cut back and in 1907–1908 and in 1911–1913 the balances on combined earnings were again favorable.

TABLE 24. NET BALANCES ON TRADE AND BUSINESS SERVICES IN RELATION TO TOTAL TRADE, ANNUAL AVERAGES IN QUINQUENNIAL PERIODS, 1841–1913

| | Total trade | Net balance on trade, business services, and other current items | | | Total trade | Net balance on trade, business services, and other current items | |
| | | Amount | Per cent of total trade | | | Amount | Per cent of total trade |
	£ mill.	£ mill.	%		£ mill.	£ mill.	%
1841–1845 ..	142.4	− 1.6	−1.1	1881–1885 ..	695.0	− 3.2	−0.5
1846–1850 ..	170.0	− 4.8	−2.8	1886–1890 ..	688.1	+ 3.4	+0.5
1851–1855 ..	238.1	− 3.7	−1.6	1891–1895 ..	705.3	−41.9	−5.9
1856–1860 ..	332.0	+ 9.7	+2.9	1896–1900 ..	788.0	−59.9	−7.6
1861–1865 ..	402.0	+ 0.2	+0.0	1901–1905 ..	908.9	−63.9	−7.0
1866–1870 ..	527.5	+ 9.7	+1.8	1906–1910 ..	1117.9	− 5.6	−0.5
1871–1875 ..	658.1	+24.6	+3.7	1911–1913 ..	1328.0	+18.2	+1.4
1876–1880 ..	640.5	−31.5	−4.9				

NET BALANCE OF PAYMENTS: FOREIGN INVESTMENT AND
INVESTMENT INCOME

This more favorable turn in the British balances earned on trade and services after 1842 brought in its train much larger credits on the net balance of payments available for investment abroad. In the first place, drafts on investment income for the balancing of Britain's international accounts were correspondingly reduced from the proportions of the last protectionist years, and when surpluses again developed, as they did almost consistently through the twenty years 1855–1874, these surpluses plus the whole of the interest and dividends were added to the stock of capital abroad. In the second place, investment income itself grew at a very rapid rate, mainly from the immense increase in the principal, but also from improvement in the regularity and therefore in the average rate of the interest and dividend receipts. By the later years of the century, when more rapid growth of imports brought about large deficits on trade and services, the income from the capital already exported easily covered these deficits and invariably provided substantial credit balances for further investment abroad.

The improvement in the balance of payments is evident from the very start of the more liberal fiscal policy. By the estimates presented in Chapter III, the average annual deficit on trade and services in the first five years, 1843–1847, was cut to one third that of 1838–1842. At the same time, investment income increased, thanks to resumption of interest and dividend payments which had been in default as well as to the returns on new investment. The net balances on current account, available for investment abroad, jumped to an average of about £ 7.2 millions a year. It was the best quinquennium since that ending in 1825 and it was accomplished in spite of extremely heavy grain imports in 1847 which produced the biggest deficit thus far on trade and services. In 1847, in spite of relatively large exports of gold, there was probably a small deficit in the net balance of payments, but it was the last to 1914. By the late 1850's, when the average of the duties was falling fast, surpluses on trade and services and ever-increasing income from accumulating investment was producing annually huge sums which were added to the stock of British capital abroad. From 1842 to 1873 inclusive, the British had exported approximately £ 787 millions of new capital, that is, about five times the amount accumulated by 1842. To this new investment made over these thirty-two years, net surpluses on trade and services (*i.e.*, after deducting for deficit years) contributed some £ 174 millions, or 22 per cent. Interest and dividend income, which was a little over £ 6 millions in the poor year 1842 and was close to £ 52 millions in 1873, supplied the balance of £ 613 millions.[20]

It is a remarkable record of what could be accomplished by the British economy when potential energies were thrown into gear with the opportunities of the age. It is the more amazing when one considers the immense capital development which must have occurred in Britain itself to supply the demands of the export trade and of home consumption without much if any inflation of prices. Yet capital for fixed equity investment abroad became rather cheaper even in this period of heavy demand, thanks to three main (and no doubt several subsidiary) factors: the sufficiency and regularity of supply of new capital, the competition of investment agencies, and the reduction of risks. Reduction of risks, in turn, was a by-

[20] From the estimates presented in Table 4. If calculated in the same way over the longer period to 1913, including the "Great Depression" years when deficits on trade and services offset the earlier surpluses, the whole immense increase in capital placed abroad after 1842 — in all over £ 3800 millions — would be attributable to interest and dividend income. But it may also be said that it was the capital from the earlier surpluses on trade and services, growing at compound interest, which provided the margin over later deficits.

product of growing experience on the part of lenders and borrowers alike, of the rising prosperity and productivity generally in the areas into which this new capital poured, and, not least, of the greater ease with which debts could be serviced when credit flowed more steadily to debtor areas and when imports moved more freely into the creditor nation without burden of heavy tax penalties.

The gains for Britain were obviously considerable. There was the stimulus to the development of her export industries and to her economic life in general, all accomplished without serious inflationary tendencies. The new capital went largely into productive enterprises, or into transportation and communication facilities, either by direct investment or through government loans, and so brought permanent improvement in purchasing power in the borrowing area with some likelihood of continuing markets for British goods. The income from the growing reservoir of capital abroad soon became, as indicated above, the prime source of new funds, and this gave steadier continuity to British foreign investment as well as better cover for deficits on trade and services in poor years. Even through the "Great Depression" period, interest and dividend income was always sufficient to meet the deficits on trade and services and to leave substantial margins for further investment. Moreover, because this capital became cheaper, more steadily available, more easily serviced and therefore generally less burdensome to the borrowers, it was more secure. There were no great waves of frustration and default as in 1830–1833 and 1841–1842 to undermine the spirit of contract-keeping. In the long run, the average rate of return was rather higher too, because the income actually received held up better through the downswings of ensuing business cycles. Defaults and repudiations were fewer and, in the aggregate, capital gains amply made up for what losses were suffered. If the average annual rate of return rarely reached the 6 per cent or so of the first years of high demand and high risk after the Napoleonic Wars, it apparently did not again fall as low as in the depression periods after 1825 and 1836.

The main trends in average rates of return on British foreign investment through the century are shown in Table 25 with data selected at regular five-year intervals from the detailed estimates constructed for Table 4. The amounts shown under "net investment abroad" are the net balances, that is after allowances for foreign investment in the United Kingdom, accumulated by the close of each preceding year, while the amounts shown under "interest and dividends" represent the estimated net balance of this class of income, similarly after income allowance for foreign investment in the United Kingdom, for the year cited. The rate of return is calculated on these values in order to allow a short interval for investment of new credits. The years selected show the range of fluctuation fairly well, with but two exceptions. The average rate of return in 1830–1831 could hardly have been more than 3.5 per cent, and in 1849 it probably dipped to about 4.2 per cent.

TABLE 25. FOREIGN INVESTMENT OF THE UNITED KINGDOM AND AVERAGE RATE
OF RETURN, IN SINGLE YEARS AT FIVE-YEAR INTERVALS, 1817–1912

	Net invest-ment abroad	*Interest and dividends*			*Net invest-ment abroad*	*Interest and dividends*	
		Amount	*Average rate of return*			*Amount*	*Average rate of return*
	£ mill.	*£ mill.*	*%*		*£ mill.*	*£ mill.*	*%*
1817 ...	25	1.5	6.0	1867 ...	523	28.2	5.4
1822 ...	60	3.6	6.0	1872 ...	764	44.3	5.8
1827 ...	100	5.4	5.5	1877 ...	1088	55.5	5.1
1832 ...	113	4.3	3.8	1882 ...	1255	62.8	5.0
1837 ...	148	8.6	5.7	1887 ...	1576	79.5	5.0
1842 ...	157	6.3	4.0	1892 ...	2005	94.7	4.7
1847 ...	193	10.6	5.5	1897 ...	2252	97.0	4.3
1852 ...	218	10.9	5.3	1902 ...	2431	109.1	4.5
1857 ...	270	16.2	6.0	1907 ...	2760	143.8	5.2
1862 ...	394	19.9	5.3	1912 ...	3568	186.9	5.2

Source: Table 4.

Investment income, then, was a major element in British balance of payments. The growth, and the relationship to fluctuating balances on trade and services, are summarized in Table 26 as annual averages in five-year periods from the detailed construction described in Chapter III. The average annual amount shown under "net balances on current account" should represent fairly closely the amount of new capital available for export in each period.

BRITISH AGRICULTURE

British agriculture is often regarded as the victim of the free-trade policy. In certain respects it does represent the other side of the shield and warrants some attention. It had once been able to produce surpluses for export, but the rapid growth of population had closed this period in its history by the end of the eighteenth century, and ensuing scarcities, which became acute in poor harvest seasons during the war period, had pushed prices of most farm produce high above those prevailing in foreign markets. Acreage under cultivation was expanded by enclosure bills and other means, and the agricultural interests had secured the passage of the stiff Corn Law in 1815 in an effort to hold prices near scarcity levels, arguing that high prices were needed to stimulate production and give the nation security in food supply. There can be no doubt that British food production increased under this regimen. By the mid-thirties, possibly a little over half of Britain's total area of 56.8 million acres was either under active cultivation or in meadow and pasture, and acreage in wheat was close to its height. But, to judge by the tapering off of enclosure bills, the limits of profitable expansion of acreage had about been reached. Yet population continued to grow — by 11 per cent in the United Kingdom as a whole and by 14 per cent in Great Britain itself in the single decade from 1831 to 1841 — and urban development, roads, and railroads were bound to subtract something from the arable land available.

TABLE 26. THE NET BALANCE OF PAYMENTS OF THE UNITED KINGDOM, ANNUAL AVERAGES IN QUINQUENNIAL PERIODS, 1841–1913

	Trade, services, and other current items	Interest and dividends	Net balance on current account
	£ mill.	£ mill.	£ mill.
1841–1845	− 1.6	+ 7.5	+ 5.9
1846–1850	− 4.8	+ 9.5	+ 4.7
1851–1855	− 3.7	+ 11.7	+ 8.0
1856–1860	+ 9.7	+ 16.5	+ 26.2
1861–1865	+ 0.2	+ 21.8	+ 22.0
1866–1870	+ 9.7	+ 30.8	+ 40.5
1871–1875	+24.6	+ 50.0	+ 74.6
1876–1880	−31.5	+ 56.3	+ 24.9
1881–1885	− 3.2	+ 64.8	+ 61.6
1886–1890	+ 3.4	+ 84.2	+ 87.6
1891–1895	−41.9	+ 94.0	+ 52.0
1896–1900	−59.9	+100.2	+ 40.3
1901–1905	−63.9	+112.9	+ 49.0
1906–1910	− 5.6	+151.4	+145.8
1911–1913	+18.2	+187.9	+206.1

Source: Table 4.

In poor harvest years, the Corn Laws made protection a very costly business for the nation at large; and the time was rapidly approaching when, with the growth in population, it would be costly in good harvest years also. Already, by 1838–1842, as we have seen in Chapter V, an average of 1.09 bushels of wheat per person, or 19.4 million bushels in all per year, had been required from abroad. In the next series of poor harvests, beginning in 1845, almost twice as much wheat was needed as well as multiplied quantities of other grains. This finished the Corn Laws. They were swept out in 1846 without substitute other than a mere registration duty of 1s. a quarter (8 bushels) on wheat which applied until 1869.

The record of British agriculture when thus thrown on its own falls into sharply contrasting periods: first prosperity, then catastrophe, followed by only modest recovery through rather slow reorientation.

The first period lasted through 1874, nearly thirty years. Far from collapsing when left to stand on its own feet with no price advantage other than that entailed in the registration duty and in proximity to the market, British agriculture flourished with the rest of the economy to a very satisfactory degree for an old industry whose only further expansion must come from more efficient methods of production. The market was a swiftly growing one. Although population increase was less rapid in this period than in the preceding thirty years,[21] general prosperity and good employment raised purchasing power at a faster rate. British consumers proved easily able to absorb both the larger production at home and ever-growing imports from abroad. *Gazette* prices of wheat, which had averaged 57.9s. a quarter for the decade 1836–1845, fell off a little with better harvests after 1848, but probably fell no faster than British unit production costs when yields were high. They averaged 53.9s. in 1846–1855, 50.3s. in 1856–1865, and 54.7s. in 1866–1875. In fact, the opening of the British market had tended much more strongly to raise world prices of cereals and of most transportable foodstuffs up towards British levels than to bring British prices down to former levels abroad. Thus both British consumers and foreign producers gained by the change without hurt to British farmers in this first period.

The challenge of self-dependence under such favorable circumstances roused farmers and landlords to energtic efforts towards more efficient cultivation, once it was clear to them that the new order was permanent. Lord Ernle has called the years from 1853 to 1862 the golden age of English agriculture. Various improvements were extensively applied and

[21] For the United Kingdom as a whole, it was only 17.8 per cent from 1841 to 1871 in contrast to 43.8 per cent from 1811 to 1841. For Great Britain alone, however, the increase from 1841 to 1871 was 40.7 per cent in contrast to 54.8 per cent in the preceding thirty years. In Ireland, population fell 34 per cent in the second period after rising 24 per cent in the first.

there were ample supplies of capital for the purpose.[22] Indeed, the tide ran high for yet another decade. Acreage under active cultivation increased until 1872. Rents advanced and land values rose. It may be doubted if the British farmer and landlord were ever in a better business position for quite so long a period; probably never before in time of peace.

The second period was one of extreme deterioration in prices and of delay in adapting to changing conditions. It began in 1875 with a discouraging succession of poor harvests, in all, seven out of nine. Hardly less grievous to the British farmer, and contrary to most past experience, the losses incurred through poor yields were compounded by falling prices, for, in all too perfect synchronization, world production of grains began to surge upward at a rate greatly in excess of population growth. Railway building in the New World, and later in Russia, opened great low-cost hinterlands to development and world supply.[23] Freight rates and handling charges on the shipping lanes also fell in these decades, thus reducing the margin of advantage which the British farmer had enjoyed by proximity to his markets. The decennial average of British *Gazette* prices of wheat dropped to 43.8s. a quarter in 1876–1885; and in 1886–1895 it was only 29.7s., 46 per cent below the average (54.7s.) for 1866–1875. In October, 1894, the quarter dipped to 17.7s., 68 per cent below the average for 1866–1875. Wheat was an extreme case. Prices of other grains dropped less drastically while those of meat and dairy products fell even less than average prices.[24]

The brunt of this swift expansion of supply and prolonged depression

[22] Lord Ernle (R. E. Prothero), *English Farming Past and Present* (London, 1927), pp. 346–373.

[23] Harvested acreage in wheat in the United States alone almost trebled from 1866 to 1892, rising from 15.4 million acres to 43.0 million. American wheat production expanded from an annual average of 234 million bushels in 1866–70 to 423 million in 1876–80, and to 576 million bushels in 1891–95. In 1891 it had reached 677 million bushels. Prices fell so precipitately that, in spite of this immense increase in production, the value of the wheat crops to American farmers rose very little. Calculating with 1 December prices, we can put the value at about $333 millions a year in 1866–70, and about $351 millions a year in 1891–95 (although only $265 millions in the price trough year 1894). The rate of increase in American production of other grains was rather more rapid, but the total fall in prices was less severe, ranging from 37 to 44 per cent for barley, oats, and corn, in contrast to 60 per cent for wheat from 1866–70 to 1891–95, perhaps because these other grains were more largely used within the United States for animal feed. Meat prices held up better than average prices.

In the next two decades up to 1913, the rate of increase in production tapered off in the United States. In the case of wheat, production rose only 21 per cent from 1891–95 to 1911–13, but, with considerable recovery in prices, was worth much more — averaging about $567 millions a year in the latter period. The preceding calculations are made from crop and price data in *Historical Statistics of the United States*, pp. 106–107.

[24] See table showing the different rates of change in British prices of various commodities from 1871–75 to 1894–98 in Layton and Crowther, *Study of Prices*, p. 88, and discussion, pp. 81–102.

of prices fell on European farmers. Many states, most notably Germany, soon applied strong protective measures. But, because the problem was primarily one of oversupply, these steps probably contributed to the further price decline in the rest of the world. By restricting markets they aggravated the difficulties of farmers in the few states which remained open, of which Britain was the chief.

Under such circumstances, only the most efficient British farmers could compete in wheat or other grain production. Land under active cultivation in Great Britain fell from the high mark of 17.1 million acres in 1872, 3.6 million acres of this in wheat, to barely 13.4 million acres in 1913, of which only 1.8 million were still in wheat. Agricultural population declined in almost exact proportion.[25] It is testimony to the tenacity of British farmers that the decline was not more drastic. Yet this same tenacity rendered them, in general, a little slow to abandon wheat and other grains in favor of a husbandry better suited to close range supply of urban dietary needs and tastes. However, the fact that, by 1913, acreage in permanent pasture and meadow had risen by five million acres, that is, more than the loss in acreage under active cultivation since 1872, suggests the development of dairying and meat production that had taken place in these forty-one years.

The British Government also was slow to take up and perform an important, indeed, a necessary role, that of fostering agricultural education and research. In 1889, fifteen years after the decline started, the government did set up a Board of Agriculture and made a small grant-in-aid — only £ 5,000 a year at the start — to agricultural and dairy schools. But significant assistance to agricultural research had to wait another twenty years. The laissez faire or individualist element in free trade was overdone. Laissez faire has its virtues but, like all systems, it requires harmony and balance. It certainly demands a high level of individual education and technical knowledge for full success, requirements which assign important educational and research functions to the state. This was especially true in the case of an industry that, like British agriculture, was so largely carried on in units of small and medium size.

The prosperity of the preceding period in industry, commerce, and in agriculture itself, also cost British farming something in this depression period. It multiplied the number of wealthy businessmen eager to acquire

---

[25] *Statistical Abstract for the United Kingdom.* Some of this decline in agricultural population must be attributed to increased use of laborsaving machinery, some to the lesser manpower requirements of pasture and meadow which absorbed all of the loss in acreage under active cultivation and gained, in addition, by over a million acres. Pasture and meadow was 12.6 million acres in 1872 and 17.6 million acres in 1913.

country estates with rather less thought for production and profit than for prestige and pleasure.[26] Agricultural prosperity, too, had contributed to push up land values and rentals to levels which were quite uneconomic later. Assessed income from land in England and Wales reached a peak at £ 51.6 millions for the fiscal year 1879/1880, after the blow had begun to fall. The recession of rents from this level was decidedly slow — testimony, in this case, to the tenacity of British landlords. By 1912/1913, assessed income from land had fallen only 29 per cent, to £ 36.8 millions which, as John H. Clapham has interestingly pointed out, was the amount shown in the last year of the old income tax in the inflated year of Waterloo.[27] Prices of wheat averaged only 32.1s. a quarter for the 1912 crop, 41 per cent below the 1866–1875 average. But since there was then no difficulty in letting holdings,[28] we may conclude that British farming had adjusted and was again profitable.

NATIONAL SECURITY: INTERDEPENDENCE AND NATIONAL UNITY

Even before this decline in British wheat farming had set in, the question was sometimes raised whether Britain's free-trade policy sacrificed national security to opulence. Indeed, even before the Corn Laws and the Navigation Acts were repealed, the protectionists, holding that a large merchant marine and self-sufficiency in food supply were vital to security, had been fond of citing the warning of the foremost philosopher of free trade on the dangers of preferring opulence. Opulence, in the sense in which Adam Smith used the term, certainly followed the new policy. But the nation, with its growing population and its specialized industries, continued to rely more and more on foreign sources for its foodstuffs and raw materials and on foreign markets for its own export products. Still more cotton factories and steel mills sprang up, while mine-heads and railway lines crowded corn fields and pasture lands. With each extension of industry and population, Britain became more and more dependent on the rest of the world. Yet one may doubt whether, with her enhanced economic strength, she was, on balance, rendered less secure. Still more may one doubt whether any security advantage was lost which protectionism could have retained.

[26] See the interesting history of Crawley in Hampshire by Norman Scott B. Gras and Ethel Culburt Gras, *The Social and Economic History of an English Village* (Cambridge, Mass., 1930), especially pp. 123–141.

[27] John Harold Clapham, *An Economic History of Modern Britain*, III (London, 1938), 94; and Supplement to the Twenty-fourth Report of the Commissioners of Inland Revenue, *Parl. Pap.*, 1881 [2979], XXIX, 160–165; and Fifty-seventh Report, *Parl. Pap.*, 1914 [7572], XXXVI, 106.

[28] Clapham, *Modern Britain*, III, 94.

Once the issue is put in this form the answer becomes clear enough. Britain had gained little in strength, or in international friendship, that could be attributed to the protectionism of her postwar years; and she was certainly becoming progressively more dependent on the rest of the world before 1842. Thereafter, continued growth of population meant that sufficient supplies of home-grown food could have been produced, if at all, only by increasingly costly concentration of effort which must have detracted from the rest of the economy and which could hardly have coped with bad seasons. Even with the bumper crops of the early 1850's, more foreign grain was taken than in the poor years 1838–1842. Against the rising needs of the population and the persistent hazard of crop failures, the only genuine security was to develop production and supply from abroad, and this could not be called suddenly into being in the quantities coming to be required in poor harvest years. Reduction of population to levels compatible with domestic food production was scarcely practicable and, in any case, could not have improved Britain's security position. Not only would it have meant loss of manpower, but also, in its collateral economic consequences, must have entailed considerable sacrifice of industrial potential. Even if it did not bring some reversion towards a subsistence economy, it must certainly have checked or arrested the developing industrial and market economy which was Britain's economic strength. There was no security gain to be found in this direction when other nations were beginning to industrialize.

Clearly the course for Britain was to develop her already specialized economy more efficiently for the better employment of her people, drawing in her foodstuffs and raw materials as needed from abroad. Security required dependable markets and sources of supply, adequate shipping and handling facilities, and open sea lanes. With the possible exception of the sea lanes, these were economic matters that called for the application of economic good sense. The matter of open sea lanes was, perhaps, the special task of diplomacy and, in crises, of the navy; but both diplomacy and, if it came to that, naval action were, if anything, rendered easier by free-trade policy which promoted mutuality of commercial interests. Greater economic interdependence was not likely to promote unfriendliness among trading partners unless policies and practices were unfair or offensive.

By and large, British free-trade policy promoted, far better than protectionism, most of these economic essentials for security. It fostered development of ample, diversified, and generally friendly sources of supply, and it contributed to building better markets for British products and fuller development of British industrial potentials which were important to her strength and security in this industrial age. The expansion of trade supplied the basis for the growth and improvement of her shipping, and it multiplied the business of her merchants and insurance brokers. The great reserves of capital accumulated and invested abroad directly or indirectly in productive enterprise, under conditions in which repayment was not made too difficult by Britain itself, generally evoked some consciousness of mutual interest and rarely required special action to enforce contract-keeping. As two world wars have shown, these resources could be drawn on when the need arose.

In domestic affairs, too, British free-trade policy contributed to national security. It allayed class bitterness and promoted national unity. Class relationships in Britain had shown many signs of deteriorating under the strains and stresses which followed the Napoleonic Wars. Free trade, with the income tax, was not the only solvent applied to class conflict. The reforms that had been made in parliament, in local government, in criminal law, and in many other fields by the mid-thirties had done much on the political side, but they left the economic sphere virtually untouched. The lopsided and burdensome fiscal system which, as we have seen, developed during the war remained to frustrate economic development and social contentment. The load of indirect taxation, and not least the Corn Laws, which seemed with the lengthening years of peace to be much less the buttress of national security than a mainstay of the privileged landed classes, were still there for all to feel in their effects upon the cost of living. Each successive trade depression had brought a louder outcry against high food prices. This is not to say that there was any immediate danger of violent revolution in 1842. Britain was a highly decentralized land accustomed to decision by vote counting, a method in which the Chartists, too, could put their faith if it included manhood suffrage and secret ballot. But there was acute class division and class bitterness. The strains of 1847–1848 might have proved very serious indeed under the old system.

What is certain is that a corner was turned and in time. The fiscal causes for dissatisfaction and bitterness were removed or alleviated. The very fact that the income tax was accepted by a parliament wholly representative of the propertied classes, and that the repeal of the Corn Laws was sponsored by persons like Sir Robert Peel, Sir James Graham, and Lord Aberdeen, themselves owners of large landed estates, revived confidence that narrow class interest could yield to considerations of national welfare. And these reforms created precedents for dealing with other problems.

Very important, too, was the fact that the ensuing economic growth and prosperity, widely ascribed to the new course, brought improvement in the condition of the working class and thereby calmed class feeling and reintegrated the national society. Employment was generally better and, with the economy expanding as it did, there was far readier absorption of displaced groups into new occupations. One hears no more of such grievous cases as those of the tens of thousands of handloom weavers who, as late as 1842, had been trying in vain to make a living in competition with machine production. Money wages, which had been nearly stationary for some years, improved considerably after 1850 and, since cost of living was generally lower,[29] real wages rose more. And if bread was not always cheaper in the mid-century years — the four-pound loaf was actually higher in price in 1847, in 1854–1856, and in 1867 than in 1838–1842 — nevertheless it was, in Peel's words, the sweeter because "no longer leavened by a sense of injustice."

Under these circumstances, it is not surprising that radical agitation diminished appreciably in Britain. The sharp depression of 1847–1848 threw all Europe west of Russia into political turmoil. In Britain, the Chartists brought forth another monster petition in 1848 — their last — but, with the quartern loaf down again to only 7½d., it was a relatively quiet and good-humored affair. It was in this age, with all its problems of adjustment to swiftly developing urban industrialism, that the British won their fame for law observance and orderly process. For all the disparities of wealth and position which still stratified their society, there were few serious symptoms thereafter of class bitterness, let alone of class warfare. This central feature of the new Marxian dialectic never quite rang true to British ears.

[29] There does not appear to be any good series on cost of living which spans the mid-century; but by linking the index of retail prices by which George H. Wood and Layton calculated real wages from 1850 on — Layton and Crowther, *Study of Prices*, pp. 263–267 — with Tucker's index of cost of living for the London artisan — *Journal of the Statistical Association*, 31:73–84 (1936) — one can get a rough clue to the trends. Tucker's numbers averaged 107 (1850 = 100) both in 1831–35 and in 1841–45, but were 115 in 1838–42, and reached 122 in 1847. To continue with Wood's retail prices (also 1850 = 100), the numbers fell off to 97 in 1851–52, rose to 126 in 1855–56 during the Crimean war, declined to 106 by 1864, then went up gradually, reaching 122 by the boom year 1873. During the "Great Depression" they fell off to a low of 83 in 1896, then rose gradually to 103 by 1913. According to Wood, average weekly wage rates at full time rose to 116 (1850 = 100) in 1855–56, to 124 in 1864, and 154 in 1873. In 1896, the index was 168 and in 1913, 198. Real wages, then, had risen to each of these check points after 1850, excepting only the momentary dip during the Crimean war.

The growth in national income in the United Kingdom was apparently somewhat more rapid, in per capita and in real income terms as well as in the aggregate, than was this rise in wage levels. See P. Deane, "Contemporary Estimates of National Income in the Second Half of the Nineteenth Century," *Economic History Review*, 10:451–461 (April

WORLD TRADE

The value of world trade multiplied over and over during the nineteenth century. Although few countries kept records of the values of their exports and imports on any systematic or uniform basis in the first half of the century — and some kept none at all — estimates have been made of aggregates at various points which, with the firmer computations of later years, should give a broad approximation to the rates of development. These constructions are put together, with some modification for the early years, in Table 27, and an attempt is made, somewhat schematically, to distinguish between export and import values. The former are generally valued f.o.b. and should, therefore, have lower values than imports commonly taken c.i.f. In adjusting the values, the ratio is assumed to have been approximately 46–54 in the earlier years of the century. The disparity presumably diminished as freight rates and other costs fell and as methods of recording changed. By 1913 it was about 48.5–51.5.

TABLE 27. THE GROWTH OF WORLD TRADE IN THE NINETEENTH CENTURY: ESTIMATED AGGREGATE VALUES, DISTINGUISHING EXPORTS AND IMPORTS, IN SELECTED YEARS, 1800–1913

		Total trade	Exports f.o.b.	Imports c.i.f.
		£ mill.	£ mill.	£ mill.
1800	..	320	150	170
1820	..	340	155	185
1840	..	560	260	300
1850	..	800	370	430
1860	..	1,450	680	770
1872–1873	..	2,890	1,360	1,530
1895–1899	..	3,900	1,870	2,030
1913	..	8,360	4,055	4,305

Sources: To 1840, from Clive Day, *A History of Commerce* (New York, 1923), p. 271, but increased by the difference between British "official" and market value of net imports, namely, £40 millions in 1800, £20 millions in 1820 and in 1840. No adjustment was needed in 1850. It is assumed that the declared values of British exports were used in preparing these estimates. If "official" values of British exports were used, the values cited above should be revised upwards in 1800 by £15 millions, and downwards in 1840 by £50 millions, and in 1850 by £100 millions. Growth from 1800 to 1840 would, therefore, be rather slower than indicated here.

Beginning in 1860, the total values are those compiled from various sources by A. E. Overton in the *Encyclopaedia Britannica*, 14th ed., XXII, 350.

If these estimates for the early part of the century are reasonably close to the mark, the value of total world trade expanded more than twenty-five-fold between 1800 and 1913. But what is particularly interesting in relation to our subject is the great quickening of the rate of growth after

1957); and A. R. Prest, "National Income of the United Kingdom, 1870–1946," *Economic Journal*, 58:58–59 (March 1948).

1840. By that year, aggregate value had risen only about 75 per cent over 1800. Part of the cause for this relatively slow increase in values was, of course, the postwar deflation of prices. Volumes, if computed by use of British export and net import prices, which may exaggerate world price change in this period, rose perhaps 290 per cent or, on an average, a little over 7 per cent a year. Over the next three decades, however, the rate became much faster. Up to 1872–1873, the average annual rate of increase in volume was around 13 per cent, nearly twice as rapid as in the preceding forty years. In terms of values, it was about 13.6 per cent a year, nearly eight times faster than in the preceding deflationary period.

As with the quickening of British development in the same mid-century decades, many factors undoubtedly contributed [30] to this striking change of pace in world trade. What are particularly relevant to our theme are certain relationships which point to the conclusion that British tariff changes played a significant part in this remarkable expansion of world commerce.

British trade constituted a huge proportion of world trade through the early and middle years of the nineteenth century. Even if we count only domestic exports and net imports against these world trade estimates, which appear to include general imports and all exports before 1895, the British total ran to 27 per cent of the world total in 1800, 24 per cent in 1840, and 19 per cent in 1872–1873.[31]

But what is much more significant with respect to the impact of British tariff changes was the preponderant position of the British market in the export trade of other countries. It was a much stronger position than these aggregated percentages suggest. This can be shown with some approximation by a few further calculations. If we deduct the value of the British exports that are included in the estimated value of world exports in Table 27, we should have approximate values of the exports of the world outside the United Kingdom. With these, we may then compare the British net import values [32] after adjusting them to an f.o.b. basis.[33]

[30] See pp. 157–158.
[31] If British general import and all export (*i.e.* including re-exports) values are counted, the percentages respectively are: 36 per cent, 27 per cent, and 23 per cent.
[32] British general import values are of some interest also, indicating how large a proportion of the export trade of the rest of the world flowed into British ports. In the war year 1800, when virtually the whole European trade of the overseas world focused on Britain, British general imports were apparently about 55 per cent of the exports of the rest of the world; in 1840, they were about 40 per cent; in 1860, 36 per cent; in 1872–73 they were 31 per cent; and in 1913, 22 per cent.
[33] The deductions made to reduce net import values from c.i.f. to an f.o.b. basis were intended to be safely generous throughout. They descend from 15 per cent in 1800 to 13 per cent in 1840, 12 per cent in 1872–73, and 10 per cent in 1913.

The percentages shown in Table 28 indicate that the British market was extraordinarily preponderant in the early and middle years of the century. Apparently more than one third of the exports of the rest of the world found their way into the United Kingdom in 1840. Although the British share diminished gradually thereafter, it was still more than one quarter of the much larger values of 1872–1873; and it was one sixth of the multiplied values of 1913.

TABLE 28. THE PREPONDERANCE OF THE BRITISH MARKET IN WORLD TRADE: BRITISH NET IMPORTS AS PERCENTAGE OF AGGREGATE NON-BRITISH EXPORTS, IN SELECTED YEARS, 1800–1913

	Aggregate non-British exports	British net imports		
		Value c.i.f.	Deduction for freight, etc.	Approximate value f.o.b.	Per cent of non-British exports
	£ mill.	£ mill.	£ mill.	£ mill.	%
1800 ..	97	47.6	7.1	40.5	42
1820 ..	109	43.8	6.1	37.7	35
1840 ..	198	81.2	10.6	70.6	36
1850 ..	287	91.0	11.8	79.2	28
1860 ..	515	181.9	23.6	158.3	31
1872–1873 ..	1,047	306.0	36.7	269.3	26
1895–1899 ..	1,631	392.7	43.2	349.5	21
1913 ..	3.530	659.2	65.9	593.3	17

The gradual lowering of British tax barriers directly touched, then, a very large part of export goods of other countries. As we have seen (Chart 21), the duty reductions showed a fairly clear tendency to bring British net import prices before duties up to the levels inside British customs lines in this period of rapid expansion. In other words, part of the tax saving passed to foreign suppliers. Foreign prices, amid the fluctuations through these thirty or so transition years, tended upward without imposing their rise proportionately on British domestic cost levels. For example, in 1873, when average net import prices *after* British duties were nearly 15 per cent below those of 1842, average net import prices *before* duties were 7 per cent higher than in 1842. It was a wonderfully felicitous divergence of price trends. The huge increase in British demand, which more than quadrupled the volume of net imports between these dates, enjoyed the stimulus of lower average domestic cost, while simultaneously providing foreign production with the incentive of higher average prices which, of course, meant relatively greater gains in foreign purchasing power. Moreover, the better prices on goods supplied to

Britain applied to other customers also, even as the gains in purchasing power extended to other markets. Trade was primed through all its increasingly multilateral channels.

The tax saving which accrued to trade grew into very sizable sums as British tariff rates were reduced and the volume of British imports expanded. A rough but illuminating approximation to the amounts that thereafter remained in trade channels as a result of purely British action — that is, apart from the moderating measures taken by other commercial states, to be summarized later — can be indicated by comparing the customs duties actually collected with what they might have been had the old rates continued in effect and had British import volume grown, somehow, just as it did. For these calculations, the average tariff rate in 1843, namely 35.8 per cent on the value of net imports, should represent the old tariff better than the rate of any of the years just preceding Peel's

TABLE 29. REDUCTIONS IN AVERAGE BRITISH CUSTOMS RATES AND THE TAX SAVINGS FOR WORLD TRADE, IN SELECTED YEARS, 1850–1913

			Net customs duties		
		Net imports	Assuming average rate of 1843 [a]	Actual collections		Tax saving
				Amount	Average rate	
		£ mill.	£ mill.	£ mill.	%	£ mill.
1850	..	91.0	32.6	22.0	24.2	10.6
1860	..	181.9	64.1	23.4	12.9	40.7
1872–1873	..	306.0	109.5	20.7	6.8	88.8
1895–1899	..	392.7	140.6	21.2	5.4	119.4
1913	..	659.2	236.0	34.0	5.2	202.0

[a] 35.8 per cent.

first reforms because that year had brought more typical takings of grain as well as some recovery in the proportions of goods bearing the higher rates after the preceding depression years. This over-all method of calculation will still minimize the extent of the duty reductions because it does not allow for the increase in the flow of goods left on high duties that followed revival of prosperity. For example, consumption of tea more than doubled by 1860 although the specific duty, successively reduced, then amounted to 90 per cent ad valorem.[34] Nevertheless, the reductions shown in the average rates on aggregate net imports (Table 29) will supply a clue to the direct influence that British tariff reform could exert on average

[34] The duty on tea was further reduced in 1863, then cut in half to 6d. a pound in 1865, or 32 per cent on the average import price in the latter year; but it was still a strong contrast to the Younger Pitt's 12½ per cent in the 1780's. In 1889 the duty was reduced to 4d. on the pound.

prices either in Britain itself or abroad. The tax savings shown will suggest the sums that remained in trade. By 1872–1873, the latter were equivalent to nearly 30 per cent on the value of British net imports. With only minor fluctuations, the tax savings remained in this high proportion through to 1913, although, of course, they multiplied further in absolute amount as volume increased.

LIBERAL TRENDS IN OTHER STATES

In the first three decades of striking British success and general world prosperity, other states also took some steps to moderate their restrictions on trade. In this respect the British example seems to have borne some of the fruit which the Committee on Import Duties had predicted for it in 1840. The difficulties in the way of extensive liberalization were very great, however. Almost everywhere, indirect taxes such as excise and import duties were the traditional mainstays of revenue, and, while income from these sources expanded with prosperity, so also did state expenditure. Nowhere among the propertied classes of town or country was there any enthusiasm for the British example of using an income tax to fill in revenue requirements. On the continent of Europe, too, political strains and tensions aroused deep feelings. The economic liberalism of free trade was commonly associated with political liberalism which demanded representative institutions and freedom of speech and of press, and it was often almost equally anathema to the privileged governing classes.

Nevertheless much was done. Although no other nation went all out for free trade to the extent that Britain did, many states did soften the duties and regulations, whether by legislation, by administrative order, or by reciprocity treaty. By the 1860's, their combined measures may have been contributing as much to stimulate world trade and economic development generally as did Britain's much more thoroughgoing program applied to her great trade and supplemented by her foreign investments.

However this may be, a distinct trend towards freer trade developed in the 1850's and 1860's. Each of the three countries ranking next to Britain in commercial importance reduced tariff barriers in significant degrees. In Germany, freer trade was one of the few liberal principles on which the eastern Prussian landed aristocracies, producing agricultural surpluses for export in these decades, could agree with the liberal western and urban classes who had contested their political predominance in 1848. Changes made in the *Zollverein* tariff were downwards after 1850, and plans were developed and put into effect for progressive reductions towards a tariff for revenue only. This program was virtually complete when Bismarck swung the Empire sharply back to a protectionist policy in 1879 after cheap grain from overseas had begun to flow in quantity. In the United States, closely linked with Britain in trade and finance, there was a discernible tendency by the late forties towards lower import duties. This culminated, in 1857, while southern cotton and tobacco interests were still strong politically, in the lowest tariff since 1816. France breached her traditional protectionism in 1860 when Napoleon III concluded the so-called Cobden Treaty providing, on a reciprocal basis, for freer trade relations with Britain. During the next seven years France contracted a whole series of reciprocity agreements with her neighbors, including one with the *Zollverein*. In many of the lesser commercial nations also, there were liberalizing tariff changes. There were few cases of tariff increases in this period.

THE "GREAT DEPRESSION" AND THE PROTECTIONIST REVIVAL

In tariff matters, the "Great Depression" was marked by revival of very active protectionism through much of the world. It was a period of disappointingly slower development in world trade. Although growth in volume continued, the general price decline which, as we have seen, was led by cereals, held down the rate of growth in values. It was also, following the Italian and German wars of unification and the American Civil War, a period of more militant nationalism and of quickened impulse to apply nationalist expedients towards economic or other ends.

The first reversal of trend among the principal commercial powers really preceded the "Great Depression." The United States emerged from the Civil War with import and excise duties raised high for revenue, with many new or expanded industrial interests, and with political balances profoundly altered. Manufacturers' excise duties were then cut back; the import duties remained until 1872 when a small general reduction was voted only to be rescinded three years later after the depression had begun.

In European countries, the change of trend waited on the decline of cereal prices in the late 1870's. At the outset, the measures taken were generally confined to duties designed to protect native agriculture. In Germany, however, the new protectionism launched in 1879 applied at once to industrial as well as agricultural goods. Bismarck made it explicitly and dramatically a reversal of policy, as indeed it was, and he rang all the changes of his theme, even asserting, in his effort to counter the influence of Britain's success in free trade, that the British were gradually returning to protectionism in order to keep the home market for themselves. The great power and prestige of Germany, and the continuing growth of her economy, made her example a formidable contrast to British free trade. Protection became the order of the next two decades. France dropped her reciprocity treaties as they expired in the 1880's and reverted to her traditional system. The three principal commercial nations standing next in order after Britain were now solidly in the protectionist camp. In world trade, the commercial weight of these three combined exceeded that of Britain by a growing margin after 1885.[35] Even a raw material-exporting country like Canada, a member of the British Empire-Commonwealth, turned to a "national policy" (1879), partly in emulation of the United States after failure to secure a new reciprocity agreement.

Whatever the long-term results of these new trade restrictions, the immediate effect was to intensify the world's "Great Depression" problem of adjusting supply and demand. Granted that production of raw materials, and most conspicuously of cereals, now expanded too rapidly for easy absorption on satisfactory terms in the markets of the world. Yet tariffs against them, or against industrial products, served only to hamper international exchange of raw materials and industrial products alike even in usual quantities, and therefore forced prices and purchasing power down further than the oversupply itself might have carried them. Tariffs certainly made it much more difficult to expand markets, which is to say, to exchange goods, on the scale demanded by the growth in production of raw materials and in production potentials for industrial goods.

In this crisis of aggravated unbalance, Britain held to her chosen policy. In spite of the extreme pressure on her agriculture — perhaps slightly intensified by the closure of other markets — and in spite of the limitations imposed upon her export industries by foreign tariffs, she did not conform to Bismarck's ill-informed or eristic prediction. She did not abandon free trade.

The soundness of this course for Britain, and the usefulness to the world at large, can hardly be in doubt. Her lot as an industrial, commercial, and creditor nation was now more irrevocably cast than in that former depression time when Peel had faced up to the problem, and she could not now retreat from the economic internationalism her acquired position demanded without incurring greater losses. Suppose, for a moment, that Britain, too, had grasped at tariff forms of aid in an effort to save her farmers in their grievous plight. Suppose she had imposed on wheat in

[35] In 1874, the total trade of Germany, France, and the United States, listed in order of magnitude, exceeded that of Great Britain (excluding re-exports) by 34 per cent; in 1885 by 32 per cent; in 1895, with the United States moved ahead of France, by 51 per cent; and in 1913 by 110 per cent. These three states together accounted for 29 per cent of world trade in 1874, for 27 per cent in 1885 and in 1895, and for 31 per cent in 1913.

1885, say, when the average *Gazette* price fell to 32.8s. a quarter, a duty of 8s. a quarter (1s. a bushel) in the hope of assuring British farmers about 40s.[36] At the very outset, this might have lifted the price of wheat in the home market by about the desired amount, but at the cost of curtailing domestic consumption of wheat or of other commodities. If this curtailment brought reduction of British imports, it would cut foreign sterling earnings for purchase of British goods or services or for payment of interest charges and so would have hurt British industry and employment and purchasing power. If it brought reduced consumption of domestic products, it would likewise have hurt home industry, employment, purchasing power. Even in the initial stage, then, a tariff on grain would have augured ill for the national economy as a whole. Soon, however, the overabundant world supply of wheat would almost certainly have forced down the world price sufficiently to clear the new barrier. In this event, one must allow for further loss in purchasing power abroad — in the Argentine, the United States, Canada, and other wheat-exporting countries. The three named were not only important trading partners of Britain but were also areas of large British investments. Their capacity to buy British goods or services, or to meet interest payments to British investors, must have fallen further. Such reduction in British earnings would either have required cuts in British imports or have reduced the credits available to the British for investment abroad, entailing, either way, further contraction of exports or of export prices. One must allow, again, that the reduction of exports would have hurt employment and purchasing power in Britain itself for both domestic and foreign commodities, including foodstuffs.[37] Furthermore, retaliatory measures by Britain's trading partners cannot be ruled out. But it is hardly necessary to attempt to follow all the ramifications of the theme in order to perceive that aid given to British agriculture in the form of a protective tariff would, without affording durable benefit to British farmers, have only aggravated the problem of the British nation as a whole, and of the

---

[36] It may be argued that if Britain had retained such a duty right along, overseas production might have developed less rapidly and this crisis of overproduction might have been less acute. But there would be a chain of correlate consequences and costs to be considered here also.

[37] Actually British imports of foodstuffs continued to grow during the period. Imports of wheat and flour rose from an annual average of 41.3 million cwt. in 1866–75 to 79.5 million in 1886–95 and to 95.5 million in 1896–1905, an increase over-all of 131 per cent. Since average *Gazette* prices of wheat fell 48 per cent to 1896–1905, the increase in value was only 20 per cent.

The volume of net imports in general rose even more rapidly, namely 157 per cent over-all from 1866–75 to 1896–1905; and the decline in net import prices was less, namely 38 per cent. Net import values rose 61 per cent.

world. The political consequences of such a course must also have been considerable.

In its main outlines, British policy made good sense. The readiness to accept imports without tax impediment, and to lend the surpluses still accruing in balance of payments, sustained the sale of British goods and services and met the interest charges on British capital placed abroad. Foreign capacity to service British loans was not seriously damaged, although the average rate of return, which can be calculated with some annual precision after 1885, fell a little below the usual 5 per cent or better in 1891–1905.[38]

Before the economic tide began to turn once more at the end of the century, protectionism was again deeply rooted in other commercial states both great and small. Strong new vested interests had developed and, by cartel arrangements and other devices as in Germany, had found ways under the tariffs to limit competition at home, yet to expand business abroad. In continental Europe, too, revived militarism, with great standing armies and masses of trained reserves that could now be summoned swiftly by telegraph to make or repel the sudden blow, inevitably added to the weight of security considerations in the determination of commercial policies. Mass armies required that virtually the whole economy of the nation be equally mobilizable in support and that vital materials be available in secure and sufficient supply. National pride or ambition often demanded more. The aims of policy were again shaped towards empire building by the urge to control resources or to deny them to rivals who were potential enemies. It was a kind of neo-mercantilism reminiscent of the imperial rivalries of the eighteenth century.

Under these circumstances, the turning of the economic tide after 1898 made little difference to the tariff history of continental Europe. The improvement in trade developed slowly at first and the sixteen years allowed in all before the war of 1914 broke were not enough to change political trends or balances. In Britain itself, free trade was vigorously challenged. Joseph Chamberlain, after a very active term as Colonial Secretary, came out strongly in the first years of the new century for a tariff plan in the name of imperial economic federation. Canada and other self-governing dominions had already accepted the principle of imperial preference, granting discounts, so to speak, from their regular tariff rates to British goods.[39] Chamberlain, manifestly concerned to fortify Britain's

---

[38] See Table 25.

[39] In order to accept, as she did in 1898, Britain had to sacrifice her trade treaties with Belgium and with the German *Zollverein* since both contained "most favored nation" clauses. Canada and Germany engaged in a tariff war on the preference issue until 1910.

security position by developing closer commercial ties with the Empire, urged a British tariff from which reciprocal preferences could be granted to the self-governing dominions.

The popular decision in the general elections of 1906 held Britain firmly to her free-trade policy. Her markets remained open and, although her share of total world trade had diminished, as we have seen, she was still the best customer for most of the trading world regardless of flag and despite lack of reciprocity. While other European nations showed no disposition to moderate their tariffs or restrictions in this period, one great overseas trading community did move promisingly, just before the war of 1914. The United States, by now the third ranking commercial power, adopted the Underwood Tariff of 1913 which cut the rates on most of the long list of dutiable goods. Simultaneously, the levying of the first federal personal income tax augured well for a reasonable test of the lower duties by covering the loss in revenue.

But American tariff reform had come too late to exert much influence on trade or on the climate of commercial opinion at home or abroad. Unlike the income tax, it did not survive the world war which, breaking within the year, closed this epoch. The distinctive policies which Britain had been able gradually to develop with so much success in the more favorable international political climate she had helped to create after the last great general war a hundred years earlier, sank under the strains and stresses of this new postwar period. For this costly war not only virtually terminated British capacity for effective political mediation or economic leadership in world affairs, but terminated it without an immediate successor. The opportunity for some continuity of development, which the victory of the allies and the swift rise of the United States might have afforded, was lost, perhaps largely because Britain's potential successor to this kind of leadership in international affairs was not then aware how much was at stake for her own welfare and was not quite ready to accept the role.

APPENDIX

THE VOLUME SERIES OF SCHLOTE AND OF THE BOARD OF TRADE

Three continuous sets of volume series for various periods prior to 1914 were available before the series presented in Chapter III were begun nearly ten years ago. Werner Schlote's series span more than a century, from 1814 through 1933. Two sets prepared by the Board of Trade reach together from 1880 to 1913 and overlap from 1900 to 1908. While the latter diverge a little — less than 2 per cent — from 1900 to 1908, both differ appreciably from Schlote in their respective periods. This circumstance suggested the need to look very closely at the methods of construction and the thoroughness of coverage.

The first Board of Trade series, from 1880 to 1908, used 1900 prices and covered exports and general imports, but not re-exports. The results were published only in over-all summary with very little definition of methods or content.[1] The second Board of Trade series, from 1900 to 1913, including re-exports as well as exports and general imports, were quite clearly defined. They were apparently carefully constructed with very comprehensive coverage of commodities. The absolute values of articles which together comprise from 75 to 89 per cent of the value of all exports, imports and re-exports, were separately calculated, and those for about half of each balance were computed from the market values by price index of a closely related commodity or groups of commodities so that only a comparatively small margin was left to the rough measurement of the general price average. In respect to the price weighting of commodities, this second Board of Trade set of volumes may be distinguished as two sets. The first, from 1900 to 1908, used directly the prices of 1900 with the annual quantities of each enumerated commodity. The second, from 1909 to 1913, used a "step by step" method, primarily in order to secure closer precision in the midst of rapidly multiplying trade classifications. The prices of each preceding year were applied to the quantities of each commodity, and results in aggregate were reduced to 1900 base.[2] This procedure has the further advantage of considerably reducing the hazards that lie in the choice of a particular year for the price weighting.

Schlote gives little information on the methods or coverage of his much more extended volume series, but he is quite explicit with respect to the price weighting. He divided the long span from 1820 to 1933 into seven periods for exports of home products and six for general imports with single year overlap for linking. For re-exports, however, the whole run was based on 1913 prices. Some of the periods are rather long in view of the considerable change which occurred in the prices and in the proportions of the commodities traded, and in one case the price base for exports and imports is not identical as, ideally, it should be. In the period 1859–1869, the choice of 1864 as the base year is particularly unfortunate since the prices of cotton and of cotton manufactures, and sympathetically of other fibres and their products, together constituting a very high proportion of British imports and ex-

---

[1] *Parl. Pap.*, 1909 [4954], CII, 53.

[2] *Ibid.*, 1914 [7432], LXXXIX, 1–37. See also *Ibid.*, 1908 [4115], XCIX, 3–6; and 1912 [6782], LXVI, 3–5.

ports, were then greatly out of line — high above the average of the period — and therefore distort the volume measurements through this period and, by linkage, in earlier years of the series also. The use of but a single price base (1913) for re-exports is a serious defect for terms of trade purposes. It renders this series dis-sonant with that on imports and therefore unsuited for determining net import volumes and prices which are logically required.[3] In trade of the United Kingdom re-exports are not to be dismissed as "of no great significance."[4] Although the pro-portions varied from time to time, they always reduced the value of net imports substantially below the general import figures. The reduction was extremely high in the earliest years of the century, sometimes as much as one quarter, fell off to as little as one tenth in the protectionist period, then recovered until it was some-times as much as one fifth and rarely as little as one eighth. Moreover, because this was a rather specialized trade involving relatively high proportions of the imports of some commodities like coffee, cotton, tin, and wool, and a low proportion of others such as the cereals, average prices often diverge radically from those of general imports so that average net import prices are also appreciably different.[5]

Schlote does not state how extensive was his enumeration of commodities. This is an important matter. If one uses a sample method, selecting, say, only the major commodities for separate treatment, one leaves to the average so set up a vast number of articles, each of which may be quite small in itself but with its own price history and, taken together, capable — as the writer discovered in early experiments on the period 1865 to 1880 — of exerting considerable influence on the over-all average. New goods coming into trade, or old goods slipping out of demand, or goods entering a mass handling phase, are particularly prone to a price history divergent from the norm (if, indeed, one can speak of a norm) and, unless the coverage is very complete and is revised for each price base period, each relatively short, their influence is likely to be missed for some time. Sampling can be useful, of course, when comprehensiveness is ruled out by one cause or another, but the sample should not be a fixed one through a long run of years. In the case of Britain, the data are sufficient to afford the surety of very broad coverage through most of the century.

The difference between the rates of change shown in Schlote's volume series and in those of the Board of Trade are considerable and lead to correspondingly large divergences in the movements of average prices computed from them. From 1880 to 1900, Schlote's export volumes rise only 30.0 per cent as against 42.6 per cent for the first series of the Board of Trade, and his general imports rise only 60.8 per cent as against 71.5 per cent. By Schlote, average export prices read 101 for 1900 (1880 = 100) as against 91 for the Board of Trade, while his general imports are 79 as against 74. Some part of these differences undoubtedly stems from the price weights used over this long span. Neither the year 1900 used by the Board of Trade nor the year 1902 used by Schlote for 1881–1902 is a very satisfactory one. In this long span such end-year weighting may exert too much downward bias in the volume series (and therefore upward bias in the price relatives). Of the two, that of the Board of Trade is somewhat better because the higher prices of 1900 were more typical of the period as a whole. But the probability of bias in the

[3] Schlote's own series on the terms of trade is based on average prices of gross imports from 1814 to 1853 and on those of gross imports of raw materials only thereafter, taken in relation throughout to average prices of exports of manufactured goods only. *British Overseas Trade*, Appendix Table 17.

[4] Schlote, *British Overseas Trade*, p. 27.

[5] See Appendix Table I. Average price movements of re-exports shown in this table may be compared with those of net imports shown in Table 8.

base year in both cases, combined with the lack of definition for both sets of series in the important matter of comprehensiveness of coverage, led me to carry my own detailed construction to 1888 on the more suitable basis of 1880 prices. The results corresponded much more closely with those of the Board of Trade than with Schlote's.

The divergences between Schlote and the very comprehensive second series of the Board of Trade are also very striking. From 1900 to 1913, Schlote's export volumes show a rise of 60.0 per cent as compared to 70.8 per cent, his general imports show 24.5 as against 32.8 per cent, and his re-exports 24.2 in strong contrast to 42.1 per cent. These differences in the rates of growth shown may be partly attributable to the opposite bias effected by the price weighting of the volume series. For the years 1902 to 1913 Schlote used as his base 1913 when the prices of almost all important commodities of British trade except coal, and iron and steel goods, which rose strongly in quantity but dropped in price, were well above the averages of the period. All in all, this end-year weighting would again tend to minimize rise in volumes a little. The Board of Trade choice of the year 1900 for the short period 1900–1908 may tend to maximize volume increase somewhat since here the prices of the goods of greatest quantity growth, again coal, iron and steel goods, were relatively high. The period for which these prices were used was a short one, however.[6] The "step by step"or chain method used by the Board of Trade from 1909 through 1913, among other advantages, should appreciably reduce, but cannot wholly eliminate, the liability to some bias in the price weighting of the volume series. It is unlikely, however, that these differences in price weightings between Schlote and the Board of Trade in this short period from 1900 to 1913 would alone produce so much divergence in results. It would seem, therefore, that differences in comprehensiveness of coverage are also major factors in the divergence.

Nevertheless, the lack of definition of the contents of Schlote and of the first Board of Trade series still left some uneasiness with respect to using the latter from 1888 to 1900. This concern was increased when Professor Charles P. Kindleberger, while preparing his study of the terms of trade of six European areas,[7] informed me that he had constructed, among others, price relatives for British exports and general imports for 1872/1900 and for 1900/1913 with end-year weighting of his sample, and that his results on both exports and imports corresponded very closely to Schlote's for these years. It seemed desirable to construct new volume series, with the utmost comprehensiveness of coverage,[8] to fill in the remaining interval from 1888 to 1900.

These new series, with the price base in 1892 near the median point of price movements and linked in 1887–1888 with the preceding ones, do not discover any uniform pattern of divergence from those of the Board of Trade with end-year weighting. Export volumes show an increase of 40.0 per cent from 1880 to 1900, that is, 2.6 percentage points less than the Board of Trade first series and with some significant variations in intervening years. General import volumes show a

---

[6] To gain some idea of the influence which the overweighting of coal might exert on the export volume series in this case, a correction was made through this period. The maximum effect was reached in 1905 when it raised the volume of aggregate exports by one half of one per cent, thereby reducing the price relative from 91.6 to 91.1 (1900 = 100). This is the effect on the aggregate of the overweighting of a single important commodity. Iron and steel goods might also raise the volume increase. On the other hand, opposite changes for several other commodities would tend to counterbalance these.

[7] *The Terms of Trade: A European Case Study* (Cambridge, Mass. and New York, 1956).

[8] See pp. 88–90.

rise of 65.8 per cent, that is, midway between the Board of Trade's 71.5 per cent and Schlote's 60.8 per cent. Re-export volumes, on the other hand, rose somewhat less rapidly than by Schlote's single and remote base year (1913) construction, namely, 28.0 per cent as compared to 30.5 per cent.

When informed of these results, Professor Kindleberger was interested to explore the matter further. Drawing from my worksheets the data for the terminal and linking years from 1872 to 1900 on his selected commodities, which comprised 43 per cent of exports and 42 per cent of general imports in 1900, he computed another set of price relatives. Since the sample is the same in each case, comparison of his first and second constructions, shown below, should indicate the contrast between results by end-year weighting according to the Paasche formula (Kindleberger I) as against period division with mid-point weighting (Kindleberger II). In Kindleberger I, the Paasche end-year weighting over this twenty-eight-year period presumably exerted a downward bias on both export and import volumes and hence an upward bias in the price relatives.[9] The difference is particularly large for exports and is probably attributable to relatively greater changes in volume relationships and prices of the selected commodities. The divergence between Kindleberger II and my own results, adjusted [10] here to conform to the practice followed in the other constructions cited, should be attributable wholly to the difference in the proportions of goods covered since in other respects they are constructed in the same way. The price relatives prepared and supplied by Professor Kindleberger compare with Schlote's and my own in 1900 as shown in Table 30. Sir Piers K. Debenham's fixed weight price relatives, which are based, as described below, on quite comprehensive coverage and weighted by the trade proportions of exports and net imports in 1889–1898, are also interesting. It is curious that, where Kindleberger I and Schlote are quite close for both exports and general imports, Kindleberger II departs further from Schlote on both than do my results. Without more detail on Schlote's coverage and procedure the explanation must remain uncertain. It may be that, by coincidence, the differences in weighting between Schlote and Kindelberger I are neatly offset by other variations such as in the flow and price change of the commodities within their samples, which presumably differed in some degree.

Some consideration should be given to two sets of fixed weight indexes which also relate to export and import prices. Differences in content and weighting naturally lead them to differ from one another and from the price relatives derived from the volume series, that is, with annually changing quantities. One is Abraham G. Silverman's indexes of export and import prices from 1880 to 1913. Silverman based these on the more important commodities of British trade, namely, those running to $\frac{1}{2}$ of 1 per cent or more of the total values of exports and general imports, and he used wholesale market prices when possible in preference to average

[9] The Fisher Ideal Index, the geometric mean of relatives, is sometimes used when there is opposite weight bias. In this instance, where Kindleberger I is constructed with a single long period and end-year weighting and Kindleberger II has two linked periods each with mid-point weighting, this formula is less appropriate. However, as a matter of interest, the relatives, which may be compared with those shown in the tabulation below, are 70.3 for exports and 66.8 for general imports.

[10] This adjustment simply involved recalculating the balance of unenumerated goods by applying the average of the enumerated, that is without reducing the great weight of cotton goods and raw cotton in exports and net imports respectively as was done in constructing Table 8. The effect of this adjustment is small in this period — for exports 69.7 as against 70.2 (1872 = 100), for general imports, 66.6 as against 66.7, and for net imports, 65.9 as against 66.1. In earlier periods, when the proportions of enumerated commodities were smaller, or when cotton prices were out of line with the average of enumerated goods, the influence was, of course, much greater than at this time.

export and import prices, applying fixed weights determined by the relative importance of his component commodities of export and of general import in 1890–1904. These indexes, as Silverman points out, are not designed to be completely representative.[11] The second is Debenham's series on exports and imports from 1870 to 1913. Here the prices throughout are the average export and general import prices published annually in the *Statistical Abstract for the United Kingdom* for articles comprising about 70–75 per cent of export values and about 80 per cent of import values. These prices are weighted according to the proportions of commodities of export and of net (not general) imports traded in 1889–1898.[12] The import series is, therefore, a weighted average of net import prices.

TABLE 30. THE PRICE RELATIVES OF EXPORTS AND IMPORTS OF THE UNITED KINGDOM BY FIVE CONSTRUCTIONS FOR THE YEAR 1900

(1872 = 100)

		Kindleberger			
	Schlote	*I Selected products with 1900 volumes*	*II Selected products with Imlah data*	*Imlah adjusted*	*Deben-ham*
Exports	76.1	75.5	65.6	69.7	70.2
General imports	69.1	68.2	65.5	66.6	—
Net imports	—	—	—	65.9	66.7

TABLE 31. PRICE RELATIVES IN TWO FIXED WEIGHT AND TWO VOLUME SERIES CONSTRUCTIONS FOR THE UNITED KINGDOM IN SELECTED YEARS, 1870–1913

(1900 = 100)

	Exports				General imports			Net imports	
	By fixed weights		By volume series						
	Silver-man	Deben-ham	Imlah	Schlote	Silver-man	Imlah	Schlote	Deben-ham	Imlah
1870 ...	—	127	129	117	—	149	141	147	152
1880 ...	101	107	109	99	125	131	126	130	131
1890 ...	93	96	96	92	100	105	104	104	106
1900 ...	100	100	100	100	100	100	100	100	100
1910 ...	101	105	98	103	122	112	116	117	110
1913 ...	111	116	106	112	126	111	118	119	109

Some idea of the effects produced by these various differences in composition and weighting can be indicated by comparing the price relatives of the several series at decennial intervals as shown in Table 31.

It is to be expected that these indexes will diverge to a considerable degree. The two fixed weight indexes differ in content and coverage, in the prices used, and in the bases selected for weighting. Also, Silverman's weighting by the proportions of general imports will produce some differences from Debenham's by net imports.

[11] *The Review of Economic Statistics*, 12:139–148 (1930).

[12] The index numbers are given in Cairncross, *Home and Foreign Investment, 1870–1913* (New York, 1953), 206; and the descriptive detail was supplied directly by Debenham.

Still more will fixed weight indexes diverge from those derived from volume series if there are any important changes in the proportions of goods traded. Debenham's prices are, in effect, comparable to my own, and his coverage of commodities is more comprehensive than Silverman's. His results are strikingly similar to mine in and near the base years and are less comparable at the ends of the series. In the last decade, when the proportions of goods actually traded changed more rapidly, strong divergence develops from mine as based on the second Board of Trade series. Here both the fixed weight indexes yield much higher numbers for exports and imports. This may be accounted for by the fact that some commodities, such as steel exports and petroleum imports, to take but two examples, grew disproportionately in volume so that their great price decline is underweighted in the fixed weight indexes. Both show, therefore, the upward bias commonly manifested in times of rapid change by indexes with weights fixed at a past date.[13] Schlote's price relatives derived from his volume series for exports are closest to Silverman's for each of the selected years shown above. For general imports, they are closer to Silverman's in 1880, but much closer to Debenham's net imports thereafter.[14]

All in all, one should be reasonably secure in using the Board of Trade volume series from 1900 to 1913. In the important matter of comprehensiveness in coverage of commodities, one would be hard put indeed to improve upon them. More precise results, then, would depend wholly upon more satisfactory price weighting than that of the year 1900 used by the Board of Trade in the run from 1900 through 1908 and would probably not alter the findings by as much as 2 per cent. Even if corrections pushed the price relatives upward by as much as 4 per cent they would still remain on the lower side of the other indexes cited above. In any case, such corrections from use of a better price weight base would probably press in the same direction for exports and net imports, although probably in different degrees, so that the effect on the numbers for terms of trade would be less significant than on the volume series and the price relatives.

[13] Kindleberger's 1900/13 relatives, using the Paasche end-year quantity weighting with selected commodities comprising, for these years, 58 per cent of the value of exports and 50 per cent of general imports, are also higher in 1913: Kindleberger, *The Terms of Trade*, p. 364. The export relative is 114, that is, intermediate between Silverman and Debenham and slightly above Schlote who, in effect, also used end-year weights here. The general import relative is 117, which is proximate to Debenham and to Schlote. Other weighting would probably effect less drastic reductions in these relatives than those shown above for the 1872/1900 samples because the interval 1900/13 is shorter and the samples form larger proportions of total exports and total imports.

[14] It is interesting but not conclusive that the shipping records on tonnage entered in cargo show a slightly stronger rise than do general import volumes by the Board of Trade series from 1900/13, i.e. 35 per cent versus 32.5 per cent. Schlote's volume series indicates 24 per cent only, hence the larger rise in his price relatives. The price movements in the Silverman and Debenham series imply still smaller increases in volume. On the export side, tonnage of shipping cleared in cargo rose 56 per cent as compared to volume increase of total exports of 65 per cent by the Board of Trade and 50 per cent by Schlote. These comparisons cannot be taken to be conclusive because neither the volume series nor the shipping records are precise measurements of cargo quantity change, the one being weighted by price, not tons or cubic yards, and the other pertaining to ship, not cargo, tonnage.

TABLE I. RE-EXPORTS OF THE UNITED KINGDOM: VALUES, VOLUMES, AVERAGE PRICES, AND PERCENTAGES OF GENERAL IMPORTS, 1796–1913

Year	Current value	Volume at 1880 prices	Volume relative	Price relative	Per cent of general imports by value
	£ mill.	£ mill.	1880 = 100	1880 = 100	%
1796 ...	8.5	5.6	9	152	21.5
1797 ...	9.3	5.7	9	163	27.0
1798 ...	11.3	6.4	10	177	22.8
1799 ...	9.4	5.4	9	174	18.5
1800 ...	14.7	9.1	14	162	23.6
1801 ...	12.9	7.9	12	163	18.8
1802 ...	12.9	9.5	15	136	23.6
1803 ...	9.1	6.0	9	152	16.9
1804 ...	11.0	6.6	10	167	19.2
1805 ...	10.0	5.4	9	185	16.4
1806 ...	9.2	5.4	9	170	17.3
1807 ...	8.3	5.2	8	160	15.4
1808 ...	6.5	4.1	6	159	12.6
1809 ...	14.3	8.2	13	174	19.4
1810 ...	12.5	7.4	12	169	14.1
1811 ...	6.7	4.4	7	152	13.2
1812 ...	9.1	6.2	10	147	16.3
1813 ...	Records destroyed by fire				
1814 ...	24.8	12.3	19	202	30.7
1815 ...	16.8	10.2	16	165	23.6
1816 ...	12.6	8.9	14	142	25.1
1817 ...	10.1	6.6	10	153	16.6
1818 ...	12.3	7.0	11	176	15.2
1819 ...	10.2	6.8	11	150	18.2
1820 ...	10.4	7.1	11	146	19.2
1821 ...	9.5	7.5	12	127	20.8
1822 ...	7.8	6.4	10	122	17.5
1823 ...	7.2	6.4	10	113	13.8
1824 ...	7.5	7.0	11	107	14.6
1825 ...	8.2	6.7	11	122	11.1
1826 ...	7.3	7.3	12	100	14.5
1827 ...	6.8	7.0	11	97	11.6
1828 ...	6.5	7.2	11	90	11.3
1829 ...	6.6	7.8	12	85	12.2
1830 ...	5.6	6.7	11	84	10.0

TABLE I. (Continued)

Year	Current value	Volume at 1880 prices	Volume relative	Price relative	Per cent of general imports
	£ mill.	£ mill.	1880=100	1880=100	%
1831 ...	6.7	7.8	12	86	10.8
1832 ...	7.3	8.6	14	85	13.9
1833 ...	6.9	7.5	12	92	11.7
1834 ...	8.0	8.9	14	90	12.4
1835 ...	9.2	10.0	16	92	13.5
1836 ...	9.3	9.6	15	97	11.0
1837 ...	9.0	10.4	16	87	12.8
1838 ...	9.2	10.1	16	91	11.5
1839 ...	10.2	9.9	15	103	11.2
1840 ...	10.0	10.3	16	97	11.0
1841 ...	9.9	11.0	18	90	11.8
1842 ...	8.4	9.7	15	87	11.0
1843 ...	7.8	10.1	16	77	11.0
1844 ...	8.0	10.5	17	76	10.1
1845 ...	9.3	11.8	19	79	10.5
1846 ...	9.2	11.7	18	79	10.5
1847 ...	11.7	14.1	22	83	10.4
1848 ...	8.4	12.7	20	66	9.5
1849 ...	12.1	17.9	28	68	11.9
1850 ...	12.0	15.3	24	78	11.7
1851 ...	12.5	16.1	25	78	11.4
1852 ...	13.0	16.3	26	80	11.8
1853 ...	16.8	18.9	30	89	11.3
1854 ...	18.6	20.4	32	91	12.2
1855 ...	21.0	22.1	35	95	14.6
1856 ...	23.4	22.3	35	105	13.6
1857 ...	24.1	21.2	33	114	12.8
1858 ...	23.2	22.9	36	101	14.1
1859 ...	25.3	24.8	39	102	14.1
1860 ...	28.6	27.0	43	106	13.6
1861 ...	34.5	32.3	51	107	15.9
1862 ...	42.2	31.8	50	133	18.7
1863 ...	50.3	34.5	54	146	20.2
1864 ...	52.2	34.7	55	150	19.0
1865 ...	53.0	38.4	61	138	19.6
1866 ...	50.0	37.9	60	132	16.9
1867 ...	44.5	38.2	60	116	16.2
1868 ...	48.1	42.5	67	113	16.3
1869 ...	47.1	41.7	66	113	16.0
1870 ...	44.5	42.6	67	104	14.7

TABLE I. (*Continued*)

Year	Current value £ mill.	Volume at 1880 prices £ mill.	Volume relative 1880=100	Price relative 1880=100	Per cent of general imports %
1871 ...	60.5	56.7	89	107	18.3
1872 ...	58.3	52.0	82	112	16.4
1873 ...	55.8	49.2	78	113	15.0
1874 ...	58.1	51.8	82	112	15.7
1875 ...	58.1	54.8	87	106	15.5
1876 ...	56.1	54.5	86	103	15.0
1877 ...	53.4	52.0	82	103	13.5
1878 ...	52.6	53.8	85	98	14.3
1879 ...	57.3	59.4	94	96	15.8
1880 ...	63.4	63.4	100	100	15.4
1881 ...	63.1	65.2	103	97	15.9
1882 ...	65.2	68.8	109	95	15.8
1883 ...	65.6	72.4	114	91	15.4
1884 ...	62.9	72.7	115	87	16.1
1885 ...	58.4	70.4	111	83	15.7
1886 ...	56.2	74.7	118	75	16.1
1887 ...	59.4	76.1	120	78	16.4
1888 ...	64.0	84.1	133	76	16.5
1889 ...	66.7	86.7	137	77	15.6
1890 ...	64.7	83.6	132	77	15.4
1891 ...	61.9	80.6	127	77	14.2
1892 ...	64.6	87.9	139	73	15.2
1893 ...	59.0	80.0	126	74	14.6
1894 ...	58.0	82.8	131	70	14.2
1895 ...	59.9	88.3	139	68	14.4
1896 ...	56.2	81.8	129	69	12.7
1897 ...	59.9	88.8	140	68	13.3
1898 ...	60.6	88.1	139	69	12.9
1899 ...	65.0	90.8	143	72	13.4
1900 ...	63.2	81.5	128	78	12.1
1901 ...	67.8	89.1	141	76	13.0
1902 ...	65.8	87.3	138	75	12.5
1903 ...	69.6	90.3	142	77	12.8
1904 ...	70.3	89.5	141	79	12.8
1905 ...	77.8	96.5	152	81	13.8
1906 ...	85.1	97.2	153	88	14.0
1907 ...	91.9	102.0	161	90	14.2
1908 ...	79.6	93.9	148	85	13.4
1909 ...	91.3	103.3	163	88	14.6
1910 ...	103.8	105.2	166	99	15.3
1911 ...	102.8	108.1	171	95	15.1
1912 ...	111.7	116.0	183	96	15.0
1913 ...	109.6	115.8	183	95	14.3

TABLE II. COTTON AND COTTON MANUFACTURES: THE NET BARTER TERMS OF TRADE OF THE UNITED KINGDOM, WITH VALUES, VOLUMES, AND AVERAGE PRICES OF EXPORTS OF COTTON YARN AND MANUFACTURES AND OF NET IMPORTS OF RAW COTTON, 1814–1880

Year	Exports of cotton yarn (little fabrication)				Exports of cotton manufactures (much fabrication)				Net imports of cotton				Net barter terms of trade	
	A Current value	B Volume at prices of 1880	C Volume relative $\frac{B_1}{B_0}$	D Price relative $\frac{A}{B}$	E Current value	F Volume at prices of 1880	G Volume relative $\frac{F_1}{F_0}$	H Price relative $\frac{E}{F}$	I Current value	J Volume at prices of 1880	K Volume relative $\frac{J_1}{J_0}$	L Price relative $\frac{I}{J}$	M Cotton yarn $\frac{D}{L}$	N Cotton manufactures $\frac{H}{L}$
	£ mill.	£ mill.	1880= 100	1880= 100	£ mill.	£ mill.	1880= 100	1880= 100	£ mill.	£ mill.	1880= 100	1880= 100	1880= 100	1880= 100
1814	2.79	0.70	6	399	17.28	2.71	4	638	5.10	1.38	4	370	108	172
1815	1.67	0.51	4	328	19.04	3.66	6	520	7.83	2.39	6	328	100	159
1816	2.63	0.87	7	302	13.04	2.57	4	507	6.88	2.24	6	307	98	165
1817	2.01	0.70	6	287	14.04	3.35	5	419	9.31	3.01	8	309	93	136
1818	2.39	0.81	7	295	16.40	3.53	6	465	12.28	3.10	11	300	98	155
1819	2.52	0.99	8	255	12.19	2.76	4	442	6.96	3.47	9	201	127	220
1820	2.83	1.27	11	223	13.71	3.49	5	393	7.68	3.72	10	206	108	191
1821	2.31	1.19	10	194	13.82	3.93	6	352	4.94	2.96	8	167	116	211
1822	2.70	1.47	12	184	14.58	4.43	7	329	4.87	3.16	8	154	119	214
1823	2.63	1.51	13	174	13.80	4.42	7	312	6.62	4.59	12	144	121	217
1824	3.14	1.86	16	169	15.32	5.05	8	303	4.69	3.45	9	136	124	223
1825	3.21	1.81	15	177	15.15	4.99	8	304	9.81	5.36	14	183	97	166
1826	3.49	2.32	19	150	10.60	3.93	6	270	4.63	3.88	10	119	126	227
1827	3.55	2.48	21	143	14.09	5.48	9	257	6.88	6.45	17	107	134	240
1828	3.60	2.79	23	129	13.65	5.45	9	250	5.23	5.34	14	98	132	255
1829	3.98	3.40	29	117	13.56	6.42	10	211	5.03	5.03	13	100	117	211
1830	4.13	3.57	30	116	15.30	6.54	10	234	6.82	6.47	17	105	110	223

Year														
1831	3.98	3.53	30	113	13.28	6.21	10	214	7.07	6.75	18	105	108	204
1832	4.72	4.18	35	113	12.68	6.87	11	185	7.28	6.81	18	107	106	173
1833	4.70	3.91	33	120	13.78	7.52	12	183	10.08	7.25	19	139	86	132
1834	5.21	4.23	36	123	15.30	8.28	13	185	11.27	7.76	21	145	85	128
1835	5.71	4.60	39	124	16.42	8.33	13	197	13.47	8.48	23	159	78	124
1836	6.12	4.87	41	126	18.51	9.46	15	196	14.34	9.39	25	153	82	128
1837	6.96	5.72	48	122	13.64	7.76	12	176	11.16	9.32	25	120	102	147
1838	7.43	6.33	53	117	16.72	10.15	16	165	14.33	12.10	32	118	99	140
1839	6.86	5.84	49	117	17.69	10.83	17	163	11.58	8.91	24	130	90	125
1840	7.10	6.55	55	108	17.57	11.56	18	152	14.78	14.14	38	105	103	145
1841	7.27	6.81	57	107	16.23	10.99	17	148	11.17	11.53	31	97	110	153
1842	7.77	7.59	64	102	13.91	10.54	17	132	11.60	12.42	33	93	110	142
1843	7.19	7.74	65	93	16.26	13.04	20	125	12.70	16.09	43	79	118	158
1844	6.99	7.65	64	91	18.82	14.80	23	127	12.37	15.25	41	81	112	157
1845	6.96	7.46	63	93	19.16	15.29	24	125	12.27	17.24	46	71	131	176
1846	7.88	8.95	75	88	17.72	14.72	23	120	8.59	10.39	28	83	106	145
1847	5.96	6.64	56	90	17.38	13.58	21	128	10.35	10.37	28	100	90	128
1848	5.93	7.50	63	79	16.76	15.59	24	108	11.54	16.37	44	70	113	154
1849	6.70	8.25	69	81	20.08	19.03	30	106	14.65	16.92	45	87	93	122
1850	6.38	7.25	61	88	21.88	19.51	31	112	16.64	14.55	39	114	77	98
1851	6.63	7.95	67	83	23.46	21.64	34	108	15.08	16.70	45	90	92	120
1852	6.66	8.10	68	82	23.23	21.56	34	108	18.93	21.03	56	90	91	120
1853	6.90	8.14	68	85	25.82	23.04	36	112	17.94	19.42	52	92	92	122
1854	6.69	8.12	68	82	25.05	23.59	37	106	17.88	19.74	53	91	90	116
1855	7.20	9.14	77	79	27.59	26.78	42	103	18.37	19.83	53	93	85	111
1856	8.03	10.03	84	80	30.21	28.69	45	105	23.10	22.68	61	102	78	103
1857	8.70	9.76	82	89	30.37	27.85	44	109	25.86	21.62	58	120	74	91
1858	9.58	11.05	93	87	33.43	31.55	50	106	26.15	22.89	61	114	76	93
1859	9.46	10.62	89	89	38.75	34.70	55	112	30.34	27.16	73	112	79	100
1860	9.87	10.90	92	91	42.15	37.86	60	111	30.37	29.76	80	102	89	109

TABLE II. (Continued)

Year	Exports of cotton yarn				Exports of cotton manufactures				Net imports of cotton				Net barter terms	
	Current value	Volume	Volume relative	Price relative	Current value	Volume	Volume relative	Price relative	Current value	Volume	Volume relative	Price relative	Cotton yarn	Cotton mfs.
	£ mill.	£ mill.	1880=100	1880=100	£ mill.	£ mill.	1880=100	1880=100	£ mill.	£ mill.	1880=100	1880=100	1880=100	1880=100
1861	9.29	9.82	83	95	37.58	34.46	54	109	30.07	25.40	68	118	81	92
1862	6.20	5.15	43	120	30.56	23.81	37	128	17.58	8.72	23	202	59	63
1863	8.06	4.11	35	196	39.52	23.49	37	168	36.18	11.83	32	306	64	55
1864	9.08	4.18	35	217	45.80	24.08	38	190	57.32	17.38	47	330	66	58
1865	10.34	5.71	48	181	46.92	27.39	43	171	47.21	18.32	49	258	70	66
1866	13.68	7.66	64	179	60.92	35.06	55	174	58.31	26.72	72	218	82	80
1867	14.87	9.33	78	159	55.97	38.10	60	147	39.56	24.63	66	161	99	91
1868	14.71	9.61	81	153	52.98	40.19	63	132	43.26	27.04	72	160	96	83
1869	14.10	9.33	78	151	53.02	39.18	62	135	45.36	25.43	68	178	85	76
1870	14.67	10.27	86	143	56.75	44.21	69	128	45.40	29.38	79	155	92	83
1871	15.06	10.68	90	141	57.75	47.03	74	123	43.98	37.90	102	116	122	106
1872	16.70	11.73	99	142	63.47	49.17	77	129	44.56	30.38	81	147	97	88
1873	15.90	11.87	100	134	61.45	48.52	76	127	48.16	34.77	93	139	96	91
1874	14.52	12.18	102	119	59.73	49.72	78	120	43.87	34.88	93	126	94	95
1875	13.17	11.91	100	111	58.60	49.47	78	118	39.67	32.81	88	121	92	98
1876	12.78	12.84	108	100	54.85	50.61	80	108	35.65	34.17	92	104	96	104
1877	12.19	12.57	106	97	57.04	53.25	84	107	31.40	31.41	84	100	97	107
1878	13.02	13.85	116	94	52.92	50.78	80	104	30.08	31.59	85	95	99	109
1879	12.11	13.02	109	93	51.86	52.40	82	99	31.86	33.95	91	94	99	105
1880	11.90	11.90	100	100	63.66	63.66	100	100	37.31	37.31	100	100	100	100

TABLE III. WOOL AND WOOLEN MANUFACTURES: THE NET BARTER TERMS OF TRADE OF THE UNITED KINGDOM, WITH VALUES, VOLUMES, AND AVERAGE PRICES OF EXPORTS OF WOOLEN YARN AND MANUFACTURES AND OF NET IMPORTS OF RAW WOOL, 1814–1880

Year	Exports of woolen yarn (little fabrication)				Exports of woolen manufactures (much fabrication)				Net imports of wool				Net barter terms of trade	
	A Current value	B Volume at prices of 1880	C Volume relative B_1/B_0	D Price relative A/B	E Current value	F Volume at prices of 1880	G Volume relative F_1/F_0	H Price relative E/F	I Current value	J Volume at prices of 1880	K Volume relative J_1/J_0	L Price relative I/J	M Woolen yarn $\frac{D}{L}$	N Woolen manufactures[a] $\frac{H}{L}$
	£ mill.	£ mill.	1880=100	1880=100	£ mill.	£ mill.	1880=100	1880=100	£ mill.	£ mill.	1880=100	1880=100	1880=100	1880=100
1814 ..	negligible	—	—	—	6.37	2.93	17	217	3.84	0.85	7	452	—	(48)
1815 ..	—	—	—	—	9.34	3.92	23	238	2.98	0.75	6	397	—	(60)
1816 ..	—	—	—	—	7.85	3.17	18	248	1.47	0.41	3	359	—	(69)
1817 ..	—	—	—	—	7.18	3.39	20	212	2.78	0.77	6	361	—	(59)
1818 ..	—	—	—	—	8.14	4.04	23	201	4.68	1.33	11	352	—	(57)
1819 ..	—	—	—	—	5.99	3.00	17	200	2.84	0.88	7	323	—	(62)
1820 ..	—	—	—	—	5.58	3.01	17	185	1.31	0.54	5	241	—	(77)
1821 ..	—	—	—	—	6.46	3.27	19	198	2.01	0.91	8	221	—	(90)
1822 ..	—	—	—	—	6.49	3.53	20	184	2.46	1.05	9	234	—	(79)
1823 ..	—	—	—	—	5.63	3.29	19	171	2.39	1.06	9	225	—	(76)
1824 ..	—	—	—	—	6.04	3.57	21	169	2.78	1.22	10	228	—	(74)
1825 ..	—	—	—	—	6.19	3.41	20	182	5.42	2.37	20	229	—	(79)
1826 ..	—	—	—	—	4.97	3.04	18	163	1.42	0.83	7	171	—	(95)
1827 ..	—	—	—	—	5.25	3.53	20	149	2.73	1.56	13	175	—	(85)
1828 ..	—	—	—	—	5.07	3.51	20	144	2.94	1.61	13	183	—	(79)
1829 ..	—	—	—	—	4.58	3.34	19	137	2.11	1.16	10	182	—	(75)
1830 ..	—	—	—	—	4.73	3.30	19	143	3.17	1.74	15	182	—	(79)

[a] The net barter numbers for woolens are placed in parentheses through 1835 mainly as a reminder that domestic production probably supplied the greater part of British consumption of raw wool until the mid-thirties when cheaper Australian wool began to enter Britain in large volume.

TABLE III. (*Continued*)

Year	Exports of woolen yarn				Exports of woolen manufactures				Net imports of wool				Net barter terms	
	Current value	Volume	Volume relative	Price relative	Current value	Volume	Volume relative	Price relative	Current value	Volume	Volume relative	Price relative	Woolen yarn	Woolen mfs.
	£ mill.	£ mill.	1880=100	1880=100	£ mill.	£ mill.	1880=100	1880=100	£ mill.	£ mill.	1880=100	1880=100	1880=100	1880=100
1831 . .	—	—	—	—	5.23	3.76	22	139	2.95	1.68	14	176	—	(79)
1832 . .	—	—	—	—	5.24	4.27	25	123	2.24	1.51	13	148	—	(83)
1833 . .	—	—	—	—	6.30	4.52	26	139	3.05	2.06	17	148	—	(94)
1834 . .	—	—	—	—	5.74	3.66	21	157	4.01	2.50	21	160	—	(98)
1835 . .	—	—	—	—	6.84	4.55	26	150	3.35	2.10	18	160	—	(94)
1836 . .	—	—	—	—	7.64	4.34	25	176	5.11	3.49	29	146	—	121
1837 . .	—	—	—	—	4.66	2.95	17	158	3.43	2.50	21	137	—	115
1838 . .	—	—	—	—	5.80	3.92	23	148	3.84	2.78	23	138	—	107
1839 . .	—	—	—	—	6.27	4.26	25	147	4.25	3.11	26	137	—	107
1840 . .	0.45	0.48	14	94	5.33	3.96	23	135	3.48	2.65	22	131	72	103
1841 . .	.55	.60	18	92	5.75	4.54	26	127	3.62	2.95	25	123	75	103
1842 . .	.64	.73	22	88	5.19	4.15	24	125	2.84	2.32	19	122	72	104
1843 . .	.74	.91	27	81	6.79	5.33	31	127	3.10	2.54	21	122	66	104
1844 . .	.96	1.02	31	94	8.21	6.29	36	131	4.06	3.50	29	116	81	113
1845 . .	1.07	1.15	34	93	7.70	6.00	35	128	5.01	4.07	34	123	76	104
1846 . .	.91	1.05	31	87	6.33	4.95	29	128	3.86	3.42	29	113	77	113
1847 . .	1.00	1.24	37	81	6.90	5.48	32	126	3.17	3.16	26	100	81	126
1848 . .	.78	1.03	31	76	5.74	4.72	27	122	3.09	3.52	29	88	86	139
1849 . .	1.09	1.45	43	75	7.34	6.71	39	109	3.34	3.53	29	95	79	115
1850 . .	1.45	1.70	51	85	8.60	8.96	52	96	3.42	3.30	28	104	82	92
1851 . .	1.49	1.80	54	83	8.38	8.81	51	95	3.91	3.83	32	102	81	93
1852 . .	1.43	1.75	52	82	8.72	9.57	55	91	5.24	4.52	38	116	71	78
1853 . .	1.46	1.71	51	85	10.17	10.17	59	100	6.92	5.91	49	117	73	85
1854 . .	1.56	1.93	58	81	9.12	9.63	56	95	5.03	4.50	38	112	72	85
1855 . .	2.03	2.51	75	81	7.72	8.08	47	96	4.65	3.85	32	121	67	79

1856 ..	2.89	3.36	101	86	9.50	9.85	57	96	6.71	4.93	41	136	63	71
1857 ..	2.94	3.03	91	97	10.70	10.97	64	98	6.91	5.15	43	134	72	73
1858 ..	2.97	2.95	88	101	9.78	9.84	57	99	7.11	5.51	46	129	78	77
1859 ..	3.08	2.80	84	110	12.05	11.32	66	106	7.68	5.74	48	134	82	79
1860 ..	3.84	3.39	101	113	12.16	11.10	64	110	8.74	6.47	54	135	84	81
1861 ..	3.55	3.37	101	105	11.12	9.77	57	114	6.10	5.14	43	119	88	96
1862 ..	3.85	3.41	102	113	13.15	10.98	64	120	8.49	6.83	57	124	91	97
1863 ..	5.09	3.99	119	128	15.49	12.88	75	120	7.60	6.28	52	121	106	99
1864 ..	5.42	3.91	117	139	18.52	13.92	81	133	11.12	8.31	69	134	104	99
1865 ..	5.11	3.84	115	133	20.13	14.64	85	138	9.04	7.09	59	128	104	108
1866 ..	4.55	3.36	101	135	21.82	15.65	91	139	12.53	9.59	80	131	103	106
1867 ..	5.74	4.64	139	124	20.15	13.99	81	144	9.77	7.81	65	125	99	115
1868 ..	6.20	5.42	162	114	19.58	14.25	83	137	8.68	8.02	67	108	106	127
1869 ..	5.54	4.70	141	118	22.68	16.16	94	140	7.96	7.64	64	104	113	135
1870 ..	4.99	4.49	134	111	21.66	16.15	94	134	10.25	9.36	78	110	101	122
1871 ..	6.10	5.53	166	110	27.18	19.66	114	138	10.23	10.21	85	100	110	138
1872 ..	6.11	5.02	150	122	32.37	22.26	129	145	9.24	9.11	76	101	120	144
1873 ..	5.39	4.39	131	123	25.35	19.60	113	129	10.65	10.62	89	100	123	129
1874 ..	5.56	4.42	132	126	22.80	18.79	109	121	10.88	10.87	91	100	126	121
1875 ..	5.1c	4.01	120	127	21.66	18.31	106	118	11.34	10.35	86	110	115	107
1876 ..	4.42	3.90	117	113	18.59	16.55	96	112	12.30	11.74	97	105	108	107
1877 ..	3.61	3.42	102	106	17.34	16.19	94	107	12.74	11.97	100	106	100	101
1878 ..	3.91	3.94	118	99	16.71	16.07	93	104	10.90	11.47	96	95	104	109
1879 ..	3.71	4.21	126	88	15.85	16.14	93	98	9.40	8.99	75	105	84	93
1880 ..	3.34	3.34	100	100	17.27	17.27	100	100	11.99	11.99	100	100	100	100

TABLE IV. EXPORTS AND NET IMPORTS OMITTING COTTON AND WOOL: THE NET
BARTER TERMS OF TRADE OF THE UNITED KINGDOM, WITH VALUES, VOLUMES,
AND AVERAGE PRICES OF EXPORTS AND NET IMPORTS, 1814–1880

Year	Exports omitting cottons and woolens				Net imports omitting cotton and wool				
	A Current value	B Volume at prices of 1880	C Volume relative	D Price relative	E Current value	F Volume at prices of 1880	G Volume relative	H Price relative	I Net barter terms of trade
			$\frac{B_1}{B_0}$	$\frac{A}{B}$			$\frac{F_1}{F_0}$	$\frac{E}{F}$	$\frac{D}{H}$
	£ mill.	£ mill.	1880= 100	1880= 100	£ mill.	£ mill.	1880= 100	1880= 100	1880= 100
1814 ..	19.0	7.5	6	253	47.1	19.8	7	233	109
1815 ..	21.6	9.1	7	237	43.7	22.0	7	199	119
1816 ..	18.1	8.1	6	223	29.3	17.7	6	166	134
1817 ..	18.6	8.7	7	214	38.8	23.5	8	165	130
1818 ..	19.5	8.7	7	224	51.4	30.3	10	170	132
1819 ..	14.5	6.9	5	210	36.1	24.6	8	147	143
1820 ..	14.3	7.7	6	186	34.8	25.0	8	139	134
1821 ..	14.1	8.1	6	174	29.2	22.5	8	130	134
1822 ..	13.2	8.8	7	150	29.5	23.6	8	125	120
1823 ..	13.3	8.5	7	156	35.8	27.9	9	128	121
1824 ..	13.9	9.3	7	149	36.2	30.2	10	120	124
1825 ..	14.3	8.2	6	174	50.2	38.0	13	132	132
1826 ..	12.5	7.7	6	162	37.0	31.8	11	116	140
1827 ..	14.3	9.7	8	147	42.4	35.6	12	119	122
1828 ..	14.4	9.8	8	147	42.6	37.6	13	113	130
1829 ..	13.6	10.0	8	136	40.4	37.2	12	109	125
1830 ..	14.0	10.7	8	131	40.3	38.8	13	104	126
1831 ..	14.5	10.9	9	133	45.3	41.9	14	108	123
1832 ..	13.6	10.7	8	127	35.7	33.2	11	108	118
1833 ..	14.7	11.8	9	125	38.9	35.9	12	108	116
1834 ..	15.2	12.1	10	126	41.4	38.2	13	108	117
1835 ..	18.1	13.3	11	136	41.9	36.4	12	115	118
1836 ..	20.7	14.2	11	146	55.6	45.5	15	122	120
1837 ..	16.5	11.8	9	140	46.5	41.6	14	112	125
1838 ..	19.7	15.2	12	140	52.8	46.0	15	115	122
1839 ..	21.0	16.5	13	127	64.8	53.7	18	121	105
1840 ..	21.0	17.5	14	120	63.0	49.5	17	127	94
1841 ..	21.8	18.0	14	121	59.3	50.8	17	117	103
1842 ..	19.9	18.5	15	108	53.6	48.1	16	111	97
1843 ..	21.3	19.7	16	108	47.4	45.2	15	105	103
1844 ..	23.6	21.3	17	111	54.4	52.8	18	103	108
1845 ..	25.2	20.9	16	121	61.9	58.7	20	105	115

TABLE IV. (*Continued*)

Year	Exports omitting cottons and woolens				Net imports omitting cotton and wool				Net barter terms
	Current value	Volume	Volume relative	Price relative	Current value	Volume	Volume relative	Price relative	
	£ mill.	£ mill.	1880= 100	1880= 100	£ mill.	£ mill.	1880= 100	1880= 100	1880= 100
1846 ..	25.0	20.1	16	124	65.6	63.4	21	103	120
1847 ..	27.6	22.9	18	121	86.8	82.0	27	106	114
1848 ..	23.6	21.2	17	111	65.2	71.9	24	91	122
1849 ..	28.4	27.6	22	103	71.3	81.6	27	87	118
1850 ..	33.1	33.3	26	99	71.0	82.4	28	86	115
1851 ..	34.5	34.9	28	99	78.0	87.1	29	90	110
1852 ..	38.0	38.6	30	98	72.8	78.2	26	93	105
1853 ..	54.6	48.5	38	113	106.8	97.5	33	110	103
1854 ..	54.8	46.2	36	119	110.9	92.2	31	120	99
1855 ..	51.2	43.7	34	117	99.5	79.5	27	125	94
1856 ..	65.2	54.9	43	119	119.3	98.2	33	121	98
1857 ..	69.4	57.7	45	120	131.0	100.8	34	130	92
1858 ..	60.9	51.5	41	118	108.2	98.7	33	110	107
1859 ..	67.1	58.5	46	115	115.9	102.7	34	113	102
1860 ..	67.9	59.6	47	114	142.8	120.0	40	119	96
1861 ..	63.6	55.2	43	115	146.8	131.0	44	112	103
1862 ..	70.2	62.8	49	112	157.5	150.5	50	105	107
1863 ..	78.4	69.3	55	113	154.8	147.2	49	105	108
1864 ..	81.6	67.4	53	121	154.3	139.5	47	111	109
1865 ..	83.3	71.6	56	116	161.8	148.0	50	109	106
1866 ..	88.0	74.1	58	119	174.5	157.6	53	111	107
1867 ..	84.2	72.2	51	117	181.4	157.5	53	115	102
1868 ..	86.2	77.5	61	111	194.6	167.3	56	116	96
1869 ..	94.6	87.1	69	109	195.1	178.0	60	110	99
1870 ..	101.5	93.4	74	109	203.1	184.6	62	110	99
1871 ..	117.0	106.1	84	110	216.3	202.5	68	107	103
1872 ..	137.6	108.1	85	127	242.6	216.9	73	112	113
1873 ..	147.1	104.4	82	141	256.6	227.9	76	113	125
1874 ..	137.0	102.6	81	134	257.2	230.8	77	111	120
1875 ..	124.9	102.6	81	122	264.8	250.6	84	106	115
1876 ..	110.0	97.7	77	113	271.1	258.4	87	105	108
1877 ..	108.7	101.9	80	107	296.8	272.9	91	109	98
1878 ..	106.3	103.7	82	103	275.2	273.3	92	101	102
1879 ..	108.0	112.8	89	96	264.5	279.4	94	95	101
1880 ..	126.9	126.9	100	100	298.6	298.6	100	100	100

INDEX

Aberdeen, Lord, 187

Absolute values. *See* Volume series

Africa, British exports to, 129–130

Agriculture, 144–146, 180–185, 195–197; acreage under cultivation, 181, 183, 184; landed interests, 118, 154, 156; the golden age, 182–183; wages, 143–144; rents, 182, 185; and assessed income, England and Wales, 185; Board of, 184. *See also* Corn; Corn Laws; Wheat

Aix-la-Chapelle, Congress of, 5

Alliance (secret) of 1815, 2

Althorp, Lord, 147

American Civil War: effect on prices, 27, 32; and tariff trends, 194

Annual Register, 119

Anti-Corn Law League, 147, 151

Artisans, skilled: forbidden to emigrate, 7; permitted to emigrate, 1824, 14; London, wages, 143–144; and cost of living, 144, 188n

Ashton, Thomas S., 66n, 144, 145

Asia, British exports to: in selected periods, 1816–1842, 129; and imports from, 130

Austria, 17; secret alliance of 1815, 2; intervention in Naples, 4, 9; loans from Britain, 10n, 11

Balance of payments, 42, 43; construction of estimates for 1816–1913, 43–67; and comparisons with other findings, 67–81; constructed series, 1816–1913, 70–75; declining margin in protectionist period, 134; and improvement in free-trade period, 177–178, 180, 181

Balance of power: in peace settlement of 1814–1815, 2–4; shaken by Prussian wars of unification, 17–19

Balance on Business Services: profits on foreign trade, 47–48, 70–75; insurance, brokerage, and shipping commissions, 48, 70–75; net balance in relation to total trade, by quinquennial periods, 1816–1845, 134; and 1841–1913, 177

Balance on current account, 64–65, 70–75, 165, 177–180 *passim*; by quinquennial averages, 1816–1845, 134; and 1841–1913, 181

Baldwin, Robert E., 102n

Bank Act of 1844, 158n

Bank of England: resumption of gold payment, 11; low gold reserves, 45–46

Baring Brothers, 57, 152

Belgium, independent, 9; British trade treaty abrogated, 197n

Bias in volume and price series, 86–88, 89, 199–204

Bismarck, Prince Otto von, 17, 18, 23, 114, 115, 193–194, 195

Board of Agriculture, established, 184

Board of Trade: estimate of shipping credits for 1901, 50n; volume series, 83n, 85–86, 87, 89, 199–204; free-trade views of officials, 146, 148, 149

Bourne, Stephen, 46, 47

Bowley, Arthur L., 69, 76–77, 143–144

Bread, wheat, 140–142; prices, 145–146, 188

British North America: trade in ships, 46; British exports to, 129. *See also* Canada

British trade. *See* Exports; Imports; Re-exports; Trade balance; Trade balance series

Bullion and specie movements, 44–46, 70–75

Cairncross, Alexander K., 76n, 83n

Canada, 15, 196; rate of return on railway investment, 61; "national policy," 195; imperial preference, 197

Canning, George, 9, 10, 12

Cape Colony, 59

Capital export. *See* Investment, British foreign

Capital gains, probably offset by losses, 63, 67

Carrying trade. *See* Shipping

Castlereagh, Lord, 2, 5, 7, 8, 9

Cattle, debate on importation, 146

Chamberlain, Joseph, 156, 197–198

Charles X, of France, overthrown, 9

Chartist movement, 15, 147, 151, 187, 188

Checks, increasing use of, 158

Clapham, Sir John H., 185

Clarendon, Lord, 10

Class bitterness and reconciliation, 152, 162, 187–188

Coal, export tax, 24n; potential foreign market, 123

Coasting trade, 52; opened to foreign ships, 154, 171

Cobden Treaty, 17, 194

Coffee: prices in 1805, 26n; in large revenue sample, 1839, 148n; important in re-export trade, 200